ENGLISH SKILLS BY OBJECTIVES

BOOK THREE

ENGLISH SKILLS BY OBJECTIVES

BOOK THREE

Writing Skills

This book is derived from
an instructional program
created by the

AMERICAN PREPARATORY INSTITUTE

Central Texas College, Killeen

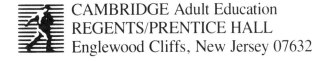

CAMBRIDGE Adult Education
REGENTS/PRENTICE HALL
Englewood Cliffs, New Jersey 07632

Cambridge gratefully acknowledges the advice and contributions of the following adult educators who reviewed the draft version of this book:

Donna Amstutz, Chicago Urban Skills Institute, Chicago, Illinois.

Janet Moore, Coordinator, A.B.E. Section, Birmingham City Schools, Birmingham, Alabama.

Denise Schultheis, Springfield Community Schools, Springfield, Ohio.

Nancy Sullivan, Jersey City Learning Center, Jersey City, New Jersey.

Project Editors: James Fina, Marjorie P.K. Weiser
Production Manager: Arthur Michalez
Managing Editor: Eileen Guerrin
Additional Editing: Gina Doggett, Rachel Kranz

Dictionary excerpts on pages 245, 250, 255. With permission.
From *Webster's New World Dictionary,* Compact School & Office Edition.
Copyright © 1982 by Simon & Schuster, Inc.

Dictionary excerpts on pages 20–22, 24, 329–332.
With permission. From *Webster's New World Dictionary,* Second College Edition.
Copyright © 1984 by Simon & Schuster, Inc.

 © 1985 by Prentice-Hall, Inc.
A Simon & Schuster Company
Englewood Cliffs, New Jersey 07632

Printed in the United States of America

10 9 8 7 6 5 4 3 2

ISBN 0-8428-0215-0

Prentice-Hall International (UK) Limited, *London*
Prentice-Hall of Australia Pty. Limited, *Sydney*
Prentice-Hall Canada Inc., *Toronto*
Prentice-Hall Hispanoamericana, S.A., *Mexico*
Prentice-Hall of India Private Limited, *New Delhi*
Prentice-Hall of Japan, Inc., *Tokyo*
Simon & Schuster Asia Pte. Ltd., *Singapore*
Editora Prentice-Hall do Brasil, Ltda., *Rio de Janeiro*

CONTENTS

INSIDE COVER CHARTS
    PARTS OF SPEECH
    PARTS OF SENTENCES
    SENTENCE PATTERNS

TO THE STUDENT

The three-book series, ENGLISH SKILLS BY OBJECTIVES, is designed to help you develop the skills that you need to write effectively. The first two books of this series introduced the grammar, or structure, of the English language. In studying them, you learned to identify the parts of speech and the parts of a sentence. Mastery of these basic grammar skills will enable you to use English correctly and effectively in your writing.

The ENGLISH SKILLS BY OBJECTIVES series consists of three books. BOOK ONE, GRAMMAR FUNDAMENTALS, introduced the basic elements of the English language. BOOK TWO, GRAMMAR AND USAGE, demonstrated how these elements come together to form meaningful sentences. This is BOOK THREE, WRITING SKILLS. In it you will learn how to use the elements of the language to present your ideas in writing. You will review the parts of speech and see how they are used to convey meaning in sentences. You will review the structure of sentences, and learn to create sentences that are interesting and accurate. Then you will learn how to combine sentences to form paragraphs, and how to organize the ideas that make up a paragraph. You will practice writing sentences and paragraphs of your own. The final units in this book will teach you some additional skills that can improve your writing: spelling rules, things you can learn from a dictionary, and the correct meanings and spellings of words that are often confused. When you complete your studies in this book, you will be able to express your ideas in writing, clearly and with confidence.

The title of this series, ENGLISH SKILLS BY OBJECTIVES, means that the material to be learned is broken into smaller "objectives" or goals for you to accomplish. Here's how the program works:

Pretest—Take the Pretest to find out what English skills you need to work on. <u>Don't worry about any questions whose answers you don't know</u>. This book will help you learn the answers. Check your answers in the separate Answer Key and then turn to the Skills Correlation Chart on pages 20–22 in the text. The Chart lists the pages in this book that you should study so that you can answer the questions you missed.

Skill Units—This book contains 11 Skill Units. Each Skill Unit is divided into smaller units called "Subskills." Each Subskill focuses on a specific part of an English language skill, thus allowing you to learn one thing at a time. You will always know what you are to learn and how you will learn it. Each Subskill starts with an objective explaining what language activity you will be able to perform after you finish the Subskill. At the end of each Subskill, there is an EXERCISE for you to complete to see how well you understand the material. If you need additional practice, you can complete a SUPPLEMENTAL EXERCISE that also includes a review of the Subskill. You can use the Subskill exercises for review at any time. At the end of each Skill Unit, there is a SELF-CHECK. Completing this exercise allows you to check your understanding of all that you have learned in the unit. Because the Self-Check has no time limit, you can take your time thinking about each question before you answer.

Posttest—Take the Posttest to review your performance in all the skills in ENGLISH SKILLS BY OBJECTIVES, BOOK THREE. Then use the Skills Correlation Chart to interpret your score on the Posttest. You will be able to go back and review the Skill Units and Subskills in which you need more practice.

When you complete this book, you will be able to communicate in writing. Your written work—essays, letters to friends, job applications—will show that you have mastered the skills required to write effectively.

LIST OF ABBREVIATIONS

The following lists the abbreviations used in the example sentences in this book:

AC	adverbial clause
Adj	adjective
Adv	adverb
Comp S	compound subject
Conj	conjunction
Conj Adv	conjunctive adverb
CP	complete predicate
CS	complete subject
DO	direct object
Ger Phrase	gerund phrase
Inf Phrase	infinitive phrase
IO	indirect object
LV	linking verb
M	modifier
N	noun
O	object
O Prep	object of the preposition
P	predicate
Part Phrase	participial phrase
P Nom or PN	predicate nominative
Prep Phrase	prepositional phrase
S	subject
V	verb

Pretest
WRITING SKILLS

Before you begin working on this book, take the following test. The test will help you find out how much you already know about writing skills. The test will also show you which parts of the book you should study most.

The test is divided into eleven parts, one part for each unit in the book. You may want to take the test all at once or one unit at a time, depending on what you and your instructor decide. When you complete the test, check your answers starting on page 1 in the Answer Key for Book Three. Then turn to the Skills Correlation Chart on pages 27 and 28 in this book and circle the numbers of any questions you miss. The chart will show you which parts of this book cover the English skills that give you the most trouble. You should study the skill units that contain the questions you miss on the test.

Skill Unit 1:   Writing Simple Sentences

Part A.   Read sentences 1–5 and do the following:
  · Circle the simple subject.
  · Circle the verb.
  · On the space provided after the sentence, tell whether the underlined word is an object, a predicate nominative, or a modifier.
Review your work to be sure you have completed each step.

EXAMPLE: (Elena and Enrico) (took) the <u>bus</u> to the station.

<u>   **object**   </u>

1.   The man in the back yard is my <u>father</u>. _____

2.   Lauren took her aging <u>aunt</u> to a restaurant for dinner.
  _____

3.   Maria and Alonzo seem <u>happier</u> than before. _____

4.   The old man bared his few remaining <u>teeth</u> in a crooked smile.
  _____

5.   <u>Fifty-seven</u> people came to the general meeting. _____

1

Part B. Underline the verbal or verbal phrase in each of the following sentences. Then identify what kind of verbal is being used by writing participle, gerund, or infinitive in the blank provided.

EXAMPLE: You shouldn't be crying over spilled milk.
    participle

6.   My sister has always wanted to live in New York.
    _____

7.   The man running for mayor is my uncle.   _____

8.   I like camping in these mountains.   _____

9.   Give me a minute to think.   _____

10.   The men working at the mill are going to the diner now.
    _____

Part C.   Underline the verb in parentheses that agrees in number with the subject.

EXAMPLE: Mathematics   (**is**, are)   my favorite subject.

11.   Most of my friends   (is, are)   married.

12.   Your scissors   (do, does)   not cut very well.

13.   Who   (is, are)   the man next to you?

14.   These fish   (swims, swim)   at the bottom of the ocean floor.

15.   Everybody   (plans, plan)   to gather at my house to talk about the strike plans.

Part D.   For each sentence, circle the subject and underline the verb in parentheses that agrees in number with the subject.

EXAMPLE: Where   (is, **are**)   (you) going?

16.   The doctor and her assistant   (has, have)   treated this illness before.

17.   (Is, Are)   the leaves on the elm tree beginning to change color?

18.   My friend Ernie, along with his brothers,   (is, are)   visiting us this week.

19.   There   (was, were)   at least twenty thousand people at the concert.

20.   The two leading roles in that movie   (was, were)   played very well.

Skill Unit 2: Writing Compound Sentences

Part A. Read each of the following compound sentences and do these steps:
 · Write S1 and S2 over the first and second subjects, respectively;
 · Underline the verbs and/or verb phrases and write V1 and V2 over them; and
 · Circle the connective and write C over it.
Review your work to be sure that you have completed each step.

<pre>
                    V1
        S1   ⌐‾‾‾‾‾‾‾¬   C S2 V2
EXAMPLE: Rudy had finished his dinner(;) he was ready to go out.
</pre>

1. I usually catch the bus into town; otherwise I get a ride with my neighbor.

2. Henry was exhausted, but he continued anyway.

3. You should join the association; members get a 15% discount on registration.

4. Margaret wanted to surprise her sister; therefore she entered the house quietly.

5. The team had won the last game, and it was ready to do well again.

Part B. Some of the following sentences are compound sentences, and some are not. Read the sentences and do these steps:
 · Rewrite the sentences on the spaces provided, adding commas or semicolons where they are needed; and
 · If a sentence does not need any additional punctuation, write no punctuation change on the space provided instead of rewriting the sentence.

EXAMPLE: Sophia wanted to rest but Natalie insisted on keeping going.
 Sophia wanted to rest, but Natalie insisted on keeping going.

6. Karl's watch stopped consequently he was late for the meeting.

_____

_____

7. The weather was bad and George decided to cancel the picnic.

_____

_____

8. Maria's answer was short and to the point.

_____

9. Tony did not get enough exercise nor was he eating well.

_____

_____

10. Peter tried to read his book but he had forgotten to bring his glasses home.

_____

_____

Part C. Correct the following run-on sentences using the conjunction or conjunctive adverb provided in parentheses.

EXAMPLE: Henry has been in an accident before, he often forgets to buckle his seat belt.   (nevertheless)
Henry has been in an accident before; **nevertheless,** he often forgets to buckle his seat belt.

11. It had been a lovely party, it was time to go home.   (and)

_____

_____

12. Sheila worked hard at making dinner, she worried about whether it would taste good.   (however)

_____

_____

13. Larry was tired, he had been walking for the past two hours. (for)

_____

_____

14. Mary Jo would be leaving in two weeks, she wanted to get everything packed.   (therefore)

_____

_____

15. Ralph had a full schedule last week, he found time to do some shopping. (nevertheless)

_____

_____

Skill Unit 3: Writing Complex Sentences

Part A. Read the following sentences. In each sentence, underline the independent clause and put brackets around the dependent clause.

EXAMPLE: **The man** [who is wearing a raincoat] **is a spy.**

1. She doesn't ride the bicycle that they gave her.

2. Mr. Quinones hired the man who wore a tie.

3. If you have time, you should visit the museum.

4. Which radio is the one that you just bought?

5. Maria, who doesn't eat meat, did not enjoy our picnic.

Part B. Read each of the following sentences and do these steps:
  · Underline the correct relative pronoun from the two given in parentheses;
  · Underline the adjectival clause;
  · On the space provided, write whether the adjectival clause is restrictive (giving essential information) or non-restrictive (adding extra information); and
  · Add commas where necessary.
Review your work to be sure you have completed each step.

EXAMPLES: The man (who's, **whose**) car is parked illegally should move it right away. **restrictive**
   My old car, (that, **which**) has 97,000 miles on it, still drives well. **nonrestrictive**

6. The firefighters (who, whom) all knew how to fight a fire approached the burning house. _____

7. The boy (that, who) delivers the newspaper was late.

_____

8. The refrigerator (which, that) makes ice is the one in the basement. _____

9. The doctor (who, that) does surgery has a lot of experience.

_____

10. I know a guy (who's, whose) wife works there.

_____

Part C.   Read the following sentences, and do these steps:
· Put brackets around each adverbial clause;
· Draw an arrow to the word the clause modifies; and
· Underline the subordinating conjunction.

EXAMPLE: [<u>Although</u> she makes a lot of noise], we like our new dog.

11.   Whenever you need my help, I'll adjust my plans.

12.   Write me a letter so that I know how you are doing.

13.   As soon as she saw George, she began to laugh uncontrollably.

14.   Paula smiled as if she knew more than she let on.

15.   I'll light the fire while you get some more wood.

Part D.   Read the following sentences and do these steps:
· Put brackets around each noun clause; and
· From the pair of choices given in parentheses, underline the words that describe the function of the clause in the sentence.

EXAMPLE: [**What you should do**] is buy a bicycle.   (**<u>subject,</u>** indirect object)

16.   John did what he wanted.   (predicate noun, direct object)

17.   Whoever wins the contest will go to Hawaii.   (subject, object of a preposition)

18.   They will give whoever wins the contest a trip to Hawaii.   (direct object, indirect object).

19.   We will sell the guitar to whomever wants it.   (predicate noun, object of a preposition)

20.   My opinion is that you should talk to a lawyer.   (indirect object, predicate noun)

Skill Unit 4:   Using Sentence Punctuation

Part A.   Put the correct punctuation at the end of each of the following sentences.

EXAMPLE: The weather is cool today.

1.   How many children do they have

2.   You've got to be kidding

3.   The economy is growing slowly

4.   What time did you get home

5.   What a wonderful day

Part B. Punctuate each of the following sentences by adding any necessary commas. If the sentence is correct as written, write C in the space provided.

EXAMPLE: Joe was born on March 22 1960 in Arlington Virginia.

_____

Joe was born on March 22, 1960, in Arlington, Virginia.

6.   The other car however was not damaged. _____

7.   Mr. Helms the mayor of the town was angry. _____

8.   We found a cozy inexpensive apartment. _____

9.   My friend Bill is an engineer. _____

10.   While driving the truck he almost fell asleep. _____

Part C. Read each of the following sentences. For each underlined phrase, use the space provided to write a phrase that uses an apostrophe and has the same meaning.

EXAMPLE: He met the captain of the ship.   **the ship's captain**

11.   We are only trying to help you. _____

12.   He took the camera that belongs to his sisters.

_____

13.   We will not go to the beach in August. _____

14.   The hero of that movie was the son of Frankenstein.

_____

15.   My father enjoys the music of Frank Sinatra.

_____

Part D. Rewrite each of the following sentences in the spaces provided, using commas, periods, quotation marks, exclamation points, and capital letters where they belong.

EXAMPLE: do you come here often asked the man
            "Do you come here often?" asked the man.

16.   people often ask me how do you stay so thin

_____

17.   i exercise i say and i eat properly

_____

18.   you need two ids to cash a check the teller said

_____

19.   did you say to her leave me alone

_____

20.   how long will it take he asked the mechanic to fix my car

_____

Skill Unit 5: Using More Sentence Punctuation

Part A. Rewrite the following sentences if necessary, adding any needed semicolons. In some cases, you will change commas to semicolons. If the sentence is correct, write a <u>C</u> in the space provided.

EXAMPLE: Henry likes his new job, the hours are better.
            <u>Henry likes his new job; the hours are better.</u>

1. The trip would be long and boring, therefore they took along plenty to read.

_____

_____

2. After the rain, however, Kevin's allergies stopped bothering him.

_____

_____

3. Ms. Lowenthal introduced the panel: Marvin Weller, a volunteer firefighter, Rita Walsh, an environmentalist, and Marilla Barbosa, a county council member.

_____

_____

4. Fred and I stayed with Larry at the emergency room, the others went home.

_____

_____

5. Since it was late, we decided to go home.

_____

_____

Part B. In some of the following sentences, the colon is used correctly; in others it is used incorrectly. Put a <u>C</u> in the space provided next to each sentence that is correctly punctuated. Put <u>I</u> in the space provided next to the sentence that is incorrectly punctuated.

EXAMPLE: When you finish: raise your hand.   <u>I</u>
            Three of my friends have birthdays in March: Juana, Ken, and Margaret.   <u>C</u>

6. The best solution was: to hire an accountant temporarily.

   _____

7. Dear Ms. Gordon:
       Thank you for your interest in . . .   _____

8. Take my advice: go by train.   _____

9. Carol's motivation was clear: she wanted to impress her new boss.   _____

10. North America includes: Canada, the United States, and Mexico.

    _____

Part C.   Rewrite each of the following sentences in the spaces provided, using dashes or parentheses where needed.

EXAMPLE: You will have to drive to Springfield about 15 miles to attend the meeting.
           You will have to drive to Springfield (about 15 miles) to attend the meeting.

11. Rhonda was not around, but as luck would have it Lenny knew how to get in.

    _____

    _____

12. The older children Mark and Wendy ate with the adults.

    _____

    _____

13. Sheila had an excuse she was moving soon.

    _____

    _____

14. Thelma was tired, hungry, and in a bad mood understandable after her ordeal.

    _____

    _____

15. The children gaped as the baseball player the one they admired so much signed autographs for them.

    _____

    _____

Skill Unit 6: Using Modifiers in Sentences

Part A. Rewrite the following sentences so that the adjectives and adverbs in parentheses clearly modify the underlined words.

EXAMPLE: When Derek <u>reached</u> safety, the tornado had passed over. (finally)

<u>When Derek finally reached safety, the tornado had passed over.</u>

1. The <u>rocks</u> scratched Brian's new shoes when he tripped.   (jagged)

   _____

2. On <u>two</u> of the exercises, she scored a passing grade.   (just)

   _____

3. The day care center <u>opened</u> at 7:00 a.m.   (usually)

   _____

4. The music they heard was being played <u>softly</u>.   (very)

   _____

Part B. The following sentences are unclear or confusing due to misplaced phrase modifiers. Rewrite each sentence to make it clear; you may add or change words as needed.

EXAMPLE: She saw the pictures her son's class had painted in the school library.

<u>In the school library, she saw the pictures her son's class had painted.</u>

5. Bill made a mess when he dropped the ice cream cone wearing his parka.

   _____

6. Felicia waved to Dolores riding her bicycle.   (Felicia's on the bike.)

   _____

7. We saw the movie about the end of the world on Tuesday.

   _____

8. Flying around the ceiling, I chased the escaped parakeet.

   _____

Part C. The following sentences are unclear due to misplaced adjective clauses. Rewrite the sentences so that they are clear.

EXAMPLE: The bookcase needs a paint job that I'll buy.
The bookcase that I'll buy needs a paint job.

9. The woman greets us cheerfully every morning who drives our bus.

_____

10. I met the man at the laundromat that has red hair.

_____

11. Helen bought a magazine at the train station that would be fun to read.

_____

12. That dog should be on a leash that always chases cars.

_____

Part D. Some of the following sentences contain dangling modifiers. If a sentence contains a dangling modifier, rewrite it. If a sentence is correct, write <u>Correct</u> in the space provided. Note that there are many possible ways to rewrite these sentences.

EXAMPLE: After eating chicken and vegetables, ice cream was for dessert.
After eating chicken and vegetables, we had ice cream for dessert.

13. Watching the baby, the telephone rang.

_____

14. Cleaning the refrigerator, the frozen food melted.

_____

15. Anthony could hear the flags flapping in the breeze.

_____

16. Groping for the flashlight, it was too dark to find the spare.

_____

Skill Unit 7:   Writing Effective Sentences

Part A.   Each of the following sets of sentences includes two sentences with incorrect parallel structure and one correct sentence. For each set, decide which sentence is correct and write C in the space provided.

EXAMPLE: Driving is cheaper than to take the train. _____

Driving is cheaper than taking the train.   __C__

To drive is cheaper than taking the train. _____

1. When Sally travels, neither postcards nor calling home are important to her. _____

When Sally travels, neither sending postcards nor calls home are important to her. _____

When Sally travels, neither sending postcards nor calling home is important to her. _____

2. Helen makes a point of being prompt and to show professionalism. _____

Helen makes a point of being prompt and showing professionalism. _____

Helen makes a point to be prompt and showing professionalism. _____

3. To go camping was a better plan than visiting relatives. _____

Going camping was a better plan than to visit relatives. _____

Going camping was a better plan than visiting relatives. _____

4. Setting deadlines is as important as meeting them. _____

To set deadlines is as important as meeting them. _____

Setting deadlines is as important as to meet them. _____

5. The party was both annoying and a bore. _____

The party was both an annoyance and boring. _____

The party was both annoying and boring. _____

Part B.   Each of the following sets of sentences includes two sentences with incorrect or inconsistent uses of verbs and one correct sentence. For each set, decide which sentence is correct and write C after it.

EXAMPLE: If Larry had arrived ten minutes earlier, he will run into Paula. _____

If Larry had arrived ten minutes earlier, he will have run into Paula. _____

If Larry had arrived ten minutes earlier, he would have run into Paula. __C__

6. Peter called his doctor and ask for an appointment. _____

Peter called his doctor and asked for an appointment. _____

Peter called his doctor and has asked for an appointment.

_____

7. Just as we were sitting down to dinner, Greg had walked in.

_____

Just as we were sitting down to dinner, Greg walked in.

_____

Just as we were sitting down to dinner, Greg walks in.

_____

8. The date of the next meeting was agreed to, and then we read the agenda. _____

We agreed to the date of the next meeting, and then we read the agenda. _____

We agreed to the date of the next meeting, and then the agenda was read. _____

9. Terry signed the letter and the envelope was sealed. _____

The letter was signed and Terry sealed the envelope. _____

Terry signed the letter and sealed the envelope. _____

10. If Bernarda would have left on time she would have arrived before sunset. _____

If Bernarda had left on time she would have arrived before sunset. _____

If Bernarda had left on time she would arrive before sunset.

_____

Part C. Read each of the following pairs of sentences. Decide which sentence shows correct pronoun reference and agreement, and put a C in the space provided.

EXAMPLE: Each of my brothers has his own opinion. __C__
Each of my brothers has their own opinion. _____

11.   When people don't get enough sleep, you can be cranky.

   _____

   When people don't get enough sleep, they can be cranky.

   _____

12.   Jana took her dog to the veterinarian, which has fleas.

   _____

   Jana took her dog, which has fleas, to the veterinarian.

   _____

13.   Everyone got a chance to call his or her family.   _____
   Everyone got a chance to call their family.   _____

14.   Jane told Jill that her speech was good.   _____
   Jill's speech was good, and Jane told her so.   _____

15.   Anyone may sign their name here.   _____
   Anyone may sign his or her name here.   _____

Part D.   The following sets of sentences contain sentences that are complete and sentences that are sentence fragments. Put a C next to sentences that are complete.

EXAMPLE: My wife, whom you met the other day. Takes her nephew to the movies. Every Friday. They always have a good time.   _____
   My wife, whom you met the other day, takes her nephew to the movies every Friday. They always have a good time.
   _C_
   My wife, whom you met the other day, takes her nephew. To the movies every Friday; they always have a good time.   _____

16.   Matthew has a puppy that wakes him up every morning. By licking his face. They take long walks in the afternoon.   _____

   Matthew has a puppy. That wakes him up every morning by licking his face. They take long walks. In the afternoon.   _____

   Matthew has a puppy that wakes him up every morning by licking his face. They take long walks in the afternoon.   _____

17.   Uncle Raoul has a restaurant. On 17th street. Recently a magazine ranked it as the best. In the neighborhood.   _____

   Uncle Raoul has a restaurant on 17th street. Recently a magazine ranked it as the best in the neighborhood.   _____

   Uncle Raoul. Has a restaurant on 17th street. Recently a magazine ranked it as the best in the neighborhood.   _____

18.   Our club, which already has 15 members. Just accepted several more. We will welcome the new members next week.   _____

   Our club, which already has 15 members, just accepted several more. We will welcome the new members. Next week.   _____

Our club, which already has 15 members, just accepted several more. We will welcome the new members next week. _____

19. Kerry was looking forward to the weekend, when he would be able to sleep late, because he had worked very hard all week.

_____

Kerry was looking forward to the weekend, when he would be able to sleep late. Because he had worked very hard all week.

_____

Kerry was looking forward to the weekend. When he would be able to sleep late. Because he had worked very hard all week.

_____

20. Margaret's next goal was to join the group of runners who were able to complete the mile. In under five minutes. _____

Margaret's next goal. Was to join the group of runners who were able to complete the mile in under five minutes. _____

Margaret's next goal was to join the group of runners who were able to complete the mile in under five minutes. _____

Skill Unit 8: Writing Unified Paragraphs

Part A. Read each of the following paragraphs. Locate the topic sentence, the sentence that sums up the details expressed by the other sentences in the paragraph. Underline the entire topic sentence. The topic sentence is not necessarily the first sentence of a paragraph.

EXAMPLE:

One of the best-kept secrets of American history is that the 32nd President of the United States could not walk. Franklin Delano Roosevelt, who was elected by a landslide in 1932, had been struck by polio in 1921 at the age of 39. In more than 35,000 photographs in an official collection, however, only two show him in a wheelchair. None of the thousands of political cartoons published during Roosevelt's 12 years as president show him as being disabled.

1. Half the fun of popcorn is popping it. At one time, people believed that popcorn kernels burst when heated because they each contain a little devil who gets so mad when he is put on the fire that he explodes with rage. Actually, what happens to popcorn is simple. Scientists have determined that the popcorn kernel has a high amount of endosperm. The kernel is like an airtight jacket surrounding a moist interior. When heated, the moisture turns to steam, which expands until the jacket explodes, and the popcorn turns inside out.

2. In 1912, the Titanic, the safest and most modern ship ever built, set out at a record-breaking speed for its maiden voyage from New York

City to Europe, carrying nearly 2,000 people, including many celebrities. The ship began receiving radio signals from other ships in the area warning of a large number of icebergs. The ship's radio operator ignored the messages, considering it more important to transmit messages from the rich and famous passengers to their friends in Europe and America. If the captain had received and listened to the warnings, he could have slowed the ship down to avoid the disastrous collision that cost over a thousand lives. The sinking of the Titanic made many people aware of the radio as a means of communication for the first time.

3. When someone uses the name Bach by itself, it usually refers to Johann Sebastian Bach, who lived from 1685 to 1750. Bach, a composer, was considered the best keyboard player of his time. Bach's fame tends to make people forget that the rest of Bach's family was also very musical. Bach's family was musically active for seven generations; Bach was of the fifth generation. Bach married twice and was the father of 20 children. Historical information is available about some 60 Bachs, almost all of whom were musicians of some importance.

Part B. Each of the following topic sentences is ineffective because it is either too narrow or too broad. In the space provided, write TN after the sentence if it is too narrow; write TB if it is too broad.

EXAMPLE: Albert Einstein developed the theory of relativity.
 TB

4. An estimated 87 percent of professional boxers suffer brain damage. _____

5. Many African countries are poor. _____

6. The scientific name of the great blue heron is *Adea herodias.*

_____

Part C. Read the following paragraphs and decide which two methods are used to develop the controlling idea. In the space provided, write 1 if the method of supplying relevant facts is used; 2 for the use of examples; 3 for contrasting or comparing; or 4 for supplying reasons showing cause or effect to explain the main idea.

EXAMPLE:
 On the East Coast, there are many advantages to traveling by train over flying or driving for a quick business trip. For example, since most city train stations are right in the center of town, you will be only minutes away from your destination when your train arrives. The main advantage over driving is that you do not have to deal with the pressures of the highway; instead you can relax, catch up on your reading, or take a nap. Finally, an advantage people often don't think about is the fact that trains have a greater energy savings per passenger mile than cars or airplanes. **1, 2**

7. The space shuttle will bring about a major change in satellite services. Because the shuttle will be available for assembly and main-

tenance activities in space, it will be possible to make satellites much larger and more advanced. At the same time, equipment on the ground will become tiny, simple, portable, and inexpensive. As a result, many more people will be able to use satellite services. _____

8. Although many people consider meat to be an excellent source of protein, the value of meat protein is about the same when compared to other foods. Meat has 20 to 25 percent protein by weight, about the same as cheese, fish, some nuts, and beans. It is true that the protein in meat is not as easily used by the human body compared to the protein in nuts, seeds, and most legumes. However, the protein found in cheese, fish, milk, and eggs is more easily used than meat protein. Seafood ranks highest in both protein content and usability of its protein. _____

9. Most Americans suffer from dental disease. Every year, statistics suggest that people in this country are getting more cavities. In other countries, where people eat less processed and refined food, tooth decay is less of a problem. Thus the American diet may be largely to blame for the growing dental health problems of Americans.

_____

Part D. Each of the following paragraphs contains a sentence that is irrelevant to the main idea of the paragraph. Read the paragraphs and underline the irrelevant sentences.

EXAMPLE:

One useful way to save money is to pay yourself first. It is nice to have a convenient bank. Set aside the same amount for your savings account each month before paying your bills. This way, you get the first crack at your own money; then you can adjust your spending to the amount of money that is left.

10. The average reader reads about 250 words a minute. Very fast readers can cover 500 or 600 words or more a minute. When you increase your reading speed, you may not remember as much information from the text as you are used to. You may like to spend your free time watching television. When you take a speed-reading course, you will learn how to increase your speed without forgetting what you read. Good speed reading is a combination of quick eye movement and effective comprehension.

11. Medical researchers are working on new approaches to allergies such as hay fever. Many allergies are brought on by breathing the proteins contained in house dust, and the pollen of ragweed, trees, and bushes. When a hay fever sufferer's body tries to defend itself from the substance, it lets off a number of different chemicals, including histamines, which cause the signs of hay fever. Antihistamines have been used for a long time to fight hay fever. Now scientists are making drugs to fight some of the other chemicals involved. The flu is another common illness.

12. You can save money on gasoline if you keep your engine tuned to the manufacturer's specifications. Many people buy and replace their own air filters, spark plugs, and other parts. People also like to wash their cars, especially in the summer. As a consumer you should be aware that replacement parts can differ in quality. For example, a company may sell two air filters. The cheaper one is made of poorer quality paper when compared to a more expensive air filter. A good quality filter is important to the performance of your engine.

Part E. Each of the following paragraphs is not unified for two of the following reasons: (1) the topic sentence is too broad or too narrow; (2) the detail sentences are not arranged in a logical order; (3) the sentences do not flow smoothly because they lack transition words or appropriate repetition; and (4) there are sentences that are unrelated to the topic sentence or contain irrelevant details. In the space provided, use the numbers to identify these problems.

EXAMPLE: Researchers have for many years tried to teach chimpanzees and gorillas to communicate using language. Some of these apes have acquired small vocabularies in sign language or symbol systems. Scientists are still debating whether apes are capable of grammar or abstract expression. A pygmy chimpanzee named Kanzi seems to communicate better than other apes. She communicates using symbols. Her abilities are similar to those of a human in the second year of life. Kanzi's performance lends support to the belief that pygmy chimpanzees are the closest living relatives of the primates that came directly before humans in evolution. Spoken language is out of the question for apes because they are physically incapable of producing the sounds of human speech.   __2, 3__

13. The first woman to be a noted film maker was Alice Guy-Blaché. The French-born director was the first woman to run a movie studio in the United States. She directed 35 films for her own company in five years. In five years Guy-Blaché supervised 350 films in production. Of course, movies were all silent then. Her company, Solax, started operations in Queens, New York, in 1910. Many women have been noted film makers. In 1985 a film festival was held in Queens to honor the 75th anniversary of Solax.   _____

14. The world's energy crisis is out of control. Some people maintain that short-term surpluses of oil will help resolve energy problems. Such surpluses provide a lot of energy for a while. No temporary surplus will ever change the fact that the amount of oil in the world is limited.   _____

15. Today there are at least 30 different kinds of gazpacho. Andalusian peasants found many ways to make up for the lack of meat and poultry in southern Spain. For example, they developed the nutritious soup called gazpacho using tomatoes, green peppers, cucumbers, olive oil, and garlic. Bread and gazpacho, which was served cold, was a cooling and adequate midday meal. Another way to escape the heat was to take a siesta.   _____

Skill Unit 9: Using the Dictionary

Part A. Alphabetize each of the following sets of words by placing 1 next to the word that should appear first in each set, 2 next to the second word, and so on.

EXAMPLE:
- **2** general
- **5** granite
- **3** genetic
- **4** gradual
- **1** gear
- **6** green

1.
- ____ proud
- ____ price
- ____ pursue
- ____ purse
- ____ pearl
- ____ punish

2.
- ____ region
- ____ attitude
- ____ memory
- ____ transport
- ____ logical
- ____ explore

3.
- ____ freeze
- ____ fear
- ____ furnace
- ____ fair
- ____ flair
- ____ friend

Part B. Choose the correct phonetic spelling for each of the following words by putting a check next to your choice.

EXAMPLE: theater
- a. ✓ thē′ ə tər
- b. ____ thē a′ tər

4. amuse
- a. ____ a myus′
- b. ____ ə myooz′

5. cough
- a. ____ kof
- b. ____ coff

6. index

a. _____ in′ deks

b. _____ en′ dex

Part C. Each of the following words is misspelled. Find the correct spelling for each word on the sample dictionary page on page 21. In the space provided, rewrite each word, showing the correct spelling and using hyphens to show syllable division.

EXAMPLE: invurse **in-verse**

7. invisable _____

8. inventorry _____

9. investegate _____

Part D. Part One: For each of the following dictionary entries, use the spaces provided to write all the different forms of the word that are given. Then in parentheses write the part of speech the dictionary entry gives for each form.

EXAMPLE:

im·i·tate (im′ə tāt′) *vt.* -tat′ed, -tat′ing [< L. *imitatus*, pp. of *imitari*, to imitate] **1.** to seek to follow the example of; take as one's model or pattern **2.** to act the same as; impersonate; mimic **3.** to reproduce in form, color, etc.; make a duplicate or copy of **4.** to be or become like in appearance; resemble [glass made to *imitate* diamonds] —**im′i·ta·ble** (-tə b'l) *adj.* —**im′i·ta′tor** *n.*

imitate (verb)

imitated (verb)

imitating (verb)

imitable (adjective)

imitator (noun)

10.

com·pat·i·ble (kəm pat′ə b'l) *adj.* [ME. < ML. *compatibilis* < LL. *compati:* see COMPASSION] **1.** capable of living together harmoniously or getting along well together; in agreement; congruous **2.** that can be mixed without reacting chemically or interfering with one another's action: said of drugs, insecticides, etc. **3.** *Bot.* that can be cross-fertilized or grafted readily **4.** *TV* designating or of a system of color transmission that produces satisfactory black and white pictures on a standard monochrome receiver —**com·pat′i·bil′i·ty, com·pat′i·ble·ness** *n.* —**com·pat′i·bly** *adv.*

_____

_____

_____

_____

invention   741   **invisible**

the mind *[to invent excuses]* **2.** to think out or produce (a new device, process, etc.); originate, as by experiment; devise for the first time **3.** [Archaic] to find; discover

in·ven·tion (in ven'shən) *n.* [ME. *inuencioun* < OFr. *invencion* < L. *inventio*] **1.** an inventing or being invented **2.** the power of inventing; ingenuity or creativity **3.** something invented; *specif.,* *a)* something thought up or mentally fabricated; esp., a falsehood *b)* something originated by experiment, etc.; new device or contrivance **4.** *Music* a short composition, usually for a keyboard instrument, developing a single short motif in counterpoint; esp., any of a group of these by J. S. Bach

in·ven·tive (-tiv) *adj.* [ME. *inventif* < ML. *inventivus*] **1.** of invention **2.** skilled in inventing **3.** indicating an ability to invent *[inventive powers]* —**in·ven'tive·ly** *adv.* —**in·ven'tive·ness** *n.*

in·ven·tor (-tər) *n.* [L.] a person who invents; esp., one who devises a new contrivance, method, etc.

in·ven·to·ry (in'vən tôr'ē) *n., pl.* **-ries** [ML. *inventorium* < LL. *inventarium* < L. *inventus:* see INVENT] **1.** an itemized list or catalog of goods, property, etc.; esp., such a list of the stock of a business, taken annually **2.** the store of goods, etc. that are or may be so listed; stock **3.** any detailed list **4.** the act of making such a list —*vt.* **-ried**, **-ry·ing 1.** to make an inventory of **2.** to place on an inventory —*SYN.* see LIST —**take inventory 1.** to make an inventory of stock on hand **2.** to make an appraisal, as of one's skills, personal characteristics, etc. —**in'ven·to'ri·al** *adj.* —**in'ven·to'ri·al·ly** *adv.*

in·ve·rac·i·ty (in'və ras'ə tē) *n.* **1.** lack of veracity; untruthfulness **2.** *pl.* **-ties** a falsehood; lie

In·ver·ness (in'vər nes') **1.** former county of N Scotland, now part of the region of Highland: also **In'ver·ness'-shire** (-shir) **2.** burgh at the head of Moray Firth: pop. 30,000 —*n.* *[often i-]* *a)* an overcoat with a long, removable, sleeveless cape *b)* the cape: also **Inverness cape**

in·verse (in vurs'; *also, for adj. & n.,* in'vurs') *adj.* [L. *inversus,* pp. of *invertere*] **1.** inverted; reversed in order or relation; directly opposite **2.** *Math.* designating or of an operation which, when applied after a specific operation, cancels it *[subtraction is the inverse operation of addition]* —*n.* **1.** any inverse thing; direct opposite **2.** *Math. a)* the result of an inversion *b)* the result obtained after dividing 1 by the given number *[the inverse of x is 1/x]* —*vt.* **-versed'**, **-vers'ing** [Rare] to invert; reverse —**in·verse'·ly** *adv.*

inverse function the function obtained by expressing the independent variable of another function in terms of the dependent variable which is then regarded as a:. independent variable

in·ver·sion (in vur'zhən, -shən) *n.* [L. *inversio* < *inversus,* pp. of *invertere*] **1.** an inverting or being inverted **2.** something inverted; reversal **3.** *Chem. a)* a chemical change in which an optically active substance is converted into another substance having no effect, or the opposite rotatory effects, on the plane of polarization *b)* the conversion of an isomeric compound to its opposite **4.** *Gram. & Rhetoric* a reversal of the normal order of words in a sentence (Ex.: "said he" for "he said") **5.** *Math. a)* the process of using an opposite rule or method *b)* an interchange of the terms of a ratio **6.** *Meteorol.* an atmospheric condition in which a layer of warm air traps cooler air near the surface of the earth, preventing the normal rising of surface air **7.** *Music a)* the reversal of the position of the tones in an interval or chord, as by raising the lower tone by an octave, etc. *b)* the recurrence of a theme, fugue subject, motive, or figure in identical intervals and note values, but consistently in the opposite direction **8.** *Phonet.* a position of the tongue in which the tip is turned upward and backward **9.** *Psychiatry* *same as* HOMOSEXUALITY —**in·ver'sive** *adj.*

in·vert (in vurt'; *for adj. & n.,* in'vurt') *vt.* [L. *invertere* < *in-,* in, to, toward + *vertere,* to turn: see VERSE] **1.** to turn upside down **2.** to change to the direct opposite; reverse the order, position, direction, etc. of **3.** to subject to inversion (in various senses) **4.** *Math.* to divide 1 by (a given quantity) —*adj. Chem.* inverted *[invert sugar]* —*n.* **1.** an inverted person or thing **2.** *Psychiatry* same as HOMOSEXUAL —*SYN.* see REVERSE —**in·vert'i·ble** *adj.*

in·vert·ase (in vur'tās) *n.* [INVERT + -ASE] an enzyme, present in certain plants and in animal intestines, which changes sucrose into dextrose and fructose

in·ver·te·brate (in vur'tə brit, -brāt') *adj.* [ModL. *invertebratus*] **1.** not vertebrate; having no backbone, or spinal column **2.** of invertebrates **3.** having no moral backbone; lacking courage, resolution, etc. —*n.* any animal without a backbone, or spinal column; any animal other than a fish, amphibian, reptile, bird, or mammal

inverted comma [Brit.] *same as* QUOTATION MARK

inverted mordent *see* MORDENT

in·vert·er (in vur'tər) *n. Elec.* a device for transforming direct current into alternating current

invert sugar a mixture of dextrose and levulose in approximately equal proportions, found in fruits and produced artificially by the hydrolysis of sucrose

in·vest (in vest') *vt.* [L. *investire* < *in-,* in + *vestire,* to clothe < *vestis,* clothing: see VEST] **1.** to clothe; array; adorn **2.** *a)* to cover, surround, or envelop like, or as if with, a garment *[fog invests the city]* *b)* to endow with qualities, attributes, etc. **3.** to install in office with ceremony **4.** to furnish with power, privilege, or authority **5.** [Rare] to vest or settle (a power or right) in a person, legislative body, etc. **6.** to put (money) into business, real estate, stocks, bonds, etc. for the purpose of obtaining an income or profit **7.** to spend (time, effort, etc.) with the expectation of some satisfaction **8.** *Mil.* to hem in or besiege (a town, port, enemy salient, etc.) —*vi.* to invest money; make an investment —**in·ves'tor** *n.*

in·ves·ti·gate (in ves'tə gāt') *vt.* **-gat'ed**, **-gat'ing** [< L. *investigatus,* pp. of *investigare,* to trace out < *in-,* in + *vestigare,* to track < *vestigium,* a track] to search into so as to learn the facts; inquire into systematically —*vi.* to make an investigation —**in·ves'ti·ga·ble** (-gə b'l) *adj.* —**in·ves'ti·ga'tor** *n.*

in·ves·ti·ga·tion (in ves'tə gā'shən) *n.* [ME. *investigacioun* < MFr. < L. *investigatio*] **1.** an investigating or being investigated **2.** a careful search or examination; systematic inquiry —**in·ves'ti·ga'tion·al** *adj.*

SYN.—**investigation** refers to a detailed examination or search, often formal or official, to uncover facts and determine the truth *[the investigation of a crime]*; **probe** applies to an extensive, searching investigation, as by an appointed committee, of alleged corrupt practices, etc.; **inquest** now refers to a judicial inquiry, especially one conducted by a coroner to determine the cause of a suspicious death; **inquisition** strictly refers to any penetrating investigation, but because of its application to the ecclesiastical inquiries for the suppression of heresy, it now usually connotes ruthless, hounding persecution; **research** implies careful, patient study and investigation from original sources of information, as by scientists or scholars

in·ves·ti·ga·tive (in ves'tə gāt'iv) *adj.* [ML. *investigativus*] **1.** of or characterized by investigation **2.** inclined to investigate Also **in·ves'ti·ga·to'ry** (-gə tôr'ē)

in·ves·ti·tive (in ves'tə tiv) *adj.* [< L. *investitus,* pp. (see INVEST) + -IVE] **1.** that invests or can invest authority, etc. **2.** of such investing

in·ves·ti·ture (-chər) *n.* [ME. < ML. *investitura* < L. *investire*] **1.** a formal investing with an office, power, authority, etc., often with appropriate symbols, robes, etc. **2.** anything that clothes or covers; vesture **3.** *Feudal Law* ceremonial transfer of land to a tenant

in·vest·ment (in vest'mənt) *n.* **1.** an investing or being invested **2.** an outer covering **3.** *same as* INVESTITURE (sense 1) **4.** *a)* the investing of money *b)* the amount invested *c)* anything in which money is or may be invested

investment fund a trust or corporation that invests in securities the funds obtained from the sale of its own shares and distributes a return to its shareholders from the income on the securities

in·vet·er·ate (in vet'ər it) *adj.* [L. *inveteratus,* pp. of *inveterare,* to make or become old < *in-,* in + *vetus,* old: see WETHER] **1.** firmly established over a long period; of long standing; deep-rooted **2.** settled in a habit, practice, prejudice, etc.; habitual —*SYN.* see CHRONIC —**in·vet'er·a·cy** *n.* —**in·vet'er·ate·ly** *adv.*

in·vi·a·ble (in vī'ə b'l) *adj.* not viable; unable to live and develop normally —**in·vi'a·bil'i·ty** *n.*

in·vid·i·ous (in vid'ē əs) *adj.* [L. *invidiosus* < *invidia:* see ENVY] **1.** *a)* such as to excite ill will, odium, or envy; giving offense *b)* giving offense by discriminating unfairly *[invidious comparisons]* **2.** [Obs.] envious —**in·vid'i·ous·ly** *adv.* —**in·vid'i·ous·ness** *n.*

in·vig·i·late (in vij'ə lāt') *vi.* **-lat'ed**, **-lat'ing** [< L. *invigilatus,* pp. of *invigilare* < *in-,* in, on + *vigilare,* to watch] [Brit.] to monitor students during a written examination —**in·vig'i·la'tion** *n.*

in·vig·or·ate (in vig'ə rāt') *vt.* **-at'ed**, **-at'ing** [IN-¹ + VIGOR + -ATE¹] to give vigor to; fill with energy; enliven —*SYN.* see ANIMATE —**in·vig'or·a'tion** *n.* —**in·vig'or·a'tive** *adj.* —**in·vig'or·a'tor** *n.*

in·vin·ci·ble (in vin'sə b'l) *adj.* [ME. *invyncyble* < MFr. *invincible* < L. *invincibilis:* see IN-² & VINCIBLE] that cannot be overcome; unconquerable —**in·vin'ci·bil'i·ty**, **in·vin'ci·ble·ness** *n.* —**in·vin'ci·bly** *adv.*

‡**in vi·no ve·ri·tas** (in vē'nō ver'ə tas, vī'nō) [L.] in wine there is truth: a quotation from Pliny the Elder

in·vi·o·la·ble (in vī'ə lə b'l) *adj.* [MFr. < L. *inviolabilis*] **1.** not to be violated; not to be profaned or injured; sacred *[an inviolable promise]* **2.** that cannot be violated; indestructible *[the inviolable heavens]* —**in·vi'o·la·bil'i·ty** *n.* —**in·vi'o·la·bly** *adv.*

in·vi·o·late (in vī'ə lit, -lāt') *adj.* [ME. < L. *inviolatus:* see IN-² & VIOLATE] not violated; kept sacred or unbroken —**in·vi'o·la·cy** (-lə sē), **in·vi'o·late·ness** *n.* —**in·vi'o·late·ly** *adv.*

in·vis·i·ble (in viz'ə b'l) *adj.* [ME. < OFr. < L. *invisibilis*] **1.** not visible; that cannot be seen **2.** out of sight; not apparent **3.** too small or too faint to be seen; imperceptible; indistinct **4.** not publicized; kept hidden *[invisible assets]* —*n.* an invisible thing or being —**the Invisible 1.**

fat, āpe, cär; ten, ēven; is, bīte; gō, hôrn, tōōl, look; oil, out; up, fur; get; joy; yet; chin; she; thin, *then*; zh, leisure; ŋ, ring; ə for a in ago, e in agent, i in sanity, o in comply, u in focus; ' as in able (ā'b'l); Fr. bāl; ë, Fr. coeur; ö, Fr. feu; Fr. mon; ð, Fr. coq; ü, Fr. duc; r, Fr. cri; H, G. ich; kh, G. doch. See inside front cover. ☆ Americanism; ‡ foreign; * hypothetical; < derived from

11.

sub·mit (-mit′) vt. -mit′ted, -mit′ting [ME. submitten < L. submittere < sub-, under, down + mittere, to send: see MISSION] 1. to present or refer to others for decision, consideration, etc. 2. to yield to the action, control, power, etc. of another or others; also, to subject or allow to be subjected to treatment, analysis, etc. of some sort: often used reflexively 3. to offer as an opinion; suggest; propose —vi. 1. a) to yield to the power, control, etc. of another or others; give in b) to allow oneself to be subjected (to treatment, analysis, etc.) 2. to defer to another's judgment or decision 3. to be submissive, obedient, humble, etc. —SYN. see SURRENDER —sub·mit′ta·ble adj. —sub·mit′tal n. —sub·mit′ter n.

_____

_____

_____

_____

_____

12.

i·den·ti·fy (ī den′tə fī′, i-) vt. -fied′, -fy′ing [LL. identificare: see ff. & -FY] 1. to make identical; consider or treat as the same [to identify one's interests with another's] 2. to recognize as being or show to be the very person or thing known, described, or claimed; fix the identity of [to identify a biological specimen] 3. to connect, associate, or involve closely [to identify a person with a school of thought] 4. Psychoanalysis to make an identification of (oneself) with someone else: often used absolutely —vi. to put oneself in another's place, so as to understand and share the other's thoughts, feelings, problems, etc.; sympathize (with) — i·den′ti·fi′a·ble adj. —i·den′ti·fi′er n.

_____

_____

_____

_____

_____

Part Two: Read the four definitions in the following dictionary entry for the noun bachelor. Then read the following sentences and choose the correct definition for each sentence by writing the number of the definition in the space next to each sentence.

bach·e·lor (bach′l ər, bach′lər) n. [ME. bacheler < OFr. bachelier < ML. baccalaris: see BACCALAUREATE] 1. orig., in the feudal system, a young knight and landholder who served under another's banner: also bach′e·lor-at-arms′ 2. an unmarried man 3. a person who is a BACHELOR OF ARTS (or SCIENCE, etc.) 4. a young male animal, specif. a fur seal, that has not yet mated —adj. of or for a bachelor —bach′e·lor·hood′, bach′e·lor·ship′ n.

EXAMPLE: __3__   The bachelors smiled for their relatives' cameras after the graduation ceremony.

13. _____   After the third broken-off engagement, Victor knew that he would probably be a bachelor for the rest of his life.

14. _____ Having gorged themselves on fish, the bachelors lay on the rocks, basking in the sun.

15. _____ After serving a number of years as a bachelor, Alfred returned to his native fiefdom.

Part E. Find each of the following words on the sample dictionary page on page 24. In the space provided, write the etymology of each word.

EXAMPLE: cable **M.E. & O.Fr. < LL. <u>capulum</u>, a cable, rope < L. <u>capere</u>, to take hold**

16. cabaret _____

17. caboose _____

18. cabin _____

Skill Unit 10: Spelling

Part A. Write each of the following words correctly by filling in the blanks with either <u>ie</u> or <u>ei</u>.

EXAMPLE: **she<u>i</u>k**

1. rel ____ ve   **2.** perc ____ ve

3. s ____ ze   **4.** v ____ n

Part B. Combine one of the prefixes in List A with a word base from List B to form the new word that best fits the meaning of each sentence. Write the word in the space provided.

List A		**List B**
Prefix	**Meaning**	**Word Base**
co	together, with	appear
dis	the opposite of	dawn
pre	before, earlier	locate
re	again	lucky
un	not, the opposite of	operate

EXAMPLE: The baker works during the **predawn** hours.

5. The job will be impossible unless we _____.

6. Many people consider 13 to be an _____ number.

7. Because of rising real estate costs, the company decided to _____ to a less expensive site.

8. The magician made the rabbit _____.

ca. 1. cathode 2. centiare 3. circa 4. *Law* case; cases

C/A 1. capital account 2. credit account 3. current account

C.A. 1. Central America 2. Confederate Army

C.A., c.a. 1. chartered accountant 2. chief accountant 3. chronological age 4. commercial agent 5. consular agent 6. controller of accounts 7. crown agent

Caa·ba (kä′ba) *same as* KAABA

CAB Civil Aeronautics Board

cab¹ (kab) *n.* [< CABRIOLET] 1. a horse-drawn carriage, esp. one for public hire 2. a taxicab 3. the place in a locomotive, motor truck, crane, etc. where the operator sits

cab² (kab) *n.* [Heb. (II Kings 6:25) *qab*, hollow vessel < *qābab*, to hollow out] an ancient Hebrew dry measure, equal to about two quarts

ca·bal (ka bal′) *n.* [Fr., intrigue, society (popularized in England from the initials of the ministers of Charles II) < ML. *cabbala*, CABALA] 1. a small group of persons joined in a secret, often political intrigue; junta 2. the intrigues of such a group; plot —*vi.* -balled′, -bal′ling to join in a cabal; plot —*SYN.* see PLOT

cab·a·la (kab′ə lə, kə bäl′ə) *n.* [ML. *cabbala* < Heb. *qabbālāh*, received lore, tradition < *qābal*, to receive, take] 1. an occult philosophy of certain Jewish rabbis, esp. in the Middle Ages, based on a mystical interpretation of the Scriptures 2. any esoteric or secret doctrine; occultism

‡ca·ba·let·ta (kä′bä let′tä) *n.* [It., dim. of *cabala*, intrigue: see prec.] the last section of an aria or duet sung in rapid uniform rhythm

cab·a·lism (kab′ə liz′m) *n.* 1. occult doctrine based on the cabala 2. any occult doctrine —**cab′a·list** *n.* —**cab·a·lis′tic** (-lis′tik) *adj.* —**cab′a·lis′ti·cal·ly** *adv.*

ca·bal·le·ro (kab′ə ler′ō, -əl yer′ō; *Sp.* kä′bä lye′rō) *n., pl.* -ros (-ōz; *Sp.* -rōs) [Sp. < LL. *caballarius* < L. *caballus*, horse: see CAVALIER] 1. a Spanish gentleman, cavalier, or knight ☆2. [Southwest] *a)* a horseman *b)* a lady's escort

☆**ca·ba·na** (kə bän′ə, -ban′ə, -bän′yə, -ban′yə) *n.* [Sp. *cabaña* < LL. *capanna*, hut] 1. a cabin or hut 2. a small shelter used as a bathhouse at a beach, pool, etc.

cab·a·ret (kab′ə rā′, kab′ə rā′) *n.* [Fr., pothouse, < MDu. *cabret* < *cambret* < OFr. dial. *camberete*, dim. of *cambre*, CHAMBER] 1. a restaurant or café with dancing, singing, skits, etc. as entertainment 2. this kind of entertainment

cab·bage¹ (kab′ij) *n.* [ME. & OFr. *caboche*, earlier *caboce*, ult. < ? L. *caput*, the head] 1. a common vegetable (*Brassica oleracea capitata*) of the mustard family, with thick leaves formed into a round, compact head on a short, thick stalk 2. an edible bud at the end of the branch on some palm trees 3. [Slang] paper money

cab·bage² (kab′ij) *vt., vi.* -baged, -bag·ing [prob. < Fr. *cabasser*, to put into a basket, steal < *cabas*, basket < VL. *capacium*, reed basket] [Brit. Slang] to steal —*n.* [prob. < the *v.*] cloth snippets appropriated by a tailor when cutting out clothes

☆**cabbage bug** *same as* HARLEQUIN BUG

cabbage butterfly a common white butterfly (*Pieris rapae*), whose green larvae feed upon cabbage and related plants

cabbage palm 1. any of several palms with terminal buds used as a vegetable: also **cabbage tree** 2. *same as* PALMETTO (sense 1): also ☆**cabbage palmetto**

cab·bage·worm (-wurm′) *n.* the larval stage of any insect that feeds on cabbage, as the caterpillar of the cabbage butterfly

cab·ba·la (kab′ə lə, kə bäl′ə) *n.* *same as* CABALA —**cab′ba·lism** *n.* —**cab′ba·list** *n.* —**cab′ba·lis′tic** *adj.*

cab·driv·er (kab′drīv′ər) *n.* a person who drives a cab: also [Colloq.] **cab′by, cab′bie** (-ē), *pl.* -bies

Cab·ell (kab′'l), **James Branch** 1879–1958; U.S. novelist

ca·ber (kä′bər, kā′-) *n.* [Gael. *cabar*] a long, heavy pole thrown in a Gaelic game to test muscular strength

Cab·er·net (kab′ar nā′; *Fr.* kȧ ber nā′) *n.* [*also* c-] any of several red wines, esp. **Cabernet Sau·vi·gnon** (sō vē nyôn′) [*also* c- s-]: originally from the Bordeaux region of France

Ca·be·za de Va·ca (kä be′thä *the* vä′kä), **Ál·var Nú·ñez** (äl′vär nōō′nyeth) 1490?–1557?; Sp. explorer in the Americas

☆**cab·e·zon** (kab′ə zän′) *n.* [Sp. < *cabeza*, a head < L. *capitium*, covering for the head < *caput*, the HEAD] any of several fishes, esp. a large sculpin (*Scorpaenichthys marmoratus*) found along the Pacific Coast of N. America

cab·in (kab′'n) *n.* [ME. *caban* < OFr. *cabane* < Pr. *cabana* < LL. *capanna*, hut] 1. a small, one-story house built simply or crudely, as of logs ☆2. any simple, small structure designed for a brief stay, as for overnight [tourist *cabins*] 3. a private room on a ship, as a bedroom or office 4. a roofed section of a small boat, as a pleasure cruiser, for the passengers or crew 5. the enclosed section of an aircraft, where the passengers sit; also, the section housing the crew or used for cargo ☆6. the living quarters in a trailer —*vt.* to confine in or as in a cabin; cramp

cabin boy a boy whose work is to serve and run errands for the officers and passengers aboard a ship

cabin class a class of accommodations on a passenger ship, below first class and above tourist class

☆**cabin cruiser** a powerboat with a cabin and the necessary equipment for living on board

Ca·bin·da (kə bin′də) exclave of Angola, on the W coast of Africa: 2,800 sq. mi.; pop. 51,000

cab·i·net (kab′ə nit, kab′nit) *n.* [Fr., dim. of *cabine*; orig. obscure] 1. a case or cupboard with drawers or shelves for holding or storing things [a china *cabinet*, a medicine *cabinet*] 2. a boxlike enclosure, usually decorated, that houses all the assembled components of a record player, radio or television receiver, etc. 3. formerly, *a)* a private council room *b)* a meeting held there ☆4. [*often* C-] a body of official advisers to a president, king, governor, etc.: in the U.S., comprised of the heads of the various governmental departments 5. [Archaic] a small, private room —*adj.* 1. of a kind usually displayed in cabinets [*cabinet* curios] 2. of or made by a cabinetmaker 3. of a political cabinet

cab·i·net·mak·er (-māk′ər) *n.* a workman who makes fine furniture, decorative moldings, etc. —**cab′i·net·mak′ing** *n.*

☆**cab·i·net·work** (-wurk′) *n.* 1. articles made by a cabinetmaker 2. the work or art of a cabinetmaker Also **cab′i·net·ry** (-rē)

☆**cabin fever** a condition of increased anxiety, tension, boredom, etc. caused by living for some time in a confined space or an isolated area, esp. in winter

ca·ble (kā′b'l) *n.* [ME. & OFr. < LL. *capulum*, a cable, rope < L. *capere*, to take hold] 1. a thick, heavy rope, now often of wire strands 2. the strong, heavy chain attached to a ship's anchor: anchor cables were formerly of rope 3. *same as* CABLE LENGTH 4. a bundle of insulated wires through which an electric current can be passed: telegraph or telephone cables are often laid under the ground or on the ocean floor ☆5. a cablegram —*vt.* -bled, -bling 1. to fasten or furnish with a cable or cables 2. to transmit by undersea cable 3. to send a cablegram to —*vi.* to send a cablegram

Ca·ble (kā′b'l), **George Washington** 1844–1925; U.S. novelist

CABLE

☆**cable car** a car drawn by a moving cable, as across a canyon, up a steeply inclined street, etc.

☆**ca·ble·gram** (-gram′) *n.* a message sent by undersea cable

ca·ble-laid (kā′b'l lād′) *adj.* made of three plain-laid ropes twisted together counterclockwise

cable length a unit of nautical measure variously equal to 720 feet (120 fathoms), 600 feet (100 fathoms), or, in the British navy, 607.6 feet (1/10 of a nautical mile): also **cable's length**

☆**cable railway** a street railway on which the cars are pulled by a continuously moving underground cable to which they are attached by a grip that can be released to halt the car

cable stitch a type of raised stitch used in knitting: it resembles ropes twisted together

ca·blet (kāb′lit) *n.* [CABL(E) + -ET] a cable-laid rope less than ten inches in circumference

☆**cable television** a television system in which a high antenna and one or more dish antennas receive signals from distant and local stations, electronic satellite relays, etc. and transmit them by direct cable to the receivers of persons subscribing to the system

cab·man (kab′mən) *n., pl.* -men (-mən) *same as* CABDRIVER

ca·bob (kə bäb′) *n.* [Ar. *kabāb*] *same as* KEBAB

ca·bo·chon (kab′ə shän′; *Fr.* kȧ bô shōn′) *n.* [Fr. < *caboche*, the head: see CABBAGE¹] 1. any precious stone cut in convex shape, polished but not faceted 2. the style of cutting such a stone

ca·bom·ba (kə bäm′bə) *n.* [ModL. < Sp.] any of a genus (*Cabomba*) of plants of the waterlily family, esp. a plant (*Cabomba caroliniana*) with submerged, finely divided leaves and rounded, floating ones, used as in aquariums

☆**ca·boo·dle** (kə bōō′d'l) *n.* [*ca-*, colloq. intens. prefix + BOODLE] [Colloq.] lot; group [the whole *caboodle*]

ca·boose (kə bōōs′) *n.* [MDu. *kabuys, kambuis* (<?), ship's galley] 1. [Brit.] a ship's galley or kitchen ☆2. the trainmen's car on a freight train, usually at the rear

Cab·ot (kab′ət) 1. **John**, (It. name *Giovanni Caboto*) 1450?–1498?; It. explorer in the service of England: discovered coast of N. America (1497) 2. **Sebastian**, 1476?–1557; Eng. cartographer & explorer: son of prec.

cab·o·tage (kab′ə tij, -täzh′) *n.* [Fr. < *caboter*, to sail along the coast < *cabo*, cape < Sp. < L. *caput*, HEAD] 1. coastal navigation and trade, esp. between ports within a country 2. air transport within a country 3. the right to engage in cabotage, esp. as granted to foreign carriers

ca·bret·ta (kə bret′ə) *adj.* [< Sp. *cabra*, goat (< L. *caper*, he-goat: see CAPRIOLE) + It. suffix *-etta*] designating or of a soft leather made from a special kind of sheepskin

ca·bril·la (kə bril′ə, kə brē′yə) *n.* [Sp., prawn, dim. of *cabra*, goat] any of various edible, perchlike fishes (family Serranidae) found off Florida, the West Indies, etc.

Ca·bri·ni (kə brē′nē) , **Saint Frances Xavier** (called *Mother Cabrini*) 1850–1917; U.S. nun, born in Italy: first U.S. citizen canonized: her day is Dec. 22

cab·ri·ole (kab′rē ōl′) *n.* [Fr.: see ff.] 1. a leg of a table, chair, etc. that curves outward and then tapers inward down to a clawlike foot grasping a ball 2. *Ballet* a leap in which one leg is extended horizontally and the feet are struck quickly together

CABRIOLE

Part C. Add the suffixes to the word bases as directed. You may have to add, drop, or change letters before the suffix can be added.

EXAMPLE: day + ly = ___**daily**___

9. big + est = _____

10. busy + ness = _____

11. use + ing = _____

12. true + ly = _____

Part D. Write the correct plural of each of the following nouns in the space provided.

EXAMPLE: passerby ___**passersby**___

13. child _____

14. tomato _____

15. scarf _____

16. rash _____

Part E. Each of the following words is incorrectly spelled. Write the correct spelling in the space provided.

EXAMPLE: diffrent ___**different**___

17. athelete _____

18. Febuary _____

19. miniture _____

20. interpret _____

Part F. Each of the following words is spelled incorrectly. Write the correct spelling in the space provided.

EXAMPLE: cemetary ___**cemetery**___

21. canidate _____

22. solem _____

23. roomate _____

24. exibit _____

Skill Unit 11: Using Frequently Confused Words Correctly

Part A. For each of the following sentences, underline the correct possessive pronoun or contraction from the pair of words in parentheses.

EXAMPLE: (Your, **You're**) kidding!

1. Owls do (they're, their) hunting at night.

2. Are you the man (whose, who's) pen I borrowed?

3. The cat lost (it's, its) way home.

4. Don't forget (your, you're) gloves.

5. I'll tell you when (its, it's) time to stop.

Part B. For each of the following sentences, underline the correct homonym from each pair in parentheses.

EXAMPLE: She ordered some (**stationery,** stationary) with Arnold's initials on it.

6. I'd like to (complement, compliment) you on a job well done.

7. If you don't behave, you won't have any (dessert, desert).

8. Pamela stood up and (led, lead) the guests in a round of songs.

9. Let me know (weather, whether) you will attend.

10. Just then a (heard, herd) of deer appeared.

Part C. For each of the following sentences, underline the correct word from each pair in parentheses.

EXAMPLE: Kevin packed enough (cloths, **clothes**) for two weeks.

11. It was so humid, I felt I could hardly (breath, breathe).

12. Marta had an easier time (than, then) Henry.

13. Despite the surprise pizza party, office (moral, morale) stayed pretty low.

14. Paula was ready to (quit, quite) last week.

15. When Janet turns 70, she will be (illegible, eligible) for retirement.

Skills Correlation Chart for Pretest

After you check your answers, look at the following chart. Circle the number of each question you missed. Then study the subskill in which the skills for the questions you missed are explained.

		Question Number	Subskill Number	Subskill Name	Page Number
Skill Unit One	WRITING SIMPLE SENTENCES	1 2 3 4 5 6 7 8 9 10 11 12 13 14 15 16 17 18 19 20	1A 1B 1C 1D	Recognizing the Parts of a Simple Sentence Identifying Verbals in Simple Sentences Making Subjects and Verbs Agree in Number Choosing a Verb to Agree With Special Subjects	pages 30–37 pages 37–46 pages 46–54 pages 54–60
		If you correctly answered 15 or fewer questions, you should study the subskills in Unit One for the questions you missed. If you correctly answered 16 or more of the questions in Unit One, go to Skill Unit Two.			
Skill Unit Two	WRITING COMPOUND SENTENCES	1 2 3 4 5 6 7 8 9 10 11 12 13 14 15	2A 2B 2C	Constructing Compound Sentences Punctuating Compound Sentences Revising Run-On Sentences	pages 64–70 pages 70–75 pages 75–81
		If you correctly answered 11 or fewer questions, you should study the subskills in Unit Two for the questions you missed. If you correctly answered 12 or more of the questions in Unit Two, go to Skill Unit Three.			
Skill Unit Three	WRITING COMPLEX SENTENCES	1 2 3 4 5 6 7 8 9 10 11 12 13 14 15 16 17 18 19 20	3A 3B 3C 3D	Identifying Dependent Clauses and Complex Sentences Using Adjective Clauses in Complex Sentences Using Adverb Clauses in Complex Sentences Using Noun Clauses in Complex Sentences	pages 85–89 pages 90–99 pages 100–105 pages 105–112
		If you correctly answered 15 or fewer questions, you should study the subskills in Unit Three for the questions you missed. If you correctly answered 16 or more of the questions in Unit Three, go to Skill Unit Four.			
Skill Unit Four	USING SENTENCE PUNCTUATION	1 2 3 4 5 6 7 8 9 10 11 12 13 14 15 16 17 18 19 20	4A 4B 4C 4D	Using Periods, Question Marks, and Exclamation Points Using Commas Using Apostrophes Punctuating Quotations	pages 115–118 pages 118–125 pages 125–130 pages 130–134
		If you correctly answered 15 or fewer questions, you should study the subskills in Unit Four for the questions you missed. If you correctly answered 16 or more of the questions in Unit Four, go to Skill Unit Five.			
Skill Unit Five	USING MORE SENTENCE PUNCTUATION	1 2 3 4 5 6 7 8 9 10 11 12 13 14 15	5A 5B 5C	Using Semicolons Using Colons Using Parentheses and Dashes	pages 137–142 pages 142–146 pages 146–152
		If you correctly answered 11 or fewer questions, you should study the subskills in Unit Five for the questions you missed. If you correctly answered 12 or more of the questions in Unit Five, go to Skill Unit Six.			
Skill Unit Six	USING MODIFIERS IN SENTENCES	1 2 3 4 5 6 7 8 9 10 11 12 13 14 15 16	6A 6B 6C 6D	Positioning Single-Word Modifiers Positioning Phrase Modifiers Positioning Clause Modifiers Correcting Dangling Modifiers	pages 156–163 pages 163–169 pages 169–172 pages 172–177
		If you correctly answered 11 or fewer questions, you should study the subskills in Unit Six for the questions you missed. If you correctly answered 12 or more of the questions in Unit Six, go to Skill Unit Seven.			

		Question Number	Subskill Number	Subskill Name	Page Number
Skill Unit Seven	WRITING EFFECTIVE SENTENCES	1 2 3 4 5	7A	Using Parallel Structure	pages 182–190
		6 7 8 9 10	7B	Using Verb Tenses and Voices Correctly	pages 190–198
		11 12 13 14 15	7C	Using Correct Pronoun Reference and Pronoun Agreement	pages 198–202
		16 17 18 19 20	7D	Avoiding Sentence Fragments	pages 202–206

If you correctly answered 15 or fewer questions, you should study the subskills in Unit Seven for the questions you missed.
If you correctly answered 16 or more of the questions in Unit Seven, go to Skill Unit Eight.

		Question Number	Subskill Number	Subskill Name	Page Number
Skill Unit Eight	WRITING UNIFIED PARAGRAPHS	1 2 3	8A	Recognizing Topic Sentences	pages 210–218
		4 5 6	8B	Writing Effective Topic Sentences	pages 218–223
		7 8 9	8C	Identifying Methods of Paragraph Development	pages 223–232
		10 11 12	8D	Recognizing Irrelevant Details	pages 232–236
		13 14 15	8E	Writing Unified Paragraphs	pages 236–241

If you correctly answered 11 or fewer questions, you should study the subskills in Unit Eight for the questions you missed.
If you correctly answered 12 or more of the questions in Unit Eight, go to Skill Unit Nine.

		Question Number	Subskill Number	Subskill Name	Page Number
Skill Unit Nine	USING THE DICTIONARY	1 2 3	9A	Finding Words in the Dictionary by Using Alphabetical Order and Guide Words	pages 244–250
		4 5 6	9B	Using the Dictionary to Pronounce Words Correctly	pages 250–254
		7 8 9	9C	Using Entry Words to Spell and Divide Words Correctly	pages 255–257
		10 11 12 13 14 15	9D	Identifying Parts of Speech and Selecting the Correct Definition	pages 257–262
		16 17 18	9E	Locating the Etymology of a Word	pages 262–264

If you correctly answered 13 or fewer questions, you should study the subskills in Unit Nine for the questions you missed.
If you correctly answered 14 or more of the questions, go to Skill Unit Ten.

		Question Number	Subskill Number	Subskill Name	Page Number
Skill Unit Ten	SPELLING	1 2 3 4	10A	Spelling Words with ie and ei	pages 266–269
		5 6 7 8	10B	Spelling Words Formed by Adding Prefixes	pages 270–273
		9 10 11 12	10C	Spelling Words Formed by Adding Suffixes	pages 274–280
		13 14 15 16	10D	Spelling Plurals	pages 280–284
		17 18 19 20	10E	Pronouncing Words Correctly to Aid Spelling	pages 284–286
		21 22 23 24	10F	Using Memory Aids to Improve Spelling	pages 286–292

If you correctly answered 18 or fewer questions, you should review the subskills in Unit Ten for the questions you missed.
If you correctly answered 19 or more of the questions in Unit Ten, go to Skill Unit Eleven.

		Question Number	Subskill Number	Subskill Name	Page Number
Skill Unit Eleven	USING FREQUENTLY CONFUSED WORDS CORRECTLY	1 2 3 4 5	11A	Identifying Possessive Pronouns and Contractions	pages 294–297
		6 7 8 9 10	11B	Distinguishing Meanings of Common Homonyms	pages 297–303
		11 12 13 14 15	11C	Learning the Difference Between Words That Are Often Confused	pages 303–306

If you correctly answered 11 or fewer questions, you should review the subskills in Unit Eleven for the questions you missed.
If you correctly answered 12 or more of the questions in Unit Eleven, you have achieved mastery.

Skill Unit 1
WRITING SIMPLE SENTENCES

What Skills You Need to Begin: You should be able to recognize and identify the different parts of speech, particularly nouns and verbs. You may refresh your memory by referring to the charts on the inside covers of this book.

What Skills You Will Learn: When you complete this skill unit, you will be able to identify the different parts of a simple sentence. You will be able to identify verbals and verbal phrases. You will also be able to identify subject-verb combinations and determine whether a subject is singular or plural. Finally, you will be able to choose verb forms that agree with their subjects in number.

Why You Need These Skills: The simple sentence is the basic building block of all writing. Once you can create a simple sentence correctly, you can begin to construct longer and more complex sentences and join these sentences together to form paragraphs, letters, and essays. In this skill unit, you will learn how to create simple sentences from subject-verb combinations and how to make sure that these combinations fit the rules of Standard English.

How You Will Show What You Have Learned: You will take the Self-Check at the end of this unit on page 60. The Self-Check consists of three parts.

In Part A, you will be given ten sets of four sentences. Above each set, a sentence part has been identified. You must decide in which sentence the underlined word or words are used as that part of a sentence.

In Part B, you will be given five sets of four sentences. Each set includes three sentences in which the verbs agree in number with their subjects and one sentence in which the verb does not agree in number with its subject. You must identify the one sentence in which the verb does not agree with its subject.

In Part C, you will write eight complete sentences. In each sentence the verb and the subject must agree in number.

If you identify the correct sentences in 8 of 10 sets in Part A, identify the incorrect sentences in 4 of 5 sets in Part B, and use subject-verb combinations correctly in 7 of 8 sentences in Part C, you will have shown that you have mastered these skills.

If you feel that you have already mastered these skills, turn to the end of the unit and complete the Self-Check on page 60.

Subskill 1A: Recognizing the Parts of a Simple Sentence

When you complete this subskill, you will be able to recognize and identify the following parts of a simple sentence: simple subject, simple predicate (or verb), objects (direct object, indirect object, object of the preposition), and modifiers.

Writing is a building process. You build paragraphs, letters, essays, and stories by putting together a series of sentences. You build sentences by putting together a series of words. Each word has a special role to play in the sentence. When you can recognize the different parts of a sentence, you will better understand how the parts work together to convey the meaning of the sentence.

Dividing Sentences into Two Parts

The definition of a **sentence** is: **a group of words that contains a subject and verb and expresses a complete thought.** Every sentence must, therefore, contain a subject and a verb. The subject is a person or thing that the sentence is about. The verb tells about the action of the subject or links the subject to another word in the sentence. You can divide sentences into two parts—the **subject,** and the verb part or **predicate.** Each part can consist of either one word or several words.

Notice how each sentence below is divided into two parts. The first part contains the subject, and the second part contains the verb. In these examples, we'll mark the subjects S and the predicates P.

S   P
Ellen / argued with her daughter.

S   P
The girl in the blue dress / is Ellen's daughter.

S   P
Ellen and her daughter / had made an agreement.

S   P
The girl / disobeyed.

The part of the sentence in which the subject is presented is called the **complete subject.** The part of the sentence in which the verb is presented is called the **complete predicate.**

Recognizing Simple Subjects

The **simple subject** of a sentence is part of the complete subject. It is the most important part. The simple subject is usually a noun or pronoun. The simple subject of a sentence always **answers the question "Who" or "What?"** The rest of the complete subject tells something about the simple subject.

Look at the following sentence. The complete subject, labeled CS, is bracketed. The simple subject is underlined.

$$\overbrace{\text{Many \underline{women} in the class}}^{\text{CS}} \text{ have jobs during the day.}$$

The simple subject—whom the sentence is about—is women. The other words in the complete subject—many and in the class—tell about, or modify, the simple subject.

In some sentences, the simple subject may be two or more words joined together as a **compound subject,** labeled below as Comp S:

$$\overbrace{\text{Flowers and trees}}^{\text{Comp S}} \text{ bloom in the spring.}$$

In this sentence, something is being said about both flowers and trees. Both nouns are part of the compound subject.

In the sentence below something is being said about both he and I. Both pronouns are part of the compound subject.

$$\overbrace{\text{He and I}}^{\text{Comp S}} \text{ play basketball.}$$

Recognizing Simple Predicates

The **simple predicate** of a sentence is part of the complete predicate. It is the most important part. The simple predicate **is a verb or verb phrase.** The rest of the complete predicate tells more about the verb.

Look at the following sentence. The complete predicate, labeled CP, has been bracketed. The simple predicate, or verb, is underlined.

$$\text{Many women in the class } \overbrace{\underline{\text{have}} \text{ jobs during the day.}}^{\text{CP}}$$

The simple predicate of the sentence is have. The complete predicate is have jobs during the day.

Just as a sentence can have two or more subjects, it can sometimes have two or more verbs or verb phrases. This is called the **compound predicate** or **compound verb** and **is made up of two or more verbs or verb phrases which tell about the action of the subject or which link the subject to another word.** In the following examples, the compound verbs have been underlined:

We worked and played at camp.

Worked and played both tell what the subject we did.

Summer and autumn <u>have come</u> and <u>gone</u>.

<u>Have come</u> and <u>gone</u> make up a compound verb telling what the compound subject <u>summer</u> and <u>autumn</u> has done.

Exercise 1 for Subskill 1A

Read each sentence. Underline the simple subject once. Underline the simple predicate twice.

EXAMPLE: The <u>carpenter</u> <u>will repair</u> and <u>repaint</u> the old cabinet.

1. Several new programs were shown on television last season.

2. This week, furniture and new appliances are on sale.

3. Many students have jobs and attend classes after work.

4. The new employees were skillful and received raises.

5. Alice and Charles wrote and directed the new play together.

Check your answers on page 7 in the Answer Key for Book Three. If you correctly underlined the simple subject and the simple predicate in all 5 sentences, continue reading. If not, review the discussion about subjects and predicates on pages 30–32. Then go on to the next section of Subskill 1A. NOTE: The skills in this exercise will be used in some of the items in the Supplemental Exercise for Subskill 1A on page 36.

Recognizing Objects

A sentence may contain several other nouns or pronouns in addition to the subject. These other nouns and pronouns usually serve as objects. They may be objects of the preposition, direct objects, or indirect objects.

A noun or pronoun that comes almost immediately after a preposition in a sentence is called the object of the preposition. A preposition and its object make up a prepositional phrase. A prepositional phrase may be part of the complete subject or the complete predicate in a sentence. In these examples, the prepositional phrases, marked <u>Prep Phrase</u>, have been bracketed and the objects of the prepositions have been underlined:

The hinges on the <u>door</u> squeaked noisily.

I poured some oil onto the <u>hinges</u>.

In the first sentence <u>door</u> is the object of the preposition <u>on</u>. In the second sentence <u>hinges</u> is the object of the preposition <u>onto</u>.

Two other types of objects usually occur in the predicate part of the sentence. These objects tell more about the action of the verb in the sentence. Look at the following sentences:

The wind rustled the trees.

I gave my nephew a new watch.

In the first sentence, <u>trees</u> explains what the wind rustled. A **noun or pronoun that receives the action of a verb is called a direct object.** A direct object answers the question: "What or who received the action of the verb?"

The second sentence contains two objects, <u>nephew</u> and <u>watch</u>. Ask yourself what was given, a nephew or a watch? Since the watch was the thing <u>I</u> gave, <u>watch</u> is the direct object. The word <u>nephew</u> explains "to whom" or "for whom" the action occurs. <u>Nephew</u> is an **indirect object** in the sentence. When an indirect object is used in a sentence, it will usually appear before a direct object. In these examples, we'll mark the indirect objects <u>IO</u> and the direct objects <u>DO</u>.

IO   DO
My father threw me the ball.

           IO   DO
The waitress handed the customer a menu.

In the first sentence, <u>ball</u> explains "what" my father threw. <u>Ball</u> is the direct object. <u>Me</u> tells "to whom" the ball was thrown. <u>Me</u> is the indirect object.

In the second sentence, <u>menu</u> is the direct object. It answers the question "What was handed?" The indirect object is <u>customer</u> because it tells "to whom" the menu was handed.

Recognizing Predicate Nominatives

A **predicate nominative is a noun or pronoun that follows a linking verb.** It identifies the subject or gives another name for the subject. Predicate nominatives most often follow the forms of linking verbs <u>be</u> (am, is, are) and <u>become</u>. In the following sentences, we'll mark the predicate nominatives <u>P Nom</u> and the linking verbs <u>LV</u>.

LV   P Nom
My third grade teacher was Ms. Smith.

The predicate nominative is the proper noun <u>Ms. Smith</u>. It gives another name for the subject <u>teacher</u>. The linking verb <u>was</u> connects the subject and the predicate nominative.

LV   P Nom
The astronaut became a national hero.

The predicate nominative is the noun <u>hero</u>. It renames the subject <u>astronaut</u>. The subject and the predicate nominative are linked by the linking verb <u>became</u>.

LV P Nom
The candidate with the most votes was you.

The pronoun you is the predicate nominative in this sentence. It renames the subject candidate. The subject is connected to the predicate nominative by the linking verb was.

Exercise 2 for Subskill 1A

One word is underlined in each of the following sentences. In the blank following each sentence, write whether the underlined word is a Predicate Nominative (P Nom), Direct Object (DO), Indirect Object (IO), or the Object of a Preposition (O Prep).

EXAMPLES: George Washington was our first President.   P Nom

The company gave the manager a generous raise.   IO

1.   The children in the schoolyard were having fun.   _____

2.   I gave you the wrong directions yesterday.   _____

3.   The young singer became an overnight sensation.   _____

4.   Todd sent his family a picture postcard from Hawaii.   _____

5.   Ann was never a member of this club.   _____

Check your answers on page 7 in the Answer Key for Book Three. If you correctly identified the underlined words in all 5 sentences, continue reading. If not, review the discussion about predicate nominatives and objects on pages 32–34. Then go on to the next section of Subskill 1A. NOTE: The skills in this exercise will be used in some of the items in the Supplemental Exercise for Subskill 1A on page 36.

Recognizing Modifiers

A sentence may also contain one or more adjectives or adverbs that tell more about the nouns and verbs in the sentence. Remember that adjectives modify nouns or pronouns by telling "what kind", "how many", "how much", or "which one." Adverbs modify action verbs, adjectives, and other adverbs. Adverbs tell "how", "where", "when", and "to what extent." Adjectives and adverbs are called modifiers. In the following examples, we'll mark adjectives Adj and adverbs Adv.

```
       Adj    S    V    Adv           Adj
The elderly woman walked slowly on the uneven sidewalk.
```

```
     Adv   S  V    Adj            Adj
Yesterday, I found a valuable antique in a thrift shop.
```

In the first sentence, elderly modifies the subject noun woman. Slowly modifies the verb walked and uneven modifies the noun sidewalk.

In the second sentence, <u>yesterday</u> modifies the verb <u>found</u>. <u>Valuable</u> modifies the noun <u>antique</u> and <u>thrift</u> modifies the noun <u>shop</u>. Each of the modifiers tells you something more about the word it modifies. NOTE: In this unit, articles (a, an, the) are not marked <u>Adj</u> even though they are always adjectives which modify nouns.

Prepositional phrases can also serve as modifiers. They may serve as adjectives and modify nouns or pronouns. Or they may serve as adverbs and modify verbs. In the following examples, the prepositional phrases are labeled <u>Prep Phrase</u>.

Prep Phrase   Prep Phrase

All <u>of us</u> are going <u>to the circus</u>.

The prepositional phrase <u>of us</u> serves as an adjective. It modifies the pronoun <u>all</u> by answering the question "Which one?" The prepositional phrase <u>to the circus</u> serves as an adverb. It modifies the verb phrase <u>are going</u> by answering the question "Where?"

Prep Phrase

The girl <u>with the pink hair</u> is going, too.

The prepositional phrase <u>with the pink hair</u> serves as an adjective. It modifies the noun <u>girl</u> by answering the question "Which one?"

Exercise 3 for Subskill 1A

Below is a chart for identifying modifiers and the words they modify. The modifiers in each sentence are given in the first column. Decide what type of modifier is being used: an adjective, an adverb, or a prepositional phrase. Then write <u>Adj</u>, <u>Adv</u> or <u>Prep Phrase</u> in the second column. In the third column, write the word that is being modified.

	Modifier	Type of Modifier	Word Being Modified
EXAMPLE:	choral	Adj	class
	to a football game	Prep Phrase	went
1.	fresh		
	completely		
2.	three		
	onto the stage		
3.	with the badge		
	police		
4.	some		
	early		
5.	impatiently		
	on the platform		

EXAMPLE: The choral group went to a football game.

1. Fresh flowers completely covered the table.

2. Three youngsters carried flags onto the stage.

3. The woman with the badge is a police officer.

4. Some workers finished the work early.

5. Passengers waited impatiently on the platform.

Check your answers on page 8 in the Answer Key for Book Three. If you correctly identified the type of modifier and the word it modified in all 5 sentences, go to Subskill 1B. If not, do the Supplemental Exercise for Subskill 1A. NOTE: The Supplemental Exercise for Subskill 1A provides practice in all the material found in this subskill. You may want to do this exercise to check your memory of all the things you have learned in this subskill.

Supplemental Exercise for Subskill 1A

This exercise provides practice in all the material found in this unit.

A simple sentence can be divided into two main parts: the subject part and the verb part, or predicate. The core of the subject part is the simple subject—a noun or pronoun that tells who or what the sentence is about. The core of the predicate is the verb, or simple predicate, that tells about the action of the subject or links the subject to another word in the sentence.

A sentence will often contain other nouns or pronouns besides the subject. These nouns or pronouns may act as objects in the sentence. They are usually objects of the preposition, direct objects, or indirect objects. Nouns or pronouns that follow a linking verb identify or rename the subject. They are predicate nominatives.

Modifiers are also often included in a sentence. Modifiers describe, or tell more about, the other words in the sentence. Adjectives, adverbs, and prepositional phrases are modifiers.

Check your ability to identify the different parts of a simple sentence by completing the following Supplementary Exercise.

Read sentences 1–10 and draw a line between the subject and predicate parts of the sentence. Label the underlined word or words in the sentence S for subject, V for verb, O for object, M for modifier, or P Nom for predicate nominative.

	S		O
EXAMPLE:	The <u>meteorologist</u> on television / predicted <u>rain</u> tomorrow.		

1. I <u>brought</u> an umbrella to work <u>yesterday</u> and <u>lost</u> it.

2. The <u>buses in my town</u> usually run late on rainy days.

3. My brother is an <u>employee</u> at a <u>firm</u> near mine.

4. I gave <u>him</u> my <u>umbrella</u>.

5. Because of the pouring rain, my <u>brother</u> and <u>I</u> were late.

6. The workers in my office usually eat lunch <u>at the coffee shop</u>.

7. Today, however, I ate a <u>sandwich</u> at my <u>desk</u>.

8. The <u>cold</u>, <u>gray</u> rain darkened the sky.

9. It was a long and dreary <u>day</u>.

10. I <u>could</u> hardly <u>wait</u> for the end of the day.

Check your answers on page 8 in the Answer Key for Book Three. If you correctly answered 8 of 10 items, go to Subskill 1B. If not, ask your instructor for help.

Subskill 1B: Identifying Verbals in Simple Sentences

When you complete this subskill, you will be able to identify verbals and verbal phrases and how they are used in simple sentences.

Some verb forms may be used as other parts of speech: nouns, adjectives, or adverbs. **When a verb form is being used as another part of speech, it is called a verbal.** There are three types of verbals: **participles, gerunds,** and **infinitives.**

Recognizing Participles

There are two verb forms that may be participial verbals: **present participles** and **past participles.** A present participle **is formed from the main form of a verb + ing.** When a present participle is used as a verb, it is always used with a form of the verb <u>be</u>:

I <u>am studying</u> now.

Jerry <u>was running</u> very fast from the fire.

A past participle is usually formed from the main form of a verb + d or ed. When a past participle is used as a verb, it is always used with a form of the verb <u>have</u>:

I <u>have</u> always <u>admired</u> her sense of humor.

Marie <u>had delivered</u> the package just in time.

Irregular verbs have past participles with various endings:

Orville <u>has burnt</u> the soup again!

Leon <u>has sung</u> in many different choirs.

When a past or a present participle is used with a helping verb, it acts as a verb. Sometimes, however, these verb forms are used without helping verbs, to modify nouns. Then they act as adjectives. A past participle or present participle that acts as an adjective is known as a **participial verbal,** or **participle.** In this unit, we shall use the term <u>participle</u> to refer to a participial verbal. The underlined words in the following examples are participles that modify the nouns that follow them:

The <u>sleeping</u> soldier dreamed of home.

The <u>falling</u> snowflakes blanketed the highway.

He repaired the <u>broken</u> vase.

The <u>delighted</u> audience cheered the band.

Look at the following two sentences. In which sentence does the underlined word act as an adjective?

    (1) He was <u>flying</u> to Detroit the next day.

    (2) Juan watched the <u>flying</u> birds.

In sentence 1, <u>was flying</u> is a verb phrase. You can tell that <u>flying</u> is being used as a verb in this sentence because it is used with the helping verb <u>was</u>. In sentence 2, <u>flying</u> acts as an adjective to modify <u>birds</u>. The verb in this sentence is <u>watched</u>. In sentence 2, the word <u>flying</u> is a participial verbal, or participle.

The following two sentences contain past participles. Can you tell which sentence uses the past participle as a verb, and which uses it as a verbal?

    (1) Gina served the <u>canned</u> fruit in a glass bowl.

    (2) Carl had <u>canned</u> some fruit the day before.

In sentence 1, <u>canned</u> is a participial verbal that acts as an adjective to modify <u>fruit</u>. The verb in this sentence is <u>served</u>. In sentence 2, <u>canned</u> is a verb. It is part of the verb phrase <u>had canned</u>.

Participial Phrases

A phrase is a group of words that doesn't contain a subject or a verb and is used as a part of speech. A phrase that includes a participle is called a **participial phrase.**

Walking to work, Terry stepped on a nail.

The participial phrase is <u>walking to work</u>; the participle in the phrase is <u>walking</u>.

Participial phrases may be used as adjectives or adverbs. In the following examples, the participial phrases are labeled <u>Part Phrase</u>.

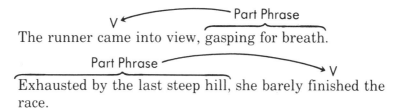

Trees blown by the wind are in constant motion.

The police spotted the car speeding on the highway.

In the first example, the participial phrase <u>blown by the wind</u> is used as an adjective to modify the noun <u>trees</u>. In the second example, the participial phrase <u>speeding on the highway</u> modifies the noun <u>car</u>.

The runner came into view, gasping for breath.

Exhausted by the last steep hill, she barely finished the race.

In the first example, the participial phrase <u>gasping for breath</u> modifies the verb <u>came</u>. In the second example, the participial phrase <u>exhausted by the last steep hill</u> modifies the verb <u>finished</u>.

Check your understanding of participles and participial phrases by doing the following exercise.

Exercise 1 for Subskill 1B

Underline the participles or participial phrases in each of the following sentences. If a sentence doesn't contain a participle or participial phrase, write X in the blank next to the line.

EXAMPLES: Elena reassured the <u>worried</u> mother.   _____

I had wanted a new dress for the party.   __X__

1. The farmers were hoping for more rain.   _____

2. We saw the plane coming down the runway.   _____

3. The waitress brought us the fried eggs.   _____

4. Shaking my head, I picked up the laughing child.   _____

5. The old car was shaking and rattling loudly.   _____

6. I didn't enjoy the party in that crowded room. _____

7. The crates damaged by the storm should be opened first. _____

8. We stretched our cramped legs after the long drive. _____

9. I awoke to the sound of a rooster crowing outside my window. _____

10. Lucia's order was filled right away. _____

Check your answers on pages 8 and 9 in the Answer Key for Book Three. If you correctly identified the participles and participial phrases in all 10 sentences, continue reading. If not, review the discussion about participles on pages 37–39. Then go on to the next section of Subskill 1B. NOTE: The skills in this exercise will be used in some of the items in the Supplemental Exercise for Subskill 1B on page 44.

Recognizing Gerunds

Like some participles, **gerunds** are verbals ending in ing. But gerunds do not function as adjectives. They function as nouns. In the following sentences, the verbs are marked V and the gerunds are underlined:

S   V
Jogging is a popular form of exercise.

V   V DO
The champion did not like losing.

V   O Prep
She bought new equipment for climbing.

V P Nom
My favorite hobby is painting.

Notice that gerunds may be subjects, direct objects, objects of prepositions, or predicate nominatives. Can you identify the gerund in the following example?

I am looking for a book on gardening.

There are two words in this sentence that end in ing: looking and gardening. However, only one of these words is used as a noun. Looking is part of the verb phrase am looking. Therefore, looking is not a gerund. Gardening is used as the object of the preposition on in the prepositional phrase on gardening. Therefore, gardening is a gerund in this sentence.

Gerund Phrases

A gerund phrase is made up of a gerund and words that relate to it. The words in a gerund phrase act together as a noun. The gerund phrases in the following examples are labeled Ger Phrase:

V   Ger Phrase
We were annoying them by talking during the show.

The gerund phrase is <u>talking during the show</u>. The entire phrase is the object of the preposition <u>by</u>. The word <u>annoying</u> is part of the verb phrase <u>were annoying</u>. Here is another example:

Ger Phrase

<u>Driving through a blizzard</u> can be dangerous.

In this example, the gerund phrase <u>driving through a blizzard</u> is the subject of the sentence. Can you identify the gerund phrase in the following example?

Frank enjoys early morning jogging.

The gerund phrase in this sentence is <u>early morning jogging</u>. The entire phrase is the direct object of the verb <u>enjoys</u>. Notice that the gerund <u>jogging</u> is the last word in the phrase. Sometimes, the gerund in a gerund phrase comes at the end.

Check your understanding of gerunds and gerund phrases by doing the following exercise.

Exercise 2 for Subskill 1B

Underline the gerunds or gerund phrases in each of the following sentences. If a sentence doesn't contain a gerund or gerund phrase, write <u>X</u> in the blank next to the line.

EXAMPLE: The campers enjoyed <u>swimming</u>. _____

1.   Suddenly, the dog began barking. _____

2.   Alex is planning on buying a new car. _____

3.   Ann likes fresh water fishing. _____

4.   Washing the dishes is the most unpleasant part of cooking.

_____

5.   Have you been looking for a new job? _____

6.   Thank you for listening to me. _____

7.   The boss was asking about you. _____

8.   I hate working late on Fridays. _____

9.   They watched TV before sleeping. _____

10.   Her job on weekends is mowing lawns and trimming bushes.

_____

Check your answers on page 9 in the Answer Key for Book Three. If you correctly identified the gerunds and gerund phrases in all 10 sentences, continue reading. If not, review the discussion about gerunds on pages 40–41. Then go on to the next section of Subskill 1B. NOTE:

The skills in this exercise will be used in some of the items in the Supplemental Exercise for Subskill 1B on page 44.

Recognizing Infinitives

Infinitives are verb forms consisting of the word <u>to</u> + the main form of the verb. The infinitives are underlined in the following examples:

Charlene helped us <u>to light</u> a fire.

<u>To sing</u> well is a wonderful talent.

The artist used charcoal <u>to draw</u>.

Infinitives may act as nouns, adjectives, or adverbs. The infinitives in the following examples act as nouns. They are marked <u>S</u> when they are subjects and <u>DO</u> when they are direct objects:

$$S$$
To succeed requires hard work.

$$S$$
To err is human.

$$DO$$
They really want to go.

$$DO$$
The baby started to cry.

Infinitives may also act as adjectives or adverbs. The infinitives in the following examples are labeled <u>Adj</u> when they act as adjectives and modify nouns. They are labeled <u>Adv</u> when they act as adverbs and modify verbs or adjectives.

N ← Adj
Mendez is the candidate to elect.

N ← Adj
She is a good person to trust.

V ← Adv
The athlete tightened his muscles to run.

V ← Adv
The artist used charcoal to draw.

Adj   Adv
He was foolish to try.

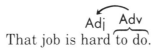

That job is hard to do.

Sometimes the word <u>to</u> in front of an infinitive is left out of a sentence. The missing <u>to</u> is said to be understood in these cases. That is, its meaning is understood even though the word isn't actually being used. Look at the following sentences:

Please help my carry the package.

Don't you dare take a chance.

The word <u>to</u> is left out of the infinitives in these sentences. It is understood that the meanings of these sentences are:

Please help me (to) carry the package.

Don't you dare (to) take a chance.

Infinitive Phrases

An infinitive phrase is made up of an infinitive and the words that relate to it. In the following sentences, the infinitive phrases are labeled <u>Inf Phrase</u>:

Inf Phrase

To play the piano well requires years of practice.

Inf Phrase

She hopes to be the new candidate.

Infinitives may act as nouns, adjectives, or adverbs. In the following example, the infinitive phrase acts as a noun:

Inf Phrase

To win the election will not be an easy task.

The infinitive phrase <u>to win the election</u> acts as a noun. In this case, it is the subject of the sentence. Infinitive phrases may also act as nouns that are direct objects:

Inf Phrase

He wanted to earn a good living.

The infinitive phrase <u>to earn a good living</u> is the direct object of the verb <u>wanted</u>.

In the following sentences, the infinitive phrases act as adjectives or adverbs:

N ← Inf Phrase

Her desire to succeed at her job never wavered.

$$\text{Adj} \overset{\frown}{\quad} \text{Inf Phrase}$$
A good budget is hard to plan quickly.

In the first example, the infinitive phrase <u>to succeed at her job</u> acts as an adjective, modifying the noun <u>desire</u>. In the second example, the infinitive phrase <u>to plan quickly</u> acts as an adverb, modifying the adjective <u>hard</u>.

Check your understanding of infinitives and infinitive phrases by doing the following exercise.

Exercise 3 for Subskill 1B

Underline the infinitives or infinitive phrases in each of the following sentences. If a sentence doesn't contain an infinitive or infinitive phrase, write X in the blank next to the line.

EXAMPLE: Carlos decided <u>to leave work early</u>. _____

1. To find a good hotel was first on their list. _____

2. She tried to find her way home. _____

3. I went to the diner on the corner for lunch. _____

4. We made a campfire to roast marshmallows. _____

5. Do you want to go to the movies? _____

6. Ed gave us a letter to mail. _____

7. Did he send a letter to you? _____

8. This Monday, Juanita is going to take her road test. _____

9. To own my own farm has been my life-long dream. _____

10. You must be at least 18 years old to enter this contest. _____

Check your answers on page 9 in the Answer Key for Book Three. If you correctly identified the infinitives and infinitive phrases in all 10 sentences, go to Subskill 1C. If not, do the Supplemental Exercise for Subskill 1B. NOTE: The Supplemental Exercise for Subskill 1B provides practice in all the material found in this subskill. You may want to do this exercise to check your memory of all the things you have learned in this subskill.

Supplemental Exercise for Subskill 1B

This exercise provides practice in all the material found in the subskill.

In Standard English sentences, some verb forms can be used as other parts of speech: nouns, adjectives, or adverbs. When a verb is used as another part of speech, it is called a verbal. Three types of verbals are participles, gerunds, and infinitives.

Participial verbals have two forms: present participles and past participles. A present participle is formed from the main form of a verb and ing. When a present participle is used as a verb, it is always used with a form of the helping verb be. A past participle is usually formed from the main form of a verb and d or ed. When a past participle is used as a verb, it is always used with a form of the helping verb have.

A past participle or present participle that acts as an adjective is a participial verbal, or participle. A participial phrase is a group of words that doesn't contain a subject or verb, but does contain a participle. Participial phrases can be used as adjectives or adverbs.

Gerunds, like some participles, are also formed by verbals ending in ing. Gerunds do not function as adjectives; they function as nouns. A gerund phrase is made up of a gerund and words that relate to it. The words in a gerund phrase act together as a noun.

Infinitives are verb forms consisting of the word to and the main form of the verb. Infinitives can act as nouns, adjectives, or adverbs. An infinitive phrase is made up of an infinitive and the words that relate to it.

Read each of the following sentences carefully. If a sentence contains a verbal or verbal phrase, underline it. Then identify what kind of verbal is being used by writing participle, gerund, or infinitive in the blank provided. If the sentence does not contain a verbal or verbal phrase, put an X in the blank provided.

EXAMPLES: My uncle is running for mayor. _____X_____

The man running for mayor is my uncle. __participle__

1. The falling snow blanketed the city. _____

2. I told the anxious child not to be afraid. _____

3. Margo was calling about the party all morning long. _____

4. Frightened by the sudden noise, our kitten ran under the couch. _____

5. Sometimes I actually enjoy cleaning my apartment. _____

6. Is Eric still looking for a job? _____

7. To go to the movies is one of my greatest pleasures. _____

8. My cousin Beatrice sells used cars. _____

9. We are considering buying one. _____

10. On icy roads, you should drive into a skid to avoid an accident. _____

11. Next summer, my family is moving to Winnipeg. _____

12. The worried mother was looking everywhere for her child.

_____

13. My favorite winter sport is skiing. _____

14. Her leg, broken by the sudden fall, would not completely heal for several weeks. _____

15. It took an hour for the water in the muddy pipes to drain.

_____

Check your answers on page 9 in the Answer Key for Book Three. If you correctly identified the verbals or verbal phrases in 12 of 15 sentences, go to Subskill 1C. If not, ask your instructor for help.

Subskill 1C: Making Subjects and Verbs Agree in Number

When you complete this subskill, you will be able to choose verb forms that agree with their subjects in number.

Forming sentences that are meaningful and correct is an important skill. To form a correct sentence, you must make sure that the subject and verb in the sentence agree in number. In other words, you must use a singular subject (one) with a singular form of a verb, and you must use a plural subject (more than one) with a plural form of a verb.

Identifying Singular and Plural Verb Forms

English verbs usually have different forms with different subjects in the present tense. Most English verbs are formed according to a specific pattern. We will use the verb live to illustrate this pattern:

	Singular	Plural
1ST PERSON	I live	we live
2ND PERSON	you live	you live
3RD PERSON	he, she, it singular nouns { lives	they plural nouns { live

Note that the verb changes form only in the third person singular. The third person singular form of a regular English verb usually adds an s.

Some English verbs are irregular. The two helping verbs that you frequently use in sentences are irregular. Here are the present tense forms of the verb have:

	Singular	**Plural**
1ST PERSON	I have	we have
2ND PERSON	you have	you have
3RD PERSON	he, she, it singular nouns } has	they plural nouns } have

The verb have changes form in the third person singular to has.

Here are the present tense forms of the verb be:

	Singular	**Plural**
1ST PERSON	I am	we are
2ND PERSON	you are	you are
3RD PERSON	he, she, it singular nouns } is	they are plural nouns } are

The forms of the verb be are am in the first person singular, is in the third person singular, and are in all other cases.

When we are concerned about the number of a verb, we almost always refer to the third person forms, in which the singular is different from the plural in the present tense. Throughout this unit, we will use the terms **singular verb** and **plural verb** to mean the third person forms.

Choosing a Verb to Agree with a Noun or Pronoun

A singular subject requires a singular form of a verb. The singular forms of verbs end in s or es:

    S   V
Jane searches the classified ads every day for a new car.

      S V
My dog likes to bark at cars.

Notice that the subject in these examples is a singular noun and the verb form ends in s or es. The subjects and verbs in these sentences agree in number.

A plural subject requires a plural form of a verb. The plural forms of verbs do not end in s:

S   V

They search the classified ads every day for a new car.

S   V

My dogs like to bark at cars.

The subjects and verbs in these sentences agree in number.

In a verb phrase, only the helping verb needs to agree in number with the subject. Helping verbs that are singular usually end in s. Helping verbs that are plural do not end in s. The helping verbs in the following examples have been underlined:

SINGULAR: Fred is working hard.   Rudy was shopping.

  PLURAL: They are working hard.   Rudy and Tom were shopping.

SINGULAR: Fred has been working hard.

  PLURAL: They have been working hard.

Notice that only the first helping verb in a verb phrase needs to agree with the subject.

To be sure that your subjects and verbs always agree, first determine whether your subject is singular or plural. Then choose the verb form that agrees with the subject. If the subject is third person singular (he, she, it, or a singular noun), the verb must be singular (end in s or es). If the subject is third person plural (they or a plural noun), the verb must be plural (not end in s or es).

Exercise 1 for Subskill 1C

Read each sentence and do the following:

- Find the subject and write it on the line provided.

- Write whether the subject is singular or plural.

- Underline the verb form that agrees with the subject.

EXAMPLE: The new uniforms (is, are) hanging in the closet.

              uniforms—plural

1. She (like, likes) her new job more than her old one.

_____

2. Jim and Marie (play, plays) baseball on Friday nights.

_____

3. Children (has, have) often played in this park.

    _____

4. He (enjoy, enjoys) diving.

    _____

5. They (was, were) listening to old Beatles albums all night.

    _____

Check your answers on page 10 in the Answer Key for Book Three. If you correctly answered all 5 items, continue reading. If not, review the discussion about subject-verb agreement on pages 46–48. Then go on to the next section of Subskill 1C. NOTE: The skills in this exercise will be used in the Supplemental Exercise for Subskill 1C on page 53.

Special Singular and Plural Nouns

It is easy to tell whether most nouns are singular or plural. Plural nouns are usually formed by adding s or es to the ends of singular nouns:

> SINGULAR: book   chair   dog
> PLURAL: books   chairs   dogs

Sometimes, however, it is not easy to tell whether a noun is singular or plural. It is important to know whether a noun is singular or plural so you can choose the right verb to agree with it.

Nouns That Always End in s

The following nouns always end in s but are singular in meaning:

> measles   mumps   mathematics   civics   news

For example, measles is a singular noun; it is one disease. Mathematics is a singular noun; it is one subject. Use a singular verb to agree with these nouns:

> Mathematics is my favorite subject.

On the other hand, the following nouns are used in the plural form only:

> scissors   tongs   shorts   pants

You'll have no problem with these words if you remember that scissors and tongs have two handles, and that trousers and shorts have two legs. Use a plural verb to agree with these nouns:

> The scissors are on the table.

Nouns That Always Have the Same Form

A few nouns—usually the names of animals—have the same form for the singular and plural.

sheep   deer   trout   moose

Although these words are spelled the same in the singular and plural, their number depends on whether you refer to one, or more than one. Use a singular verb with one of these nouns when the meaning of the noun is singular. Use a plural verb when the meaning of the noun is plural:

> SINGULAR: One sheep is in the meadow.
> PLURAL: Many sheep are in the meadow.

Collective Nouns

A collective noun names a group or collection of persons or things that are considered as one unit:

herd   team   class   jury   crowd   audience

Collective nouns are singular when the group is thought of as a unit, but plural when the context of the sentence shows that members of the group are thought of as individuals acting separately.

> SINGULAR: The herd of cattle is stampeding.
> PLURAL: The herd of cattle are receiving their shots.

In the first sentence, herd is singular because it refers to a single unit. The singular verb is agrees with the subject. In the second sentence, herd refers to a number of individual animals that make up that herd. Therefore, herd is plural, and the plural verb are is used with it.

> SINGULAR: The jury was deliberating.
> PLURAL: The jury were shaking their heads in
>   bewilderment.

In the first sentence, jury is thought of as one unit, so jury is singular, and the singular verb was is used. In the second sentence, the several members of the jury are being thought of as individuals. In this case, jury is plural. The plural verb were is used to agree with the subject.

Exercise 2 for Subskill 1C

Underline the verb that agrees with the subject in each sentence.

EXAMPLE: Trout (is, are) abundant in the lakes of Minnesota.

1. The entire class (was, were) promoted to the next grade.

2. The class (is, are) bringing their donations for the charity drive.

3. Mumps (is, are) a common childhood disease.

4. Those deer always (drinks, drink) at this stream.

5. Your shorts (is, are) in the top drawer.

Check your answers on page 10 in the Answer Key for Book Three. If you chose the correct verbs in all 5 sentences, continue reading. If not, review the discussion about special singular and plural nouns on page 49 and page 50. NOTE: The skills in this exercise will be used in some of the sentences in the Supplemental Exercise for Subskill 1C on page 53.

Singular and Plural Pronouns

A pronoun is a word that takes the place of a noun. Like nouns, then, pronouns can be singular or plural. Three groups of pronouns that are often used as subjects of simple sentences are personal pronouns, interrogative pronouns, and indefinite pronouns. You should learn to recognize which pronouns are singular and which are plural so you can choose the right verb to agree with them. Personal pronouns take the place of specific persons or things. Interrogative pronouns ask about persons or things.

	Singular	Plural
Personal pronouns 1st person 2nd person 3rd person	I you he, she, it	we you they
Interrogative pronouns	who	who
	what	what

Note that the pronouns you, who, and what have the same form in both the singular and the plural. The pronoun you always takes a plural verb even if the meaning of you is singular. The pronouns who and what, however, take singular verbs when their meanings are singular and plural verbs when their meanings are plural. In the following sentences, you, who, and what are used as singular and plural pronouns.

SINGULAR: You are an honest man.
PLURAL: You are excellent workers.
SINGULAR: Who is that woman?
PLURAL: Who are those people?
SINGULAR: What is your name?
PLURAL: What are the answers to the problems?

Indefinite pronouns refer to people or things that are not specified or clearly identified. Indefinite pronouns can be singular or plural. Some indefinite pronouns can be either singular or plural, depending on the noun to which they refer. The following chart illustrates the indefinite pronouns that are singular, plural or both:

Indefinite Pronouns			
Singular		**Plural**	**Singular or Plural**
other	nothing	both	all
another	anything	few	any
everybody	something	many	more
anybody	everything	others	most
nobody	each	several	none
somebody	either		some
one	neither		
anyone	little		
someone	much		
everyone	no one		

Notice that pronouns ending in other, body, one, and thing are singular. These pronouns take singular verbs:

> Everything is in its place.
> Everyone is at his or her desk.

Notice that the meanings of the plural indefinite pronouns each implies "more than one." The plural pronouns take plural verbs:

> Both are invited to the dance.

> Several of the witnesses are present.

> Many have cast their votes.

The indefinite pronouns all, none, any, more, most, and some may be singular or plural, depending on the noun they refer to.

> All of the cake was eaten.

All refers to cake. Cake is singular; therefore, all is singular in this sentence, and the singular verb was is used.

> All of the tickets were sold.

All refers to tickets. Tickets is plural; therefore, all is plural in this sentence, and the plural verb were is used.

Check your understanding of singular and plural pronouns by completing the following exercise.

Exercise 3 for Subskill 1C

Underline the verb that agrees with the subject in each sentence.

EXAMPLE: You   (is, <u>are</u>)   the smartest person in the class.

1.   Who (is, are) your favorite actors?

2.   Who (was, were) the first person to walk on the moon?

3.   Everyone (is, are) going to the picnic.

4.   Several (is, are) riding bicycles.

5.   Most of the coffee (has, have) been drunk.

6.   Most of the guests (has, have) gone.

7.   Each (has, have) earned a black belt in karate.

8.   You (run, runs) very fast.

9.   Nobody (want, wants) to go swimming.

10.   Some of the insurance money (is, are) being used to buy a new car.

Check your answers on page 10 in the Answer Key for Book Three. If you correctly answered all 10 items, go to Subskill 1D. If not, do the Supplemental Exercise for Subskill 1C. NOTE: The Supplemental Exercise for Subskill 1C provides practice in all the material found in this subskill. You may want to do this exercise to check your memory of all the things you have learned in this subskill.

Supplemental Exercise for Subskill 1C

This exercise provides practice in all the material found in this subskill.

In Standard English sentences, a verb must agree with its subject in number. You must use a singular verb with a singular subject and a plural verb with a plural subject. Here is a good hint to help you choose verbs that agree with subjects: Nouns that end in <u>s</u> or <u>es</u> are usually plural; verbs that end in <u>s</u> or <u>es</u> are always singular.

Sometimes, it is difficult to tell whether a noun is singular or plural. Some nouns that end in <u>s</u>, like <u>mumps</u>, <u>measles</u>, <u>mathematics</u>, and <u>civics</u>, are actually singular in meaning and therefore take singular verbs. Some nouns that end in <u>s</u>, like <u>scissors</u> and <u>pants</u>, are plural in form, even when they refer to one item. These nouns take plural verbs. Nouns like <u>sheep</u>, <u>fish</u>, and <u>deer</u> have the same form whether they are singular or plural. And some nouns, called collective nouns, can be singular or plural, depending on whether you are considering the group as a whole or are considering the individual members of the group. To choose a correct verb to agree with these nouns, you must consider the meaning of the noun in the sentence.

Pronouns can also be singular or plural. The personal pronouns I, he, she, and it are singular. The personal pronouns we and they are plural. The pronoun you and the interrogative pronouns who and what may be considered singular or plural. However, you always takes a plural verb while who and what take a singular or plural verb depending on their meanings in the sentence. Indefinite pronouns that end in other, body, one, and thing are singular and take singular verbs. Indefinite pronouns that imply "more than one," such as both, few, many, and several are plural and take plural verbs. Indefinite pronouns such as all, any, none, and some can be either singular or plural depending on the nouns they refer to in a sentence. When their meanings are singular, they take singular verbs. When their meanings are plural, they take plural verbs.

Underline the verb that agrees with the subject in each sentence.

EXAMPLES: The floor   (has, have)   been tiled.
            Who   (is, are)   those people with the sunglasses and trench coats?

1. Both   (is, are)   too tired to go with you.

2. The steel scissors   (is, are)   in the sewing box.

3. None of the ice cream   (is, are)   left.

4. Many deer   (is, are)   going hungry this year.

5. The entire team   (was, were)   booed off the field.

6. No one   (has, have)   seen the moose.

7. That moose   (is, are)   hiding behind the bushes.

8. Stan   (is, are)   going to bring the potato chips.

9. What   (is, are)   the matter with you?

10. You   (is, are)   obviously too tired to go out tonight.

Check your answers on page 10 in the Answer Key for Book Three. If you chose the correct verb in 8 of 10 sentences, go to Subskill 1D. If not, ask your instructor for help.

Subskill 1D: Choosing a Verb to Agree with Special Subjects

When you complete this subskill, you will be able to choose the right verb to agree with compound subjects and with subjects that are not obvious.

Choosing a Verb for a Compound Subject

Generally, use a plural verb with two subjects that are joined by and.

V
Allen and Ronnie are good friends.

On rare occasions, a compound subject with and requires a singular verb.

V
Ham and eggs is my favorite breakfast.

Use is if you are referring to a single breakfast order called "ham and eggs." Use are if you are referring to two separate grocery items to be purchased:

V
Ham and eggs are going up in price.

When two subjects are joined by or, nor, either-or, neither-nor, or not only-but also, the verb should agree in number with the subject closest to the verb.

V
Either Tom or Mary has been adjusting the television set again.

Has is a singular verb. It agrees in number with the singular noun Mary. Either Tom or Mary is a compound subject; it is not a plural subject. Tom and Mary would require a plural verb because two subjects joined together by and form a plural subject. Or indicates a choice of just one subject or the other.

V
Either Tom or his sisters have been adjusting the TV again.

Either Tom or his sisters is a compound subject. The choice is to make the verb agree with the single noun Tom or with the plural noun sisters. Since sisters is closest to the verb, the verb must agree with sisters.

V
Neither his sisters nor Tom has touched the TV set.

Has agrees with the simple subject closest to it, Tom, which is a singular noun.

Practice choosing verb forms with compound subjects by completing the following exercise.

Exercise 1 for Subskill 1D

Read each sentence and do the following:

- Find the subject and write it on the line provided.

- Indicate whether it is singular or plural.

- Underline the Standard English verb form that agrees with the subject.

EXAMPLE: You and your brother (is, <u>are</u>) good in marksmanship.

<u>   You and your brother–plural   </u>

1. Mary or Sue (have, has) your book.

_____

2. Macaroni and cheese (are, is) my favorite dish.

_____

3. Randy and I (play, plays) tennis all day.

_____

4. Neither his father nor his grandparents (was, were) born in this country.

_____

5. Either Nancy or I (drive, drives) the children to school most mornings.

_____

Check your answers on pages 10 and 11 in the Answer Book for Book Three. If you correctly answered all 5 items, continue reading. If not, review the discussion about agreeing with compound subjects on page 54. Then go on to the next section of Subskill 1D. NOTE: The skills in this exercise will be used in the Supplemental Exercise for Subskill 1D on page 59.

Choosing a Verb to Agree with Subjects That Are Not Obvious

A sentence does not always begin with a subject. In some sentences, the verb appears before the subject. Other sentences have words that come between the subject and the verb. These sentences still require that the subject and the verb agree in number. You must be sure that you always know what the subjects of your sentences are, so you can be sure that your subjects and verbs agree.

Inverted Sentences

Although most sentences follow a subject-first pattern, sometimes the verb or part of the verb comes before the subject. Inverted sentences do not begin with a subject. However, as long as you know "who" or "what" is doing the action in the sentence, you will know which word is your subject and whether you should use a singular or plural verb with it:

Under the willow trees (stands, stand) a strange house.

Which verb in the above example should be used to agree with the subject? First, find the subject. Who or what will be standing? Although the word house is at the end of the sentence, the house will be standing and not the trees. House is a singular noun, so you need a singular verb to agree with it. The singular form of stand is stands. The sentence should read:

Under the willow trees stands a strange house.

The most common inverted sentences are questions. In a question, the subject is usually found between the helping verb and the main verb. Remember that the helping verb must agree with the subject. Look at the following examples. Notice that the helping verbs agree with the subjects in number.

V   S   V
Is the Captain preparing his report?

V   S   V
Are your friends coming to dinner?

V   S   V
Where are you going to go?

Another type of inverted sentence begins with here or there. Here and there are never subjects. The subjects of sentences that begin with here or there are found after the verbs:

V   S
Here is your library book.

V   S
Here are your library books.

V   S
There goes Mark in his new car.

V   S
There go Mark and Jeannette in their new car.

Prepositional Phrases

An object of a preposition can never be a subject:

The color of the uniforms (is, are) green.

Which verb should be used to agree with the subject? First, find the subject. There are two words in this sentence that might be the subject: color and uniforms. Of the uniforms is a prepositional phrase that modifies color. Uniforms is the object of the preposition of. The object of a preposition can never be a subject. The subject in this sentence is <u>color</u>. <u>Color</u> is a singular noun, so the sentence needs a singular verb to agree with it. The sentence should read:

> The color of the uniforms is green.

It's a good idea to overlook all prepositional phrases when choosing a verb to agree with the subject. Remember from Subskill 1A that a prepositional phrase generally serves as a modifier; its function is to add descriptive information to the sentence.

Interrupters

An interrupter is a phrase that contains additional information but does not serve as a modifier. It should not be confused with the subject.

> The teacher, as well as the students, is going on a field
> trip.

The subject is <u>teacher</u>, not <u>students</u>. The verb <u>is going</u> is singular to agree with the singular subject <u>teacher</u>. <u>As well as the students</u> is a sentence interrupter. A sentence interrupter is often joined to the subject by such words as <u>along with</u>, <u>plus</u>, <u>accompanied by</u>, <u>together with</u>, <u>as well as</u>, or <u>including</u>. A sentence interrupter is always set off from the rest of the sentence by commas.

It's a good idea to overlook all interrupters when choosing a verb to agree with the subject. The words in a sentence interrupter cannot be part of the subject.

Titles as Subjects

A part of a title can never be the subject. The full title of any work would be the subject. The full title of a work is singular and takes a singular verb:

> *The Screwtape Letters* is one of my favorite books.

The Screwtape Letters, not just *Letters*, is the subject. *The Screwtape Letters* is one book. It is singular. Therefore, the singular verb <u>is</u> is used to agree with it.

Check your ability to choose a verb to agree with subjects that are not obvious by doing the following exercise.

Exercise 2 for Subskill 1D

Underline the subject in each sentence. Then underline the verb in parentheses that agrees with the subject.

EXAMPLE: What time   (<u>does</u>, do)   the <u>train</u> arrive in St. Louis?

1. *Star Wars*   (has, have)   revived many people's interests in science fiction movies.

2. At the entrance to the vault (stand, stands) several armed guards.

3. The boats on the Erie Canal (was, were) once drawn by horses and mules.

4. There (is, are) usually forty-six strings in a harp.

5. The Prime Minister, accompanied by his advisors, (is, are) attending the conference in Geneva.

Check your answers on page 11 in the Answer Key for Book Three. If you correctly answered all 5 items, go to the Self-Check. If not, do the Supplemental Exercise for Subskill 1D. NOTE: The Supplemental Exercise for Subskill 1D provides practice in all the material found in this subskill. You may want to do this exercise to check your memory of all the things you have learned in this subskill.

Supplemental Exercise for Subskill 1D

This exercise provides practice in all the material found in this subskill.

A compound subject with two or more words connected by and usually takes a plural verb unless the compound subject is considered a single item. A compound subject with two or more words connected by or, nor, either-or, neither-nor, or not only-but also takes a singular or plural verb depending on the number of the word that is closest to the verb.

Most sentences follow a pattern in which the verb follows the subject. Some sentences, however, follow an inverted pattern in which the verb or part of the verb comes before the subject. In these sentences, identify the subject by asking "Who?" or "What?" is performing the action. Then choose the appropriate verb to agree with it. In choosing a verb to agree with a subject, ignore any prepositional phrases or sentence interrupters that come between the subject and the verb. When the title of a work is the subject of a sentence, a singular verb should be used with it. Do not consider only part of the title to be the subject.

Underline the subject in each sentence. Then underline the verb in parentheses that agrees with the subject.

EXAMPLE: The telegraph and the electric doorbell (work, works) on similar principles.

1. Where (has, have) they put the sale items?

2. The news from the Middle East (was, were) not encouraging.

3. There (go, goes) my father to see the doctor.

4. Rice and beans (make, makes) up most of the family's diet.

5. The building superintendent, along with the landlord, (make, makes) the rules for the apartment house.

6. On a high chair beside the Christmas stockings (was, were) sitting a little old gentleman in a fur coat.

7. *Lord of the Rings* (is, are) my favorite book.

8. In autumn, the leaves on the trees in my backyard (turn, turns) red and gold.

9. Not only Belle but also her brothers (is, are) close to their mother.

10. (Is, Are) you going early to the party?

Check your answers on page 11 in the Answer Key for Book Three. If you correctly answered 8 of 10 items, go to the Self-Check. If not, ask your instructor for help.

SELF-CHECK: SKILL UNIT 1

Part A. Above each set of four sentences, a sentence part has been identified. Circle the letter before the sentence in which the underlined word or words are used as that part of the sentence.

EXAMPLE: Modifier:
   a.   We wanted to <u>play</u> for a while.
   b.   Their <u>play</u> school closed for the summer.
   c.   We can <u>play</u> for only a short time.
   d.   We enjoyed the <u>play</u> very much.

1.   Predicate nominative:
   a.   The man and woman were <u>newlyweds</u>.
   b.   They were obviously a <u>newlywed</u> couple.
   c.   The <u>newlyweds</u> made an attractive couple.
   d.   A couple of <u>newlyweds</u> arrived at the hotel.

2.   Object of a preposition:
   a.   In the lounge stood <u>Hector</u>.
   b.   He stood in the lounge with <u>Hector</u>.
   c.   I saw <u>Hector</u> standing in the lounge.
   d.   We gave <u>Hector</u> directions to the lounge.

3.   Direct Object:
   a.   <u>Drinking cold milk</u> is refreshing.
   b.   He was <u>drinking cold milk</u> with his meals.
   c.   The man <u>drinking cold milk</u> was coughing.
   d.   I enjoy <u>drinking cold milk</u> every morning.

4. Indirect Object:
   a. Lola gave the <u>puppy</u> a bath.

   b. The <u>puppy</u> was given a bath by Lola.

   c. Lola bathed the <u>puppy</u>.

   d. Lola bought a bathtub for the <u>puppy</u>.

5. Modifier:
   a. The express <u>train</u> pulled into the station.

   b. We pulled into the <u>train</u> station.

   c. I take the <u>train</u> to the last station.

   d. The station was filled with <u>trains</u>.

6. Subject:
   a. <u>Laura</u> and <u>Susan</u>, please report to the office.

   b. The women sitting in the office were <u>Laura</u> and <u>Susan</u>.

   c. <u>Laura</u>, along with <u>Susan</u>, reported to the office.

   d. After a while, <u>Laura</u> and <u>Susan</u> reported to the office.

7. Verb:
   a. <u>Running</u> and <u>jumping</u> are good exercises.

   b. I find <u>running</u> and <u>jumping</u> exhausting.

   c. He had been <u>running</u> and <u>jumping</u> in the gym.

   d. They enjoy <u>running</u>, but <u>jumping</u> is too strenuous.

8. Object of a preposition:
   a. Al saved money by <u>eating at home</u>.

   b. <u>Eating at home</u> saved Al money.

   c. Al prefers <u>eating at home</u>.

   d. I found Al <u>eating at home</u> yesterday.

9. Subject:
   a. It was not easy <u>to solve</u> the problem without a calculator.

   b. <u>To solve</u> the problem without a calculator was not easy.

   c. I tried <u>to solve</u> the problem without a calculator.

   d. <u>To solve</u> the problem, I used a calculator.

10. Modifier:
    a. She had a <u>frightened</u> look on her face.

    b. She was <u>frightened</u> by the look.

    c. She <u>frightened</u> others with her look.

    d. She didn't want to <u>frighten</u> anyone.

Part B. Each set of four sentences contains three correct simple sentences and one simple sentence in which the subject and verb do not agree in number. Identify the incorrect sentence by circling the letter that precedes it.

EXAMPLE: a.   Everybody in the family knows how to play an instrument.

b.   The senators are voting on the tax reform act.

c.   The girls or their mother plan to attend the sewing class.

d.   *Stars and Stripes Forever* is a famous American march.

11.   a.   The entire group are arriving on the 8:45 train.

b.   Everyone is doing his or her job.

c.   Each of the magazines costs seventy cents.

d.   Every man in the medical unit was overweight.

12.   a.   My cousins and their father were here today.

b.   Much of the food was stolen.

c.   These scissors are too dull to cut paper.

d.   John, as well as his parents, are going to California.

13.   a.   Either Randy or his wife is wrong.

b.   The team is flying to Dallas.

c.   No news is good news.

d.   A mob of angry, violent people are outside the door.

14.   a.   Where are my new pants?

b.   Only one of his many poems were published.

c.   Neither the scientist nor his assistant was able to work the problem.

d.   In the center of the Gulf of Mexico lie the ruins.

15.   a.   All of the bananas were bruised.

b.   The most important part of all our trips was coming home.

c.   Physics, as well as civics, are taught in summer school.

d.   Here come some of my favorite actors.

Part C. Write eight complete sentences. If you like, your sentences may form a paragraph describing someone you know. Your eight sentences should show an understanding of subject-verb agreement.

_____

_____

_____

_____

_____

_____

_____

_____

Check your answers for Part A and Part B on pages 11–13 of the Answer Key for Book Three. Have your instructor check Part C. If you identified the correct sentences in 8 of 10 sets in Part A, identified the incorrect sentences in 4 of 5 sets in Part B, and used subject-verb combinations correctly in 7 of 8 sentences in Part C, you have shown that you have mastered these skills. If not, ask your instructor for help.

Skill Unit 2

WRITING COMPOUND SENTENCES

What Skills You Need to Begin: You need to be able to write simple sentences (Skill Unit 1).

What Skills You Will Learn: After you complete this skill unit, you will be able to identify the elements of compound sentences. You will be able to differentiate between compound sentences and other types of compounds and to use punctuation correctly. You will also be able to revise run-on sentences.

Why You Need These Skills: Now that you know how to use subjects and verbs correctly in short simple sentences, you should learn how to write sentences that are longer and more complex. In this unit and in Unit 3 you will learn how to combine two or more ideas into the same sentence. When you write, "The brakes squealed" and then write, "The car skidded to a halt," you have written two simple sentences. When you write, "The brakes squealed, and the car skidded to a halt," you have combined the two ideas into one compound sentence. Using both compound sentences and simple sentences will make your writing more interesting and less choppy.

How You Will Show What You Have Learned: You will take the Self-Check at the end of this unit on page 81. The Self-Check consists of two parts. If you correctly answer 12 of 15 items in Part A and 4 of 5 items in Part B, you will have shown that you have mastered the skills in this unit.

If you feel that you have already mastered the skills of writing and punctuating compound sentences correctly, turn to the end of this unit and complete the Self-Check on page 81.

Subskill 2A: Constructing Compound Sentences

When you complete this subskill, you will be able to identify compound sentences. You will recognize that compound sentences consist of two or more independent clauses joined by coordinating conjunctions, conjunctive adverbs, and/or semicolons.

In Skill Unit 1, you learned that a sentence is a group of words that expresses a complete thought. All sentences must have a subject (tells who or what a sentence is about) and a verb (tells what the subject is or does). In every sentence, the subject and verb must agree in number.

All of the sentences that you studied in the last skill unit were simple sentences. They had one subject–verb combination. In this skill unit, you will study and write more complicated types of sentences, called **compound sentences.** Compound sentences are made up of two or more simple sentences joined together by means of a connecting word and proper punctuation and/or by a semicolon (;).

A simple sentence used as part of a compound sentence is called an **independent clause.** An independent clause is a group of words that contains a subject and a verb. It expresses a complete thought and can stand by itself. That is why it is called independent. A compound sentence is made up of two or more independent clauses. Look at the following sentences:

$$\text{SIMPLE SENTENCE:} \quad \overset{\text{S}}{\text{Today}} \,\overset{\text{V}}{\text{is}} \text{ a beautiful day.}$$

$$\text{SIMPLE SENTENCE:} \quad \overset{\text{S}}{\text{I}} \,\overset{\text{V}}{\overbrace{\text{am going}}} \text{ for a walk.}$$

$$\text{COMPOUND SENTENCE:} \quad \overset{\text{S}}{\text{Today}} \,\overset{\text{V}}{\text{is}} \text{ a beautiful day; therefore, } \overset{\text{S}}{\text{I}}$$
$$\overset{\text{V}}{\overbrace{\text{am going}}} \text{ for a walk.}$$

In the compound sentence, <u>Today is a beautiful day</u> is an independent clause. So is <u>I am going for a walk</u>. The two independent clauses are joined by <u>therefore</u>, a conjunctive adverb, or connective.

Notice that each independent clause contains a subject (<u>Today</u>, <u>I</u>) and a verb or verb phrase (<u>is</u>, <u>am going</u>). Also notice that a semicolon is used before the conjunctive adverb <u>therefore</u>, and a comma is used afterwards.

The following sections will discuss how coordinating conjunctions, conjunctive adverbs, and/or semicolons link independent clauses into compound sentences.

Coordinating Conjunctions as Connectives

One of the ways to join independent clauses is to use a comma and then a connecting word called a **coordinating conjunction.** The coordinating conjunctions include <u>and</u>, <u>yet</u>, <u>for</u>, <u>nor</u>, <u>so</u>, <u>or</u>, and <u>but</u>. The prefix <u>co</u> in coordinating means <u>equal with</u> or <u>together with</u>.

The chart on page 66 defines the purposes for using specific coordinating conjunctions and offers examples of each connective in use in compound sentences. Notice that a comma is used before the conjunction in each compound sentence.

Conjunction	Purpose	Example
and	to add information	I put in a new battery, <u>and</u> the clock began running.
but, yet	to show contrast	I put in a new battery, <u>but</u> the clock still didn't work.
nor, or	to show an alternative	The clock is broken, <u>or</u> the battery is dead.
for	to show a reason	I bought a new clock, <u>for</u> the old one was broken.
so	to show a result	Union and management couldn't reach an agreement, <u>so</u> the union went on strike.

Conjunctive Adverbs as Connectives

Another way to join independent clauses into a compound sentence is by using a semicolon plus a **conjunctive adverb.** Some of the most common conjunctive adverbs are: <u>furthermore, in addition, so, however, nevertheless, otherwise, consequently, therefore,</u> and <u>thus.</u>

The following chart defines the purposes for using specific conjunctive adverbs, and offers examples of each in use in compound sentences. Notice that a semicolon is used before the conjunctive adverb, and a comma follows.

Conjunctive Adverb	Purpose	Example
furthermore, in addition, besides	to add information	I buy very little on credit; <u>furthermore</u>, I pay my bills promptly.
however, nevertheless	to show contrast	I usually pay my bills promptly; <u>however</u>, this month I was low on funds.
otherwise	to show an alternative	Pay your bills promptly; <u>otherwise</u>, you may get a bad credit rating.
consequently, so, therefore, thus	to show a result	I always pay my bills promptly; <u>therefore</u>, I have a good credit rating.
finally, later, next, then	to show a sequence in time	I went to the store; <u>then</u>, I returned home.

Semicolon as a Connective

A **semicolon** (;), can join independent clauses to form a compound sentence. You should use this method when you want to show that the two clauses are closely related or when writing simple statements without a need for showing a contrast, alternative, or a result.

SIMPLE SENTENCE:	The walls of my room are painted light blue.
SIMPLE SENTENCE:	The ceiling is painted white.
COMPOUND SENTENCE:	The walls of my room are painted light blue; the ceiling is painted white.

Exercise for Subskill 2A

Below is a chart for analyzing the compound sentences in this exercise. Read sentences 1–10 on page 68 and do the following:

- Find the subject and verb or verb phrase in the first independent clause. Write them in the first and second columns.

- Locate the connective (words and/or punctuation) used to join the two independent clauses. Write the connective in the third column.

- Find the subject and verb or verb phrase in the second independent clause. Write them in the last two columns.

Review your work to be sure you have completed each step.

	Subject 1	Verb 1	Connective	Subject 2	Verb 2
EXAMPLE:	dogs	perform	, for	they	are
1.					
2.					
3.					
4.					
5.					
6.					
7.					
8.					
9.					
10.					

EXAMPLE: Dogs perform tricks more readily than cats, for they are especially interested in pleasing people.

1. Cats are independent animals; however, dogs need their masters' affection and attention.
2. Cats will catch mice or rats, but they do this mostly for fun and not to please people.
3. People have many misconceptions about cats and dogs; consequently, they misinterpret the animals' actions.
4. Puppies and kittens do not learn by imitation; they learn by participation.
5. The mother takes her offspring along, and she allows it to participate in an activity.
6. The mother urges her baby to take part in the activity, so it learns by doing.
7. People consider cats to be natural hunters; however, research has proved differently.
8. A young kitten and a mouse were put together in a cage, yet the kitten did not harm the mouse.
9. The kitten and mouse became good friends; they played together happily.
10. Kittens should learn to hunt mice with their mothers; otherwise, this skill may not develop.

Check your answers on page 13 in the Answer Key for Book Three. If you correctly identified the subjects, verbs, and connectives in all 10 sentences, go to Subskill 2B. If not, do the Supplemental Exercise for Subskill 2A.

Supplemental Exercise for Subskill 2A

A compound sentence contains two or more independent clauses. Each independent clause is a simple sentence that contains a subject and a verb. The two independent clauses are joined together in one of three ways:

(1) by a comma plus a coordinating conjunction such as <u>and</u>, <u>but</u>, <u>or</u>, <u>so</u>, or <u>yet</u>.
(2) by a semicolon plus a conjunctive adverb followed by a comma. Some conjunctive adverbs are <u>therefore</u>, <u>however</u>, <u>nevertheless</u>, <u>furthermore</u>, and <u>consequently</u>.
(3) by only a semicolon, if the two independent clauses are very closely balanced.

Check your ability to identify the elements of compound sentences by completing the following Supplemental Exercise.

Use the chart on page 69 for analyzing the compound sentences in this exercise. Read each sentence and do the following:

· Find the subject and verb or verb phrase in the first independent clause. Write them in the first and second columns.

· Locate the connective (words and/or punctuation) used to join the two independent clauses. Write the connective in the third column.

· Find the subject and verb or verb phrase in the second independent clause. Write them in the last two columns.

Review your work to be sure you have completed each step.

	Subject 1	Verb 1	Connective	Subject 2	Verb 2
EXAMPLE:	John	slipped	, and	he	twisted
1.					
2.					
3.					
4.					
5.					
6.					
7.					
8.					
9.					
10.					

EXAMPLE: John slipped on the broken pavement, and he twisted his ankle.

1. Bill usually does not set his alarm; consequently, he is often late for work.
2. The soldiers were weary, but they would not surrender.
3. We left early for the meeting; however, we were delayed by an accident on the expressway.
4. You can help me with the dishes, or you can vacuum the living room carpet.
5. Ellen wouldn't answer my phone calls; furthermore, she wouldn't accept my letters.
6. The professor lectured for 40 minutes; I took eight pages of notes.
7. My car ran out of gas on the highway, for I did not look at the gas gauge.
8. The storm severed power lines in the neighborhood; in addition, many trees were toppled by the heavy winds.
9. The closet was overstuffed with heavy coats; therefore, the door would not close tightly.
10. The baby has his mother's blue eyes; he has his father's dimples.

Check your answers on page 13 in the Answer Key for Book Three. If you correctly identified the subjects, verbs, and connectives in 8 of 10 sentences, go to Subskill 2B. If not, ask your instructor for help.

Subskill 2B: Punctuating Compound Sentences

When you complete this subskill, you will be able to punctuate compound sentences in which independent clauses are joined with coordinating conjunctions, conjunctive adverbs, and/or semicolons.

Punctuation Inside Compound Sentences

The sentences you studied in Unit 1 were simple sentences. They contained one subject–verb combination. Simple sentences do not always require any special internal punctuation. Compound sentences, on the other hand, require internal punctuation.

SIMPLE SENTENCE:	The teller counted out my money.
SIMPLE SENTENCE:	I put the stack of bills into my wallet.
COMPOUND SENTENCE:	The teller counted out my money, and I put the stack of bills into my wallet.

Some people confuse compound sentences with simple sentences containing other types of compounds. Therefore, they do not use the proper punctuation when they write the compound sentence or the simple sentence. To avoid confusing compound sentences with other types of compounds, study the following methods for punctuating compound sentences.

Punctuating Compound Sentences Containing Coordinating Conjunctions

The following pattern shows the parts of a compound sentence formed by using a coordinating conjunction:

$$S1 + V1 - Comma + Conj. - S2 + V2$$

Notice how the compound sentence on page 71 fits this pattern. Also notice the punctuation used inside the sentence.

<pre>
        S1   V1   Conj S2   V2
A new job opened at the plant, and I applied for the
position.
</pre>

Simple sentences that contain a compound subject or a compound verb may also include a conjunction, such as <u>and</u>, <u>but</u>, <u>or</u>, or <u>nor</u>. However, these simple sentences are punctuated differently from compound sentences. Make sure that you can tell the difference between a compound sentence and a simple sentence that contains a compound subject or compound verb.

The following pattern shows a simple sentence that contains a compound subject:

$$S1 + S2 - V$$

The following pattern shows a simple sentence that contains a compound verb:

$$S - V1 + V2$$

Notice that only the compound sentence (shown in the first pattern) requires inside punctuation: a comma. It is placed between the two independent clauses but before the coordinating conjunction.

Look at the three sentences below. Decide which one fits the pattern of a compound sentence. The other two are simple sentences with compound parts.

                S   V1   V2
(1) My mother likes spinach and serves it often.

            S1 V1   S2 V2
(2) I hate the taste of spinach, but I eat it anyway.

            S1   S2   V
(3) Spinach and broccoli are my least favorite
        vegetables.

Sentence 2 is a compound sentence. I hate the taste of spinach is an independent clause. I eat it anyway is also an independent clause. The two clauses are connected by a comma plus the coordinating conjunction but.

Now look at sentence 1. My mother likes spinach expresses a complete thought. It contains a subject and verb. However, serves it often does not contain a subject, so it is not an independent clause. Sentence 1 fits the pattern of a simple sentence with a compound verb. Notice that there is no comma needed before the word and.

Look at sentence 3. It fits the pattern of a simple sentence with a compound subject. Once again, no comma is needed before the word and.

Punctuating Compound Sentences Formed by Using Conjunctive Adverbs

The following pattern shows the parts of a compound sentence formed by using a conjunctive adverb to join the independent clauses:

$$S1 + V1 - \text{Semicolon} + \text{Conjunctive Adverb} + \text{Comma} - S2 + V2$$

Notice how the compound sentence on page 72 fits this pattern. Also notice the punctuation used inside the sentence.

      S   V   V   Conj Adv   S   V

I have lost 20 pounds; consequently, I need a new wardrobe.

When you use a conjunctive adverb in a compound sentence, you will usually follow the conjunctive adverb with a comma. One main exception to this rule involves the use of the conjunctive adverb <u>then</u>. This word is usually not followed by a comma.

The hard jab stunned the boxer; then he fell to the mat.

Now compare the two sentences below:

              S   V   V   S

(1)   John had done fairly well on the test; however, he

        V   V

    was tired from the long hours of study. (compound sentence)

              S   V

(2)   This game, however, is too difficult for you to play. (simple sentence)

Sentence 1 contains two independent clauses:

          S   V   V

         John had done fairly well

         and

         S   V   V

         he was tired from long hours of study.

The semicolon, conjunctive adverb, comma combination makes a three-part connective between the two clauses. All three parts must be used when a conjunctive adverb joins the two independent clauses.

Sentence 2 also contains the word <u>however</u>, but you can see that in this sentence <u>however</u> is not used to connect two clauses in a compound sentence. Instead, it is used as an ordinary adverb in a simple sentence. Notice there is no semicolon used before the word <u>however</u> in this case. <u>However</u> is separated from the rest of the sentence by commas.

Make sure you can recognize when a conjunctive adverb is being used to connect the parts of a compound sentence, so that you can punctuate these compound sentences correctly.

Punctuating Compound Sentences Formed By Using a Semicolon Alone

Sometimes the ideas in two independent clauses are very closely related or totally balanced. You can create a special effect by using only a semicolon to connect the two independent clauses, omitting either a coordinating conjunction or a conjunctive adverb. The additional words are not needed to show how the two clauses are related to each other. You should use this method only if the relationship between the two independent clauses is very clear.

The following pattern shows this type of compound sentence:

$$S1 + V1 — Semicolon — S2 + V2$$

Notice how the following compound sentences fit this pattern:

        S1   V1
(1) He speaks German, Russian, and Japanese

        S2   V2
fluently; he must have lived abroad for
many years.

        S1   V1   S2 V2
(2) No one likes him; he is an outcast from society.

NOTE: Occasionally a semicolon is used to separate two independent clauses that are joined by a coordinating conjunction. This occurs when several commas (usually two or more) are needed within one or both of the clauses to clarify meaning.

> Mrs. Johnston, my neighbor, went home immediately;
> but by the time she arrived, the burglar, who had
> been frightened by her dog, had fled.

To check your ability to recognize compound sentences and to punctuate them correctly, complete the following exercise.

Exercise for Subskill 2B

Some of the sentences below are compound sentences, and some are not. Rewrite the sentences on the lines provided and put commas or semicolons where they are needed. Remember that each part of a compound sentence must contain a subject and a verb. Some sentences may not need any punctuation. If so, write No punctuation change on the line below the sentence.

EXAMPLE: I needed to shop for groceries today but I didn't have time.

      I needed to shop for groceries today, but I didn't
      have time.

1. The door was locked and she had left her key in the room.

2. I gave the doll to Joan then Mary began to demand one too.

3. We fished in the morning however in the evening we loafed and read.

_____

_____

4. Put that chair in the corner or by the door.

_____

_____

5. I like the taste of melon but it gives me indigestion.

_____

_____

6. All the men but two had arrived and were hard at work.

_____

7. I am interested in improving my education consequently I may be able to get a better job.

_____

_____

8. Max had never been to New York nor did he care much to go now.

_____

_____

9. You are a good person and a hard worker.

_____

10. You are a hard worker you are sure to get a promotion soon.

_____

_____

Check your answers on page 14 in the Answer Key for Book Three. If you correctly answered all 10 items, go to Subskill 2C. If not, complete the Supplemental Exercise for Subskill 2B.

Supplemental Exercise for Subskill 2B

Here are the three patterns that compound sentences usually follow. Notice the placement of punctuation marks in each pattern.

S1 + V1 — Comma + Coordinating Conj. — S2 + V2

S1 + V1 — Semicolon + Conjunctive Adverb + Comma — S2 + V2

S1 + V1 — Semicolon — S2 + V2

Also notice that each compound sentence contains at least two subject–

verb combinations. Don't be confused by simple sentences that contain compound subjects or compound verbs; they are not compound sentences.

Apply what you have learned about punctuating compound sentences by completing the following exercise.

Complete the following sentences by writing in any necessary commas (,) or semicolons (;). Do not use unnecessary punctuation.

EXAMPLE: I wasn't feeling well so I spent the day in bed.
I wasn't feeling well, so I spent the day in bed.

1. Beth wrote to Karen however Karen did not answer her letter.

2. Water the lawn early in the morning or late in the evening to conserve water.

3. I read the book I don't plan to see the movie.

4. Are you going to Chicago for Christmas or have you decided to stay home?

5. My sister and my aunt are coming to spend the holiday with me.

6. He was usually an excellent student nevertheless he did not study and failed the exam.

7. I plan to eat dinner early and go to bed.

8. He needed help on his project but she was too busy to assist him.

9. Mr. Jamison, the man I told you about, will not be able to come but his sister, who is also an architect, will be there at 2:00 p.m.

10. Help me find my watch otherwise I may never find it.

Check your answers on page 14 in the Answer Key for Book Three. If you correctly punctuated 8 of 10 sentences, go to Subskill 2C. If not, ask your instructor for help.

Subskill 2C: Revising Run-on Sentences

When you complete this subskill, you will be able to recognize run-on sentences and correct them.

So far in this unit you have learned how to recognize compound sentences and how to punctuate them correctly. One error that writers sometimes commit when they attempt to write a compound sentence is a run-on sentence. A run-on sentence consists of two independent clauses that are run together with no punctuation between them or with the wrong punctuation.

Notice these two run-on sentences:

```
        S    V    V              S   V    V
```
My uncle was born in Vietnam, he has become an
American citizen.

```
S    V                 S  V    V
```
I received my green card I can remain in this country.

In the first run-on example, the two independent clauses are joined with a comma alone. This is incorrect. When you use a comma to join two independent clauses, you must also use a coordinating conjunction (and, but, or, nor, for, yet, so).

In the second run-on example, no punctuation has been used to connect the two independent clauses. There are several ways to correct this run-on. You could insert a period after card. You could also use a comma plus a coordinating conjunction, a semicolon plus a conjunctive adverb, or a semicolon alone. You will learn when to use each of these methods in the examples below.

Using End Punctuation to Correct a Run-on Sentence

If the two independent clauses in a run-on sentence seem to express two separate ideas, you should probably divide the run-on into two separate sentences. You can do this by inserting end punctuation (a period, question mark, or exclamation point) between the two clauses.

RUN-ON: I bought snow tires yesterday, they cost $65 each.

CORRECTION: I bought snow tires yesterday. They cost $65 each.

Using a Semicolon to Correct a Run-on Sentence

If the two independent clauses in a run-on are very closely related, you can join them with a semicolon in order to show their close relationship and balance. Don't overuse this method for correcting run-ons.

RUN-ON: Wind whistled through the trees rain pounded on the roof.

CORRECTION: Wind whistled through the trees; rain pounded on the roof.

Using a Comma and a Coordinating Conjunction to Correct a Run-on Sentence

You should never use a comma alone to join independent clauses in a compound sentence. Use a coordinating conjunction after the comma to show the relationship between the two clauses.

RUN-ON: My uncle was born in Vietnam, he has become an American citizen.

CORRECTION: My uncle was born in Vietnam, but he has become an American citizen.

The coordinating conjunction <u>but</u> shows that there is a contrast between the events described in the two independent clauses.

Using a Semicolon, Conjunctive Adverb, and Comma to Correct a Run-on Sentence

You can also correct a run-on sentence by joining the two independent clauses with a conjunctive adverb. (You can look back at the chart listing conjunctive adverbs in Subskill 2A, page 66.) The conjunctive adverb will clarify how the two clauses are related to each other. You should use a semicolon before the conjunctive adverb and usually use a comma after the conjunctive adverb.

RUN-ON: I received my green card I can remain in this country.

CORRECTION: I received my green card; therefore, I can remain in this country.

The conjunctive adverb <u>therefore</u> shows that the idea in the second independent clause is a result of the idea in the first independent clause.

Now study the following to see how these four different methods can be used to correct the same run-on sentence.

RUN-ON: The telethon has been most successful it has raised many dollars to help handicapped children.

CORRECTION 1: The telethon has been most successful. It has raised many dollars to help handicapped children. (two separate sentences)

CORRECTION 2: The telethon has been most successful; it has raised many dollars to help handicapped children. (independent clauses joined with a semicolon)

CORRECTION 3: The telethon has been most successful, for it has raised many dollars to help handicapped children. (joined with a comma plus the coordinating conjunction <u>for</u>)

CORRECTION 4: The telethon has been most successful; consequently, it has raised many dollars to help handicapped children. (joined by a semicolon, conjunctive adverb, and comma)

Check your ability to revise run-on sentences by completing the following exercise.

Exercise for Subskill 2C

Correct each of the run-on sentences on pages 78 and 79 in any one of these ways:

- Insert end punctuation to divide the run-on sentence into two sentences.
- Use a semicolon to join the independent clauses into one sentence.
- Use a comma and a coordinating conjunction to join the independent clauses into one sentence.
- Use a semicolon with a conjunctive adverb followed by a comma to join the independent clauses into one sentence.

EXAMPLE: I will go on vacation this year, I will make money at the same time.

I will go on vacation this year. I will make money at the same time.

I will go on vacation this year; I will make money at the same time.

I will go on vacation this year, but I will make money at the same time.

I will go on vacation this year; however, I will make money at the same time.

NOTE: Examples are given to show how a run-on sentence can be corrected using each of the four methods. However, you are to give only one corrected version of each sentence.

1. He could do the math problems he couldn't explain his solutions to his instructor.

   _____

   _____

2. There are many good television sets on the market, choosing the right one is difficult.

   _____

   _____

3. He packed all of his things he moved out yesterday.

   _____

   _____

4. Mother is an excellent cook she would rather eat in a restaurant.

_____

_____

5. The school day is very long, I manage to stay alert.

_____

_____

6. Where did you go the weather was lovely.

_____

_____

7. I applied my brakes just in time, I avoided crashing into the car in front of mine.

_____

_____

8. Ms. Logan left for the day, she won't be in until next Tuesday.

_____

_____

Ask your instructor to evaluate your work. If you correctly completed 7 of 8 items, go to the Self-Check. If not, do the Supplemental Exercise for Subskill 2C.

Supplemental Exercise for Subskill 2C

Run-on sentences consist of two independent clauses that are improperly joined together or incorrectly punctuated. You can correct a run-on sentence in four different ways:

CORRECTION 1: Insert end punctuation to divide the independent clauses into separate sentences.

CORRECTION 2: Join the independent clauses with a semicolon.

CORRECTION 3: Join the independent clauses with a comma plus a coordinating conjunction.

CORRECTION 4: Join the independent clauses with a semicolon plus a conjunctive adverb followed by a comma.

Correct each of the following run-on sentences by using one of the four methods listed above that you think best suits the sentence, and write your correct sentence on the lines provided.

EXAMPLE: My new watch runs fast, I'm taking it back to the store.

My new watch runs fast. I'm taking it back to the store.

My new watch runs fast; I'm taking it back to the store.

My new watch runs fast, so I'm taking it back to the store.

NOTE: Examples are given to show how a run-on sentence can be corrected using each of the four methods. However, you are to give only one corrected version of each sentence.

1. Pieces of driftwood washed up onto the beach, I used them to build a table.

   _____

   _____

2. The boat capsized in the storm the Coast Guard saved all of the passengers.

   _____

   _____

3. Mother's Day is the second Sunday in May, Father's Day is the third Sunday in June.

   _____

   _____

4. My kitchen is very small the appliances are nearly brand new.

   _____

   _____

5. My landlord intends to raise the rent I must find a new apartment.

   _____

   _____

6. The classified ads list lots of apartments, most of them are out of my price range.

   _____

   _____

7. The copying machine broke down again, we are using carbon paper to make copies of those letters.

_____

_____

8. A mature mind is a motivated mind, learning is a valuable experience at any age.

_____

_____

Ask your instructor to evaluate your sentences. If you satisfactorily corrected at least 7 of 8 run-on sentences, go to the Self-Check. If not, ask your instructor for help.

SELF-CHECK: SKILL UNIT 2

Part A. Read each of the following sentences carefully. Decide whether the punctuation used in each underlined part is correct. Then, choose the correct answer from the list of choices after each sentence. Circle the letter next to your choice.

EXAMPLE: She studied very <u>hard, consequently she</u> performed well on the test.
  a. correct as written
  b. hard, consequently, she
  c. hard, consequently; she
  (d.) hard; consequently, she

1. We have put in an order for new <u>supplies and they</u> should be here this week.
  a. correct as written
  b. supplies, and, they
  c. supplies, and they
  d. supplies and, they

2. He caught the <u>ball, but</u> then dropped it.
  a. correct as written
  b. ball but
  c. ball; but
  d. ball, but,

3. The children had never seen an <u>elephant; however, they</u> were not frightened.
  a. correct as written
  b. elephant, however, they
  c. elephant however they
  d. elephant, however; they

4. Joe will come at four <u>o'clock, and pick</u> you up.
   a. correct as written
   b. o'clock, and, pick
   c. o'clock and, pick
   d. o'clock and pick

5. Sal has to work <u>nights, otherwise, he</u> cannot afford to go to school.
   a. correct as written
   b. nights, otherwise; he
   c. nights; otherwise, he
   d. nights; otherwise he

6. We had never before been in the <u>jungle therefore we</u> were all a little nervous.
   a. correct as written
   b. jungle; therefore, we
   c. jungle, therefore, we
   d. jungle, therefore; we

7. Martin was a good <u>worker, nevertheless he</u> lost his job.
   a. correct as written
   b. worker, nevertheless, he
   c. worker; nevertheless, he
   d. worker; nevertheless; he

8. I am interested in improving my <u>education, and in</u> getting a better job.
   a. correct as written
   b. education and in
   c. education and, in
   d. education; and, in

9. The work was <u>interesting; the</u> pay was excellent.
   a. correct as written
   b. interesting, the
   c. interesting: the
   d. interesting the

10. The teacher was <u>pleased but</u> the boy was not satisfied with himself.
    a. correct as written
    b. pleased, but,
    c. pleased, but
    d. pleased; but,

11. He had done pretty <u>well, however, he</u> felt he could do better.
    a. correct as written
    b. well; however, he
    c. well however he
    d. well, however; he

12. There must be one person in <u>charge; otherwise, there</u> will be chaos.
    a. correct as written
    b. charge, otherwise, there

        c. charge; otherwise there
        d. charge, otherwise there

13. The air was cool in the <u>morning but by</u> the afternoon the temperature was 90°.
        a. correct as written
        b. morning, but, by
        c. morning; but by
        d. morning, but by

14. You must take one tablet in the <u>morning, and another</u> in the evening.
        a. correct as written
        b. morning and another
        c. morning and, another
        d. morning, and, another

15. You may take the test <u>again, however, you</u> should restudy the material.
        a. correct as written
        b. again; however you
        c. again; however, you
        d. again, however; you

Part B. In each of the following items, connect the two independent clauses to form a compound sentence. Use either coordinating conjunctions or conjunctive adverbs and correct punctuation as you rewrite the sentences. The independent clauses may be used in any order.

16. I want a color television set with remote controls.
I can't afford it.

      _____

      _____

17. There was a terrible traffic jam on the freeway this morning.
Some people were half an hour late to work.

      _____

      _____

18. The team played hard.
Their opponents won the game.

      _____

      _____

19. Don owns twelve pairs of shoes.
He just bought two new pairs of boots.

      _____

      _____

20. Bill is often late to work.
   He makes up for it by staying past quitting time.

   _____

   _____

Check your answers for Part A on page 14 in the Answer Key for Book Three. Ask your instructor to evaluate Part B. If you satisfactorily completed 12 of 15 items in Part A and 4 of 5 items in Part B, you have shown that you have mastered these skills. If not, ask your instructor for help.

Skill Unit 3
WRITING COMPLEX SENTENCES

What Skills You Need to Begin: You need to be able to write simple sentences (Skill Unit 1) and compound sentences (Skill Unit 2).

What Skills You Will Learn: When you complete this skill unit, you will be able to identify a complex sentence. You will be able to distinguish between an independent clause and a dependent clause. You will be able to identify three types of dependent clauses: adjective clauses, adverb clauses, and noun clauses. You will be able to write correctly punctuated sentences using each type of clause.

Why You Need These Skills: In Skill Unit 2, you learned how to combine ideas in compound sentences in order to add variety to your writing. Another way to make your writing more interesting is to use complex sentences. Once you understand how to write all three kinds of sentences—simple, compound, and complex—you can use a variety of sentence patterns in all your writing.

How You Will Show What You Have Learned: You will take the Self-Check at the end of this unit on page 112. The Self-Check contains 20 items. If you correctly answer 16 of 20 items, you will have shown that you have mastered these skills.

If you feel that you have already mastered these skills, turn to the end of this unit and complete the Self-Check on page 112.

Subskill 3A: Identifying Dependent Clauses and Complex Sentences

When you complete this subskill, you will be able to identify independent clauses and dependent clauses. You will also be able to identify complex sentences, in which both types of clauses appear.

How Complex Sentences Are Formed

An **independent clause** contains a subject and a verb and can stand alone as a simple sentence. The following sentence consists of one independent clause:

A woman gave me this book.

A **dependent clause** also contains a subject and a verb, but it cannot stand alone as a sentence. Look at the following dependent clause:

whom I know

Notice that this dependent clause has the subject I and the verb know. The other word in the sentence is whom. What person does whom refer to? The reader has no way of knowing. Because something is missing, the clause cannot stand by itself. It is incomplete, a sentence fragment.

The full meaning of the dependent clause becomes clear only when it is combined with an independent clause, as the following example demonstrates:

A woman [whom I know] gave me this book.

Notice what happens when the clause whom I know is added to the independent clause A woman gave me this book. The dependent clause now identifies or further describes the subject woman. The sentence takes on a more definite meaning. A sentence made up of an independent clause plus one or more dependent clauses is called a **complex sentence.**

Now look at this dependent clause:

when I was on vacation

Notice that the clause contains a subject, I, and a verb, was. However, it does not express a complete thought. The reader is left wondering what the writer meant to communicate.

Once again, the full meaning of the dependent clause becomes clear only when it is combined with an independent clause:

[When I was on vacation,] a woman gave me this book.

The dependent clause now tells when the action in the independent clause took place. Together, the dependent clause and the independent clause form a complex sentence.

Some complex sentences contain more than one dependent clause. The following complex sentence contains one independent clause and two dependent clauses:

[When I was on vacation,] a woman [whom I know]
gave me this book.

Using Dependent Clauses to Subordinate Ideas

A dependent clause is also called a **subordinate clause** because its function is secondary, or subordinate, to the independent clause of a complex sentence. You can, for example, remove dependent clauses from a sentence and still be left with a complete sentence. If, however, you remove the independent clause, you are left with a sentence fragment.

Dependent clauses help to express ideas and relationships clearly. Look at the following sentences:

This stereo will be sold for $385.
It replaces the older model.

As these sentences are written, they stand apart from each other and thus give equal weight or emphasis to the price and the replacing of the stereo. But when these sentences are joined together by making one of them a dependent clause, the thought expressed in the dependent clause becomes secondary, or subordinate, to the thought expressed in the main, or independent, clause.

This stereo, which replaces the older model, will be sold for $385.

Here, the clause which replaces the older model is the dependent, or subordinate, clause. In this example, emphasis is given to the price, not the replacing, of the stereo. If the dependent and independent clauses are interchanged, the emphasis of a sentence is altered:

This stereo, which will be sold for $385, replaces the older model.

Notice here that the replacing—not the price—has become the main idea of the sentence.

A dependent clause is not always less important than the main clause. The information contained in the dependent clause can be as important as the information in the main clause. Consider the following sentence:

All dogs that bite people will be kept indoors.

If the subordinate clause that bite people is removed from the above sentence, the true meaning of the sentence is lost. In this example, the subordinate clause is vital to the meaning of the sentence.

Exercise for Subskill 3A

Part A. Read the following ten clauses. In the blanks provided, write whether each clause is dependent or independent.

EXAMPLE: Time flies.   ___independent___

1. Whom I met. _____

2. I love cream cheese. _____

3. Who is that tall guy? _____

4. Whose address I have. _____

5. Which I saw yesterday. _____

6. We will be home soon. _____

7. When I get a chance. _____

8. I've seen that play. _____

9. The end is near. _____

10. If he calls you. _____

Part B. Look at the following complex sentences. In each sentence, underline the independent clause. Put brackets around the dependent clause.

EXAMPLE: <u>I just finished the book</u> [that you liked so much].

11. The waiter who is serving us is an old friend of mine.

12. The poster that you gave me looks great in my bedroom.

13. I don't know anyone who would eat raw fish.

14. Because it was raining, we cancelled the picnic.

15. A person who looks for trouble usually finds it.

16. The first interview that I had resulted in a job.

17. I'll turn on the TV when the game starts.

18. I won't go to the show unless you go with me.

19. He is the man whom I met in Atlanta.

20. This clock, which once belonged to my grandfather, keeps perfect time.

Check your answers on pages 14 and 15 in the Answer Key for Book Three. If you correctly answered all 20 items, go to Subskill 3B. If not, do the Supplemental Exercise for Subskill 3A.

Supplemental Exercise for Subskill 3A

A dependent clause is a group of words that contains a subject and a verb but cannot stand alone as a complete sentence. An independent clause expresses a complete thought and can stand alone as a sentence. The combination of a dependent clause and an independent clause is called a complex sentence.

Part A. Read the following ten clauses. In the blanks provided, write whether each clause is <u>dependent</u> or <u>independent</u>.

EXAMPLE: Flowers bloom.   <u>independent</u>

 1. Whom she liked.   _____

 2. Where we ate today.   _____

 3. Baseball is my sport.   _____

 4. Whose book I took.   _____

 5. Run on home.   _____

 6. If she writes you.   _____

 7. Please work overtime.   _____

 8. Whose lunch this is.   _____

 9. The door closed.   _____

10. Which I just borrowed.   _____

Part B. In the following complex sentences, underline the independent clause. Put brackets around the dependent clause.

EXAMPLE: <u>No one</u> [who lives here] <u>drives a blue car.</u>

11. She is a boss who expects everyone to work hard.

12. There are many people who have never been out of their home state.

13. The card that I will turn over next is the ace of hearts.

14. When you see her, tell her I said hello.

15. The article that I mentioned was in yesterday's paper.

16. The woman whose purse you found lives near my bus stop.

17. She might not get angry if you have a good explanation for your behavior.

18. The tomato, which is now a part of our diet, was once considered poisonous.

19. Which apartment is the one that you live in?

20. After our friends left, we washed the dishes.

Check your answers on page 15 in the Answer Key for Book Three. If you correctly answered 16 of 20 items, go to Subskill 3B. If not, ask your instructor for help.

Subskill 3B: Using Adjective Clauses in Complex Sentences

When you complete this subskill, you will be able to recognize dependent clauses that function as adjectives. You will be able to choose the correct relative pronoun to begin an adjective clause. You will be able also to correctly punctuate sentences with adjective clauses.

Subordinate Clauses as Adjective Clauses

An adjective is a word that modifies or describes a noun. Adjectives tell "what kind," "how many," or "which one." Look at the following sentence:

The black poodle jumped through the small hoop.

Black and small are both adjectives. Black modifies the noun poodle, and small modifies the noun hoop. Both adjectives answer the question "What kind?"

Sometimes a dependent clause is used instead of a single word to modify a noun. A dependent clause that functions as an adjective is called an **adjective clause.** An adjective clause generally answers the question "Which one?" about the noun it modifies.

Look at the following complex sentence:

The ship [that sank at sea] was an oil tanker.

In this example, the dependent clause is that sank at sea. The entire clause serves as an adjective that modifies the noun ship. It answers the question "Which one?"

An adjective clause closely follows the noun that it modifies. In these examples, we'll mark the subjects S and the verbs V.

$$\text{S} \qquad \text{S} \underbrace{\quad \text{V} \quad}_{} \qquad \text{V}$$
The country [that I would like to visit] is Mexico.

In this example, note that the independent clause is The country is Mexico. The adjective clause that I would like to visit closely follows the noun country, which it modifies. The adjective clause describes or tells something about the noun country. It answers the question "Which one?" Note that the adjective clause that I would like to visit contains a subject and verb but cannot stand alone as a sentence.

Here's another example:

$$\text{S} \quad \text{V} \qquad \overset{\frown}{\quad} \text{S} \quad \text{V}$$
I visited my cousin [who lives in New Jersey].

The arrow is used to indicate that the dependent clause modifies the noun cousin. The adjective clause tells something about the cousin by answering the question "Which one?"

Adjective Clauses Start With a Relative Pronoun

Adjective clauses are often called **relative clauses** because they are usually introduced by the relative pronouns who, whom, whose, which, or that. These pronouns connect the adjective clause to the noun or pronoun that the clause modifies. In the examples below, each adjective clause is enclosed in brackets and each relative pronoun is underlined. An arrow is drawn from the relative pronoun to the noun it modifies.

A man [whom I know] was elected mayor.

ADJECTIVE CLAUSE:	whom I know
SUBJECT:	I
VERB:	know
RELATIVE PRONOUN:	whom
INDEPENDENT CLAUSE:	A man was elected mayor.
SUBJECT:	man
VERB:	was elected

The adjective clause modifies the noun man. It tells something about the man by answering the question "Which one?"

Many people [who visit New York City] tour Ellis Island.

ADJECTIVE CLAUSE:	who visit New York City
SUBJECT:	who
VERB:	visit
RELATIVE PRONOUN:	who
INDEPENDENT CLAUSE:	Many people tour Ellis Island.
SUBJECT:	people
VERB:	tour

The adjective clause modifies the noun people. It tells something about the people.

Exercise 1 for Subskill 3B

Each of the following sentences contains an adjective clause. For each sentence, do the following:

· Put brackets around the adjective clause.

· Underline the relative pronoun that begins each clause.

· Draw an arrow from the clause to the noun that it modifies.

Check your work to make sure you have completed each step.

EXAMPLE: The book [that I need] is on the top shelf.

1. The woman who helped you is named Sarah.

2. The new stadium, which we saw last night, is huge.

3. He is a person whom you can trust.

4. The dress that she liked was too expensive.

5. The boy whose front tooth is missing is her son.

Check your answers on page 15 in the Answer Key for Book Three. If you correctly answered all 5 items, continue reading. If not, review the discussion about recognizing adjective clauses on pages 90–91. Then go on to the next section of Subskill 3B. NOTE: The skills in this exercise will be used in some of the sentences in the Supplemental Exercise for Subskill 3B on page 98.

Choosing the Correct Relative Pronoun

Choosing the correct relative pronoun to begin an adjective clause can be confusing. Some relative pronouns are used to refer to people. Others are used to refer to things. The following guidelines show the correct relative pronouns for different situations.

Who/Whom

Who and whom are relative pronouns that refer to people. Use who as the subject of a sentence or dependent clause. Use whom as a direct object, an indirect object, or an object of a preposition.

You will remember that a direct object tells who or what receives the action of a verb. An indirect object tells to whom or for whom an action is done. In this example, we'll mark the indirect object IO and the direct object DO.

S   V   IO   DO

That man gave my brother a free hamburger.

In the above example, hamburger is the direct object of the verb gave. It tells what the man gave. Brother is the indirect object. It tells to whom the man gave the hamburger.

An object of a preposition is a noun or pronoun that follows a preposition. Prepositions are words such as as, to, for, at, above, across, toward, under, during and with. In this example, we'll mark the object of the preposition O Prep.

S   V   DO   O Prep

That man gave a free hamburger to my brother.

In the above, the word brother is the object of the preposition to.

Like all clauses, an adjective clause contains a subject and a verb. The relative pronoun who can be used as the subject of an adjective clause. Look at the following example:

The man [who gave me a hamburger] owns a restaurant.

ADJECTIVE CLAUSE:	who gave me a hamburger
SUBJECT:	who
VERB:	gave
DIRECT OBJECT:	hamburger
INDIRECT OBJECT:	me

INDEPENDENT CLAUSE:	The man owns a restaurant.
SUBJECT:	man
VERB:	owns
DIRECT OBJECT:	restaurant

In this example, who is the subject of the adjective clause. The clause modifies the noun man.

In addition to a subject and verb, an adjective clause may also contain a direct object, an indirect object, or an object of the preposition.

Although the words who and whom are similar, who is always used as the subject of a sentence or clause. Whom, on the other hand, is always used as an object.

Look at the following example:

A woman [whom I know] gave me a bad check.

ADJECTIVE CLAUSE:	whom I know
SUBJECT:	I
VERB:	know
DIRECT OBJECT:	whom
INDEPENDENT CLAUSE:	A woman gave me a bad check.
SUBJECT:	woman
VERB:	gave
DIRECT OBJECT:	check
INDIRECT OBJECT:	me

In this example, whom serves as the direct object of the adjective clause. The entire adjective clause modifies the noun woman.

Here is another example of the use of whom in an adjective clause:

The person [for whom I placed the order] still owes me money.

ADJECTIVE CLAUSE:	for whom I placed the order
SUBJECT:	I
VERB:	placed
DIRECT OBJECT:	order
OBJECT OF THE PREPOSITION:	whom

INDEPENDENT CLAUSE:	The person still owes me money.
SUBJECT:	person
VERB:	owes
DIRECT OBJECT:	money
INDIRECT OBJECT:	me

The adjective clause modifies the noun person. The relative pronoun whom serves as an object of the preposition within the clause.

Whose

The relative pronoun whose should not be confused with the contraction who's, which stands for who is. Whose is the possessive case of the word who. Unlike the relative pronoun who, whose may refer to either a person or a thing.

The possessive case of a word indicates ownership. For example, in the phrase my apartment, my is a possessive pronoun. The word my indicates ownership of the apartment. The following examples show how the relative pronoun whose is used:

The man [whose pen you borrowed] went home for the day.

In the above example, the adjective clause whose pen you borrowed modifies the noun man. The relative pronoun whose indicates that the man owns the pen.

The tree [whose leaves are yellow] will be cut down.

In the above example, the adjective clause whose leaves are yellow modifies the noun tree. The relative pronoun whose indicates that the leaves belong to the tree.

Which/That

Which and that are relative pronouns used to refer to things. As a general rule, which is used to provide extra information about a thing. A relative clause that starts with which is usually set off by commas.

My bicycle, [which I bought last year], needs oil.

In this example, which is used to begin a clause that provides extra information. The information which I bought last year is not vital to the sentence. It seems almost incidental.

The relative pronoun that is used in a clause that helps to identify a particular thing. Often, the information in a clause that starts with that may seem more essential to the sentence. A clause starting with that describes the particular thing being spoken of. The entire clause answers the question "Which one?" Such an identifying clause can be smoothly absorbed into the sentence without any extra punctuation and should not be set off by commas.

The bicycle [that squeaks] needs oil.

In this example, the relative pronoun that is used to introduce an adjective clause that pinpoints or identifies which bicycle is being referred to. Notice that no commas are used to set off the clause. You will learn more about punctuating adjective clauses in the next section. NOTE: Sometimes you will see the relative pronoun that used to refer to a person. This usage is acceptable, but who or whom is always a better choice.

ACCEPTABLE: The man [that owns the store] is my uncle.
BETTER: The man [who owns the store] is my uncle.

Apply what you have learned by doing the following exercise.

Exercise 2 for Subskill 3B

Underline the correct relative pronoun in each sentence.

EXAMPLE: The boy (who, whom) lifted the carton is strong for his age.

1. Steve is someone (who, whom) I respect.

2. Mary, (whose, who's) horse won the blue ribbon, is my riding instructor.

3. That old house, (that, which) I think should be torn down, has been crumbling for years.

4. The woman with (who, whom) I shared a ride is my neighbor.

5. The first person (which, who, whom) reaches the finish line will be the winner.

Check your answers on page 15 in the Answer Key for Book Three. If you answered all 5 items correctly, continue reading. If not, review the discussion about relative pronouns in adjective clauses on pages 92–94. Then go on to the next section of Subskill 3B. NOTE: The skills in this exercise will be used in some of the sentences in the Supplemental Exercise for Subskill 3B on page 98.

Punctuating Sentences With Adjective Clauses

Adjective clauses that limit or pinpoint the word that modify are called **restrictive clauses.** Restrictive clauses supply necessary information about who or what is being talked about. They are not set off by commas.

People [who own cars] should have them inspected regularly.

The adjective clause who own cars is restrictive. It supplies the information that is needed to pinpoint to whom the sentence refers. The advice given in the sentence does not apply to all people, only to people who own cars. Commas are not used in the sentence because they would break the flow of the sentence and confuse the reader.

Adjective clauses that do not limit or pinpoint the word they modify are called **nonrestrictive.** Nonrestrictive clauses supply extra information about the words they modify. These clauses are set off by commas. The commas tell the reader that extra information is being given.

People, [who all share the same basic needs], should
help one another more.

In this sentence, the adjective clause is not used to pinpoint or limit the subject people. Instead, it is used to make a generalization about people.

Study these additional examples of restrictive and nonrestrictive adjective clauses:

The used car [that she bought] is in good condition.

The clause that she bought is restrictive. It supplies necessary information to pinpoint or identify exactly which used car is under discussion. No commas are used.

That used car, [which I think was overpriced], is going
to need a lot of repairs.

The clause which I think was overpriced does not pinpoint which used car is being talked about. It merely supplies extra information about that used car. The commas are signals that tell the reader that extra information is being given about the used car.

Summary of Subskills 3A and 3B

· An adjective clause is a dependent clause. It contains a subject and verb, but it is a sentence fragment.

· An adjective clause functions as an adjective. It describes a noun or pronoun and usually answers the question "Which one?"

· An adjective clause closely follows the noun it modifies.

· Adjective clauses are often called relative clauses because they usually start with one of the relative pronouns: who, whom, whose, which, or that.

· The relative pronouns who and whom are used to introduce adjective clauses that refer to people. Use who when the clause needs a subject. Use whom when the clause needs an object.

· The relative pronouns that and which are used to introduce adjective clauses that refer to animals and things. That is used to introduce clauses that identify or pinpoint the word they modify. Which is used to introduce clauses that add extra information.

· The relative pronoun whose shows possession. It can be used for either people or things. Do not confuse whose with who's, the contraction of who is or who has.

· Adjective clauses that pinpoint or identify the words they modify are called restrictive clauses. Restrictive clauses are not set off by commas. Adjective clauses that provide extra information are called nonrestrictive clauses. Nonrestrictive clauses are set off by commas.

Apply all that you have learned about adjective clauses by doing the following exercise.

Exercise 3 for Subskill 3B

Part A. For each of the following sentences, underline the adjective clause and add commas where necessary.

EXAMPLES: A person who has been drinking alcoholic beverages should not drive a car.
A person <u>who has been drinking alcoholic beverages</u> should not drive a car.

The woman next door who works at Sears is my friend.
The woman next door, <u>who works at Sears</u>, is my friend.

REMEMBER: If an adjective clause adds additional but nonessential information, it should be set off by commas.

1.   The hat that she wore to the concert was not new.

2.   Her new hat which she had worked so hard to buy was still on the bus somewhere between Boston and New York.

3.   A child who is treated considerately will probably be considerate of others.

4.   The backyard which was quite large was the children's playground.

5.   We put the food in the refrigerator which was the only cool place in the house.

6.   Mr. Anderson's house which stood on a hill was one of our favorite meeting places.

7.   The apartment that they live in now is not nearly as large as their old one.

8.   The only cable that would work in my computer could not be found in town.

9.   This lamp which was made in England has a very small base.

10.   A driver who is not used to these roads could easily get lost.

Part B. Rewrite each of the sentence pairs on page 98 as a complex sentence with an adjective clause. In each case, subordinate the sentence that is underlined. Be sure to choose the correct relative pronoun and to use commas where necessary.

EXAMPLE: **a.**   The movie was too long.
b.   <u>I saw the movie.</u>

The movie that I saw was too long.

11. **a.** A lady was once an opera singer.
    b. I know the lady.

    _____

12. **a.** Mrs. Byrne still writes to my mother.
    b. Mrs. Byrne was our neighbor in Columbus.

    _____

    _____

13. **a.** That new show is going off the air.
    b. I happen to like the show.

    _____

    _____

14. **a.** The woman plays in the local orchestra.
    b. The woman's trumpet was stolen.

    _____

    _____

15. **a.** The map does not show the new highway.
    b. I gave you the map.

    _____

    _____

Check your answers on pages 15 and 16 in the Answer Key for Book Three. If you correctly answered at least 12 of 15 items, go to Subskill 3C. If not, do the Supplemental Exercise for Subskill 3B.

Supplemental Exercise for Subskill 3B

This exercise provides practice in all the material found in this subskill.

Review the Summary on page 96. Then do the following exercise.

Part A. Underline the adjective clause in each sentence and add commas where necessary.

EXAMPLES: A story that is exciting can be read in one evening.
A story that is exciting can be read in one evening.

Angel Martin who has a blazing fast ball struck out eleven batters.
Angel Martin, who has a blazing fast ball, struck out eleven batters.

1. My dining room table which is made of walnut has a split leg.

2. Ralph Ortiz who once lived next door to me has been elected councillor.

3. A child who reads poorly usually has difficulty with other lessons, too.

4. The person who wins the contest will receive a free trip to Europe.

5. Hollyhocks which should be transplanted in late May show a lively variety of colors.

6. The members of the bowling team who ranged in age from seventeen to fifty brought back souvenirs from their tournament.

7. My only sister who moved to Tulsa last year calls me at least once a month.

8. Anyone whose grade is 70% or over will pass.

9. People who break their word cannot be trusted.

10. All those suggestions which were given in a spirit of helpfulness were read by my boss.

Part B. Rewrite each of the following sentence pairs as a complex sentence with an adjective clause. In each case, subordinate the sentence that is underlined. Be sure to choose the correct relative pronoun and to use commas where necessary.

EXAMPLE: a. Washington is very humid.
b. Washington was built on a swamp.

Washington, which was built on a swamp, is very humid.

11. a. The man was in an accident.
b. The man's wrist is broken.

12. a. The woman should do something.
b. She is in charge.

13. a. My Aunt Helen is coming to visit me.
b. I really like Aunt Helen.

14. a. That record is scratched.
b. A friend gave it to me.

15. a. The car should be stopped.
b. It went through that red light.

Check your answers on page 16 in the Answer Key for Book Three. If you answered 12 of 15 items correctly, go to Subskill 3C. If not, ask your instructor for help.

Subskill 3C: Using Adverb Clauses in Complex Sentences

When you complete this subskill, you will be able to use adverb clauses in complex sentences. You will recognize the subordinate conjunctions that are used to introduce adverb clauses. You will also be able to punctuate sentences that contain adverb clauses.

Clauses That Function as Adverbs

In the last subskill, you learned that some dependent clauses function as adjectives in a sentence. Another kind of dependent clause functions as an adverb. A clause that serves as an adverb is known as an **adverb clause.**

Remember that an adverb is a word used to modify or expand the meaning of a verb, an adjective, or another adverb. For example, notice how the meaning of the independent clause she swims changes with the addition of two different adverbs. In these examples, we'll mark the adverbs Adv.

Adv
She swims quickly.

Adv
She swims poorly.

Each of the sentences above contains an adverb modifying the verb swims. In each case, the adverb answers the question "How?" Each tells "how" the woman swims. Adverbs can also answer the questions "Why?", "Where?", "When?", or "To what extent?" Consider the following sentence:

Sam looked everywhere for her.

In the above example, everywhere is an adverb. In this case, the adverb modifies the verb looked and tells "where" Sam looked.

Like single-word adverbs, adverb clauses answer the questions "How?", "Where?", "When?", "Why?", and "To what extent?" They may also answer the question "Under what condition?" Adverb clauses usually modify verbs only.

Like other dependent clauses, adverb clauses contain a subject and a verb, but they do not express a complete thought unless they are combined with an independent clause in a complex sentence.

In the following complex sentence, the independent clause is underlined and the adverb clause is in brackets:

We left the party [before you arrived.]

Notice that the dependent clause before you arrived has a subject and verb. However, the clause is a sentence fragment and does not make sense when it stands alone. The adverb clause modifies the verb left. It tells "when" we left.

In the last subskill, you learned that adjective clauses begin with a relative pronoun. Adverb clauses, on the other hand, usually begin with a **subordinating conjunction.** Here is a list of the most common subordinating conjunctions:

Common Subordinating Conjunctions

after	because	since	when
although	before	so that	whenever
as	considering	supposing	where
as if	if	though	whereas
as long as	in order that	unless	wherever
as soon as	provided	until	while

Study the following example of a complex sentence containing an adverb clause.

The accident occurred [where the two highways intersect].

ADVERB CLAUSE:	where the two highways intersect
SUBJECT:	highways
VERB:	intersect
SUBORDINATING CONJUNCTION:	where
INDEPENDENT CLAUSE:	The accident occurred.
SUBJECT:	accident
VERB:	occurred

In the above example, the adverb clause modifies the verb occurred. It tells "where" the accident occurred.

Here's another example of a complex sentence with an adverb clause:

I drove to the side of the road [because my car had a flat tire].

ADVERB CLAUSE:	because my car had a flat tire
SUBJECT:	car
VERB:	had
SUBORDINATING CONJUNCTION:	because
INDEPENDENT CLAUSE:	I drove to the side of the road.
SUBJECT:	I
VERB:	drove

The adverb clause because my car had a flat tire modifies the verb drove. It answers the question "Why?"

The adverb clause in the following complex sentence answers the question "Under what condition?"

The entire row of dominoes will fall [if you hit one of them.]

The adverb clause modifies the verb will fall. It tells what condition needs to be met in order for the row of dominoes to fall.

Punctuating Sentences With Adverb Clauses

Use a comma after an adverb clause that begins a sentence.

Wherever he goes, people know him.

If you cannot finish the work on time, please let me know.

Generally, no comma is necessary when the adverb clause comes after the independent clause.

Please let me know if you can't finish the work on time.

People know him wherever he goes.

Study these examples. Can you explain why some of the sentences have commas and others do not?

As soon as the new road is built, traffic conditions will improve.

When the doctor measured us, Bobby was taller than I was.

The adverb clauses begin the sentence, so a comma is needed after them.

Take your camera with you wherever you go on your vacation.

There will be no vacation this year unless I earn more money.

The adverb clauses end the sentence. No comma is needed.

Exercise for Subskill 3C

Part A. For each sentence, do the following:

· Identify the adverb clauses by enclosing them in brackets.

· Circle the subordinating conjunction in each clause.

· Draw an arrow to the word that is modified by each clause.

· Add commas where necessary.

EXAMPLE: Paul will leave [(when) Andy returns.]

1. Dan walked as if he could hardly move.

2. My father goes fishing when the sun sets.

3. If he gets here in time, John will lend a hand.

4. Although I have moved from that town, I still call it home.

5. The doctor came when we called her.

6. This bridge has not been repaired since it was built.

7. I watched television until I fell asleep.

8. I solved the puzzle before you did.

9. She moved to Texas after she retired.

10. She works all day unless it rains.

Part B. Rewrite each of the following pairs of sentences as a complex sentence with an adverb clause. Select an appropriate subordinating conjunction to begin each clause (refer to the chart on page 101, if needed). Remember to use a comma after an adverb clause that begins a sentence. There are several possible correct sentences for each item.

EXAMPLE: You work hard. You will get a bonus.

    If you work hard, you will get a bonus.

11. All of you push. I signal.

12. Mary laughed. I told her that joke.

13. They felt better. They played basketball.

14. I heard her call. I hurried back.

15. He left. She left.

Check your answers to Part A on pages 16 and 17 in the Answer Key for Book Three. Have your instructor evaluate your answers for Part B. If you correctly answered 12 of 15 items, go to Subskill 3D. If not, do the Supplemental Exercise for Subskill 3C.

Supplemental Exercise for Subskill 3C

An adverb clause is a dependent clause that functions as an adverb. An adverb clause usually modifies a verb. It tells "where," "when," "how," "why," "to what extent," or "under what condition."

An adverb clause begins with a subordinating conjunction. Review the most common subordinating conjunctions on page 101.

Part A.

For each sentence, do the following:

· Identify the adverb clauses by enclosing them in brackets.

· Draw an arrow to the word that is modified by each clause.

· Circle the subordinating conjunction in each clause.

· Add commas where necessary.

Check your work to make sure you have completed each step.

EXAMPLE: We will cancel the picnic [(if) it rains today.]

1. We will send out our wedding invitations as soon as they are ready.

2. Although he looked well he had a serious health problem.

3. If we have an opportunity we should stop and put chains on the tires.

4. While the potatoes are baking I can toss the salad.

5. Although you are riding your bike you will get home first.

6. After we set the table we can eat.

7. We watched the football game until my friend came home.

8. We went to the movie because there was nothing on television.

9. He acts as if he owns the whole town.

10. Please answer this letter so that I can make plans.

Part B. Rewrite each of the following pairs of sentences as a complex sentence with an adverb clause. Select an appropriate subordinating conjunction to begin each clause (refer to the chart on page 101, if needed). Remember to use a comma after an adverb clause that begins a sentence. There are several possible correct sentences for each item.

EXAMPLE: We will go to the dance. The band is great.

We will go to the dance because the band is great.

11.   You hurry. You can catch the train.

_____

12.   Robert wants that job. The job pays good wages.

_____

13.   I went to Mexico. I could practice my Spanish there.

_____

14.   Summer arrives. I plan to hike through the mountains.

_____

15.   That car is ten years old. That car has no rust on it.

_____

Check your answers to Part A on page 17 in the Answer Key for Book Three. Have your instructor evaluate your answers for Part B. If you correctly answered 12 of 15 items, go to Subskill 3D. If not, ask your instructor for help.

Subskill 3D: Using Noun Clauses in Complex Sentences

When you complete this subskill, you will be able to recognize noun clauses and identify their functions in a complex sentence. You will be able to use noun clauses correctly in complex sentences. You will also be able to use the pronouns <u>who</u>, <u>whom</u>, <u>whoever</u>, and <u>whomever</u> correctly in noun clauses.

Noun Clauses Function as Nouns

You have learned that some dependent clauses function as adjectives and others function as adverbs. A third kind of dependent clause functions as a noun in complex sentences.

Remember that a noun is the name of a person, place, or thing. Nouns can function as subjects, predicate nouns, direct objects, indirect objects, or objects of a preposition in a sentence. The following sentences will help you review these noun functions:

Steve was lying.

The noun Steve is the subject of the sentence. The subject tells who or what the sentence is about. Who was lying? Steve.

Dessert will be chocolate cake.

In this sentence, cake is a predicate nominative. A predicate nominative is a noun or pronoun that follows a linking verb and renames the subject.

I threw the ball.
I can't remember the message.
I called Sarah.

In these sentences, the nouns ball, message, and Sarah are direct objects. A direct object tells who or what receives the action of the verb. The direct objects in these sentences answer the questions "threw what?" "remember what?" and "called whom?"

I will tell Betty the news.

In this sentence the noun news is the direct object and the noun Betty is the indirect object. An indirect object tells to whom or for whom an action is done. An indirect object can occur only in combination with a direct object. The words to and for are never expressed before an indirect object.

I will tell the news to Betty.

Prepositions such as to show the relationship between one part of a sentence and another. A noun that follows a preposition is called an object of the preposition. In the example above, the noun Betty is the object of the preposition to.

Identifying Noun Clauses

Like other kinds of dependent clauses, noun clauses consist of a subject-verb combination that cannot stand alone as a sentence. Like other dependent clauses, they must be attached to an independent clause to make sense.

The following words may be used to introduce noun clauses:

who	which	where
whoever	whichever	why
whom	what	how
whomever	whatever	if
whose	whether	that
whosever	when	

Notice that the list includes the relative pronouns who, whom, whose, and that, which can also be used to introduce adjective clauses. Also notice that the list contains the words whether, when, where, and if, which can also be used to introduce adverb clauses. To identify a noun clause, you must identify how the clause functions in the sentence. Notice how the clauses in the following sentences function as nouns.

Noun Clause as Subject

[Whoever told you that story] was lying.

Notice that the noun clause itself contains a subject-verb combination. Whoever is the subject and told is the verb. Also notice that the entire noun clause functions as the subject of the sentence as a whole. Who was lying? Whoever told you that story. You could replace the entire noun clause by a noun and the sentence would still make sense: Steve was lying.

Noun Clause as Predicate Noun

The dessert will be [whatever you like.]

Notice again that the noun clause itself contains a subject-verb combination (you like). Also notice that the entire clause functions as a predicate nominative in the sentence as a whole. It renames the subject of the sentence: dessert. Dessert = whatever you like. You could replace the entire noun clause with a noun and the sentence would still make sense: The dessert will be chocolate cake.

Noun Clause as Direct Object

Notice the different kinds of noun clauses that can be used as direct objects in the following examples:

I can't remember [what you said.]
[whether they are coming.]
[why I did that.]
[where we are meeting.]
[whom you called.]
[who called you.]

Each noun clause above names something that can't be remembered. Each answers the question "can't remember what?" Each clause functions as a direct object.

Noun Clause as Indirect Object

I will tell [whoever calls me] the news.
I will tell [whomever I like] the news.

Each sentence above has the same subject and verb: I will tell. Each has the same direct object: news. Each sentence contains a noun clause that tells to whom the action will be done. Each noun clause functions as an indirect object.

Noun Clause as Object of the Preposition

> I will tell the news to [whoever calls me.]
> I will tell the news to [whomever you like.]

Again, each sentence contains the same subject, verb, and direct object. This time, however, the noun clauses function as objects of the preposition because the word <u>to</u> is expressed before each clause.

HINT: To identify a noun clause, find a subject-verb combination that cannot stand alone as a sentence. Then ask yourself whether the entire clause can be replaced by a noun. Notice that each of the noun clauses used in this section can be replaced by a noun.

Using <u>Who</u>, <u>Whom</u>, <u>Whoever</u>, and <u>Whomever</u> Correctly in Noun Clauses

In Subskill 3B, you learned to use <u>who</u> and <u>whom</u> correctly in adjective clauses. You learned to use <u>who</u> as the subject of a clause and <u>whom</u> as an object. The same rules apply to using <u>who</u>, <u>whom</u>, <u>whoever</u>, and <u>whomever</u> in noun clauses.

Use <u>who</u> or <u>whoever</u> as the subject of a noun clause. Use <u>whom</u> or <u>whomever</u> as an object. When choosing the correct pronoun for a noun clause, ignore the rest of the sentence. Look only at the noun clause. The function of the clause in the sentence does not affect the correct pronoun choice.

>   S   V
> [Whoever told you that story] was lying.

>   DO   S   V
> [Whomever you like] will be invited.

In each example, the entire noun clause functions as the subject of the sentence. However, to choose the correct pronoun, you must ignore the function of the clause in the sentence and look only at the clause itself. In the clause <u>whoever told you that story</u>, <u>whoever</u> is the subject of the verb <u>told</u>. In the clause <u>whomever you like</u>, the subject is <u>you</u> and the verb is <u>like</u>. <u>Whomever</u> is the direct object of the clause.

Now look at these sentences. In the second example, we'll mark the direct object <u>DO</u>.

>   S   V
> I will tell the news to [whoever calls me.]

>   DO   S   V
> I will tell the news to [whomever you like.]

In both sentences the noun clause is used as the object of the preposition <u>to</u>. However, to choose the right pronoun, you must ignore the function of the clause in the sentence and focus on the clause itself.

In the noun clause <u>whoever calls me</u>, <u>whoever</u> is the subject of the verb <u>calls</u>. In the noun clause <u>whomever you like</u>, <u>you</u> is the subject, <u>like</u> is the verb, and <u>whomever</u> is the direct object. NOTE: In a noun clause <u>who</u>, <u>whom</u>, <u>whoever</u>, or <u>whomever</u> may also function as predicate nouns. In the following example, we'll mark the predicate nominative PN and the linking verb LV.

PN   LV
Do you know [who he is?]

The subject of the noun clause is he. The linking verb in the clause is is. The predicate nominative who renames the subject he.

Using That to Introduce Noun Clauses

The pronoun that is often used to introduce a noun clause. In many cases, however, the pronoun that can be left out and the sentence will still make sense. Both of the following sentences contain a noun clause and are correct:

> I think [that they are coming].
> I think [they are coming].

In both sentences, a noun clause is used as the direct object of the sentence. Even when the pronoun that is not stated, it is understood to be there. That they are coming remains a dependent clause that cannot stand alone.

Punctuating Noun Clauses in Sentences

Commas should not be placed between a subject and a verb or between a verb and its objects. Because noun clauses function most often as subjects or objects, they are usually not set off by commas.

> Jack will be back to pick it up.
> [Whoever left this jacket] will be back to pick it up.

> I believe it.
> I believe [that she was telling the truth].

Exercise for Subskill 3D

Part A. Each of the following sentences contains at least one noun clause. Put brackets around each noun clause. Then, on the line below, write subject, predicate nominative, direct object, indirect object, or object of the preposition to indicate how the clause functions in the sentence.

EXAMPLE: Do you see [what I see]?

       direct object

1. Your encouragement is what I need.

   _____

2. Whoever has the winning raffle ticket will receive the prize.

   _____

3. I know that they miss us.

   _____

4. Put your books on whichever desk you'd like.

   _____

5. Give whoever answers the door the package.

   _____

6. Do you think the price is reasonable?

   _____

7. What you see is what you get.

   _____

8. When the crime occurred is not known.

   _____

9. Tell me how you did that trick.

   _____

10. She forgot where she put her keys.

    _____

Part B. Underline the correct pronoun in each sentence.

EXAMPLE: See (who, whom) is at the door.

11. She will give a receipt to (whoever, whomever) needs one.

12. I know (who, whom) you will choose.

13. I know (who, whom) was here yesterday.

14. Send an invitation to (whoever, whomever) you like.

15. They gave (whoever, whomever) volunteered a chance to do an important job.

Check your answers on page 18 in the Answer Key for Book Three. If you answered all 15 items correctly, go to the Self-Check. If not, do the Supplemental Exercise for Subskill 3D.

Supplemental Exercise for Subskill 3D

· A noun clause is a dependent clause that functions as a noun. Noun clauses can be subjects, predicate nominatives, direct objects, indirect objects, or objects of the preposition.

· To choose between who and whom or whoever and whomever in a noun clause, ignore the function of the clause in the sentence. Look only at the subject-verb combination in the clause itself.

· The relative pronoun <u>that</u> can be either stated or understood before a noun clause:

> I believe [that I can do it].
> I believe [I can do it].

Part A.   Put brackets around each noun clause. Then, on the line below, write the function of the clause in the sentence.

EXAMPLE: She told me [what I needed to know].

_____direct object_____

1. We went shopping for whatever we needed.

   _____

2. The crucial question is whether we can afford the payments.

   _____

3. What you are saying is the truth.

   _____

4. Some of the neighbors thought that we should sign a petition against the new landfill.

   _____

5. I think it's going to rain.

   _____

6. I will give whoever is in charge that message.

   _____

7. His excuse for speeding was that he was late for work.

   _____

8. They are never satisfied with what we do.

   _____

9. Whoever is the last to leave should turn out the lights.

   _____

10. She thinks he is home.

   _____

Part B.   Underline the correct pronoun in each sentence.

EXAMPLE: She will ask (whoever, <u>whomever</u>) we suggest.

11. (Whoever, Whomever) you contact should be someone trustworthy.

12. I will cheer for (whoever, whomever) wins.

13. (Whoever, Whomever) is in charge should sign the purchase order.

14. I know (who, whom) he is.

15. I don't know (who, whom) she called.

Check your answers on pages 18 and 19 in the Answer Key for Book Three. If you answered 12 of 15 items correctly, go to the Self-Check. If not, ask your instructor for help.

SELF-CHECK: SKILL UNIT 3

Part A. Rewrite each pair of sentences as one complex sentence by changing the underlined sentence to the type of dependent clause indicated in parentheses. You may have to omit a word, add a word, or change the order of the words in the original sentences. Supply any necessary commas.

EXAMPLE: The rookie joined the baseball team today. He slammed a home run his first time at bat.   (adjective clause)

The rookie who joined the baseball team today

slammed a home run his first time at bat.

1. A biologist is a person. A biologist studies living things. (adjective clause)

_____

_____

2. You want to try something. It isn't very practical.   (noun clause)

_____

_____

3. The sun is beginning to come out. It is still raining.   (adverb clause)

_____

_____

4. The woman's cat is missing. The woman posted a sign on the bulletin board.   (adjective clause)

_____

_____

5. The garden is growing very well. Mary planted the garden.   (adjective clause)

_____

_____

6. John was only sixteen. <u>He joined the work force.</u>   (adverb clause)

_____

_____

7. <u>Lisa recognized the woman.</u> Lisa did not speak to her.
(adverb clause)

_____

_____

8. <u>A woman is running for mayor.</u> I know the woman.
(adjective clause)

_____

_____

9. <u>The officers were elected.</u> The meeting was adjourned.
(adverb clause)

_____

_____

10. <u>Her sister is coming to visit on Friday.</u> She has already told me
that.   (noun clause)

_____

_____

Part B.   Underline the correct pronoun in each sentence.

EXAMPLE: Give this cash to (whoever, <u>whomever</u>) wins the carnival
lottery.

11. The clerk to (who, whom) I gave the money is not here now.

12. Anyone (who, whom) likes mysteries will like that movie.

13. The man (who's, whose) jacket is torn is my brother.

14. My new dress, (that, which) is blue and white, was very reasonably
priced.

15. (Whoever, Whomever) you invite should bring a bathing suit.

16. Tell me (who, whom) you like.

17. The person (that, which, who) lives here is a friend of mine.

18. The couch (that, which) I want is on sale.

19. Hand this paper to (whoever, whomever) opens the door.

20. The doctor (who, whom) she usually sees is out of town.

Check your answers on page 19 in the Answer Key for Book Three.
If you answered 16 of 20 items correctly, you have shown that you have
mastered these skills. If not, ask your instructor for help.

Skill Unit 4

USING SENTENCE PUNCTUATION

What Skills You Need to Begin: You need to be able to write simple sentences (Skill Unit 1), compound sentences (Skill Unit 2) and complex sentences (Skill Unit 3).

What Skills You Will Learn: When you complete this unit, you will understand most uses of punctuation. You will be able to use correct punctuation at the end of a sentence. You will be able to use commas to set off certain words or groups of words within sentences. You will be able to use apostrophes in different ways. You will also be able to use quotation marks, and punctuate sentences correctly when quotation marks are used with other punctuation marks.

Why You Need These Skills: Punctuation marks make sentences easier to understand. The ancient Greeks invented punctuation marks, but did not use them as we do today. The words period and comma are both Greek in origin. But for many centuries, no rules for punctuation existed. When most books were handwritten, often the only indication of the start of a sentence was a larger initial letter. By about the tenth century, periods or short vertical lines sometimes were used to mark a break in the flow of words. Gradually, after the printing industry began in the 15th century, a greater variety of marks became familiar. But punctuation rules, as we know them, did not become a standard practice until the middle of the 19th century.

When important punctuation marks are missing, readers can become confused. Punctuation marks are a kind of code that people have agreed to use for certain information about sentences. Think of punctuation as being something like the system of traffic signals and road signs. People who drive have agreed to this code in much the same way that writers of English have agreed to use the punctuation code. So, get your signals straight. Don't go when you are supposed to stop. Also, don't confuse a reader by putting a comma, for example, where a period would make more sense.

How You Will Show What You Have Learned: You will take the Self-Check at the end of this unit on page 135. The Self-Check contains 20 sentences. If you correctly punctuate 16 of 20 sentences, you will have shown that you have mastered these skills. You will have 30 minutes to complete the Self-Check.

If you feel that you have already mastered these skills, turn to the end of this unit and complete the Self-Check on page 135.

Subskill 4A: Using Periods, Question Marks, and Exclamation Points

When you complete this subskill, you will be able to choose the correct punctuation to put at the end of sentences and questions.

Use of the Period

The **period** is by far the most common punctuation mark for the end of a sentence. A period is used at the end of any **declarative sentence,** or any sentence that states a fact or an opinion, condition, or possibility. A period is used to end each of the following statements:

I have $25 in my wallet.
It's too cold in Minnesota.
If you finish your homework, you may go to the game.
The package may arrive during the day tomorrow.

Periods are also used to end **imperative** statements, which express commands and direct requests:

Sign on the dotted line.

Please sit down.

The period is the most basic punctuation mark because it is used to show the end of most sentences.

Use of the Question Mark

Question marks are used at the end of every sentence that is a direct question. A question mark is used to end each of the following questions:

Do you know what time it is?

Why is she laughing?

When an **indirect question** is asked, a question mark is not used:

He asked her if she would help him.

Bob wondered why his boss was late.

Use of the Exclamation Point

An **exclamation point** is generally used at the end of a sentence that expresses surprise, strong emotion, or urgency. Often these expressions of urgency are not complete sentences. They lack a subject or a verb, or both. They are called exclamations. With exclamations that begin with <u>how</u>, or <u>what</u>, an exclamation point is generally used to give even greater stress. Exclamations and exclamation points communicate the author or speaker's point of view. They are never neutral or bland:

How tall you've grown!

What a beautiful day!

The exclamation point is also commonly used with an imperative:

Hurry!

Don't sign it!

The imperative <u>Don't sign it</u> could also end with a period, in which case there would be no sense of urgency:

Don't sign it.

The exclamation point is also used with a declarative statement to show surprise or strong feeling:

You have a beautiful tan!

Do the following exercise to test your understanding of the uses of periods, question marks, and exclamation points to end sentences.

Exercise for Subskill 4A

Put the correct end punctuation after each of the following sentences.

EXAMPLE: What a gorgeous day
          What a gorgeous day!

1. Where is the post office
2. Turn left at the first intersection after the church
3. What a silly story
4. I asked him if he had time to help me
5. It may rain tomorrow
6. The sun rose at 7:35
7. How do you like the music
8. I wonder what will happen next
9. How right you are
10. Look out

Check your answers on pages 19 and 20 in the Answer Key for Book Three. If you correctly punctuated all 10 sentences, go to Subskill 4B. If not, do the Supplemental Exercise for Subskill 4A.

Supplemental Exercise for Subskill 4A

Periods, question marks, and exclamation points are used for end punctuation, showing where thoughts are completed.

· Periods are used for declarative sentences. These are sentences that state facts or opinions.

She bought a new raincoat.

· Imperative statements, or statements that make commands or requests, also end with a period.

Please be on time.

· Question marks are used with direct questions.

How old are you?

· A question mark should not be used for an indirect question.

Martha asked her son where he was calling from.

· Exclamation points are used with statements of surprise, strong emotion, or urgency. An exclamation that begins with <u>how</u> or <u>what</u> ends with an exclamation point.

What a mess!

· When an exclamation is used at the end of an imperative statement, the command or request has a sense of urgency.

Be careful!

· When an exclamation is used with a declarative statement, surprise or a strong feeling is expressed.

You have some gray hairs!

Put the correct end punctuation after each of the following sentences.

EXAMPLE: When are we going

When are we going?

1. He asked his friend to wait for him

2. What a lovely day

3. Call me when you get a chance

4. What time is it

5. My mother is an accountant

6. She wondered where her cat was

7. That's a gorgeous necklace

8. Stop that right now

9. Will Harry stop in Chicago on his way to Des Moines

10. You have some nerve

Check your answers on page 25 in the Answer Key for Book Three. If you correctly punctuated 8 of 10 sentences, go to Subskill 4B. If not, ask your instructor for help.

Subskill 4B: Using Commas

When you complete this subskill, you will be able to use commas correctly in sentences.

Separating Independent Clauses

One of the main uses of a comma is to separate **independent clauses** in a compound sentence. As you learned in Skill Unit 2, a compound sentence is made up of two or more simple sentences joined together. The sentences within the compound sentence are called independent clauses, and they are joined together by **coordinating conjunctions.** A comma should be used before any of the following conjunctions: <u>and</u>, <u>but</u>, <u>for</u>, <u>or</u>, <u>nor</u>, <u>so</u>, and <u>yet</u>. For example:

> The dachshund has a long body, but its legs are very
> short.

This compound sentence is made up of the two simple sentences <u>The dachshund has a long body</u> and <u>Its legs are very short</u>. These are joined together by the conjunction <u>but</u>, and a comma appears before <u>but</u>.

Separating Introductory Words and Phrases

The comma is used also to set off an introductory word or group of words at the beginning of a sentence. A sentence may begin with an adverbial clause, a prepositional phrase, a participial phrase, the name of the person to whom the sentence is addressed, or introductory words such as <u>yes</u>, <u>well</u>, and <u>oh</u>.

The following sentence begins with an adverbial clause labeled <u>AC</u>:

> AC
> ⏜⏜⏜⏜⏜⏜⏜
> While I was eating, the cat jumped on the table.

When a sentence begins with an adverbial clause, the clause must be followed by a comma. But if the adverbial clause comes at the end of the sentence, a comma is not used:

AC

The cat jumped on the table while I was eating.

The following sentence begins with a prepositional phrase, labeled Prep Phrase, which is set off by a comma:

Prep Phrase

At the turn of the century, ragtime was very popular.

Again, a comma is not used when the sentence is turned around:

Prep Phrase

Ragtime was very popular at the turn of the century.

The next sentence example begins with a participial phrase, labeled Part Phrase, which is set off by a comma:

Part Phrase

Thanking their hosts, they left the party.

A participial phrase takes a comma in both positions:

Part Phrase

They left the party, thanking their hosts.

Use commas to separate the name of a person being addressed from the rest of the sentence:

Mr. Miller, please process these forms.

I had a terrific time, Lenny.

Finally, the comma separates introductory words at the beginning of sentences:

Oh, that's all right!

Yes, I will go with you.

In both examples, the comma tells the reader to pause briefly before going on to the independent clause that is the main part of the sentence.

Separating Items in a Series

A list of at least three items is called a **series.** The items in a series can be nouns, adjectives, verbs, or phrases. The last two items in a series usually are joined by the conjunction and or or. Commas are used between the items in the series, but not before or after the series. Series of nouns occur in the following examples:

The cashier put the tomatoes, onions, and cabbage in the bag.

Pencils, paper, and pens are all necessary items for school.

Notice where the commas are placed.

In the following example, three adjectives are used in a series and are separated by commas:

The hall was long, dark, and damp.

Adjectives in a series preceding a noun are also separated by commas:

The old, red, wooden farmhouse creaked in the storm.

Sometimes all of the items in a series may be connected by <u>and</u>, <u>or</u>, or <u>nor</u> for emphasis. In these cases, no commas are used. For example:

We could neither see nor hear nor feel the presence of
the invaders.

In the following sentence, three phrases are used in a series:

Myron got dressed, ate his breakfast, and went to work.

The commas used in a series tell the reader when items are being listed in a sentence.

Setting Off Nonessential Words

Sentences often contain words and phrases that are not absolutely essential to their meaning. Such words can be set off by commas. For example, the word <u>however</u> is not essential to the following sentence:

The rain, however, stopped.

In the following sentence, the phrase <u>of course</u> interrupts the main idea of the sentence:

Colleen, of course, was shaken by the accident.

The commas around <u>of course</u> help the reader to focus on the main idea, which is <u>Colleen was shaken by the accident</u>.

The following two sentences show why commas must be placed around words that are unnecessary to the meaning of a sentence:

Gino was shocked by the way Tom drove his car.

Tom, by the way, drove recklessly.

In the first sentence, the words <u>by the way</u> are essential to understanding what shocked Gino. The meaning would change if these words were omitted: <u>Gino was shocked Tom drove his car</u>. The second sentence, however, would have basically the same meaning without the words <u>by the way</u>: <u>Tom drove recklessly</u>.

Separating Parts of Addresses and Dates

Commas are used to separate parts of an address, as in the following example:

We moved to Houston, Texas, last fall.

The new company is located at 5500 Main St., Houston,
Texas 76543.

Notice that no comma is used to separate the state name and the zip
code.

Use commas to separate the parts of a date used in a sentence as
follows:

June 28, 1983, is the day she started working there.

Note that the month and day form a unit that is followed by a comma,
and that the year is followed by a comma.

Setting Off Appositives

An **appositive** is a noun phrase that gives more information about
another noun in the sentence. Because the appositive can be omitted
without changing the basic meaning of the sentence, it is usually set
off by commas. The appositive immediately follows the noun it describes:

Sidney, our star football player, was injured in last
week's game.

The appositive, our star football player, explains the noun Sidney more
fully.

When an appositive is essential to clarify the meaning of the noun
it follows, it is called a **close appositive** and no comma is necessary:

My son Sidney is a star football player.

In this sentence, Sidney is a close appositive. It gives the information
that the author has more than one son by identifying the son who is
being referred to. It is son Sidney, not son Ted or son Leon. If the author
had written "My only son, Sidney," Sidney would not be essential to
the meaning of the noun and would be an appositive set off by commas.

Apply what you have learned about the correct uses of commas by
doing the following exercise.

Exercise for Subskill 4B

Read the sentences on the next page and punctuate them correctly by
adding all necessary commas. If a sentence is correct as it stands, write
C in the space provided. If you add commas, use the space provided to
state the purpose the comma or commas serve in each sentence (e.g., to
separate independent clauses, to set off an appositive, etc.).

EXAMPLE: Rhoda, however, talked to the pilot and asked many questions.

To set off non-essential word

1. While Sandra was fishing a snake bit her on the ankle.

    _____

2. It was hot outside and the air was humid.

    _____

3. The horse ran out of the corral after we opened the gate.

    _____

4. Take this report to the boss Phil.

    _____

5. The red yellow and orange leaves fell from the tree.

    _____

6. Carrie packed her car drove to the mountains and set up camp.

    _____

7. The rich black moist soil produced an abundant crop of grain.

    _____

8. We could taste and feel and see the difference between the two items.

    _____

9. On January 20 1968 they were given a new car.

    _____

10. Jack by the way went to Nevada for Christmas.

    _____

11. Our fondest dream was to win the first prize a trip to Hawaii.

    _____

12. Margie the best debater on the team lost her voice last week.

    _____

Check your answers on page 25 in the Answer Key for Book Three. If you correctly added commas to 10 of 12 sentences, go to Subskill 4C. If not, do the Supplemental Exercise for Subskill 4B.

Supplemental Exercise for Subskill 4B

Commas are used in several different ways to make sentences easier to understand.

A comma is used between the two parts of a compound sentence when the parts are joined by a conjunction such as <u>and</u>, <u>but</u>, <u>for</u>, <u>or</u>, <u>nor</u>, <u>so</u>, or <u>yet</u>.

- A comma separates an introductory word group and the complete sentence that follows. In the following example, an adverbial clause is set off from the rest of the sentence:

    If you expect to succeed, you must prepare yourself.

- When an adverbial clause comes at the end of the sentence, a comma is not needed.

- Another example of an introductory word group is the name of the person or people to whom the sentence is addressed.

    Mr. Miller and Mrs. Anderson, please come to the meeting.

- A comma is also used if the noun of address comes at the end of the sentence.

- Commas are used to separate items in a series. A series consists of at least three items, which may or may not be joined by a conjunction. The items may be adjectives, verb phrases or nouns:

    The tall, thin, well-dressed man stood at the doorway.

    She arose from her chair, smiled at the audience, and began to sing.

    The farmer planted oats, barley, and corn.

- When a conjunction is used between each item in a series, commas are not used.

    You may have peas or carrots or potatoes.

- Commas set off words that are not necessary to the meaning of a sentence.

    The coat, I believe, is mine.

- Commas set off items in dates and addresses.

    Their daughter was born on Thursday, May 6, 1983.

    We live at 1203 Broadway, Houston, Texas 77062.

- No comma is necessary between the month and the day, or between the state and the zip code.

- An appositive, or a phrase that gives more information about a noun, is usually set off by commas.

    My friend, an avid tennis player, is coming to town for the tournament.

- When the appositive gives information that is essential to the noun it describes, commas are not used.

    My brother Tony lives in Kansas.

Carefully review the explanations and examples again. Then complete the following exercise to check your understanding of the uses of commas.

Read the following sentences and punctuate them correctly by adding all necessary commas. If a sentence is correct as it stands, write C in the space provided. If you add commas, use the space provided to state the purpose the comma or commas serve in each sentence (e.g., to separate independent clauses, to set off an appositive, etc.).

EXAMPLE: Will you Gilbert do the dishes this evening?
Will you, Gilbert, do the dishes this evening?

To set off a name used in direct address

1. While they waited for the bus the boys started a fight.

_____

2. Charles brought sodas hot dogs and hamburgers to the picnic.

_____

3. Neither Pedro nor Charles nor Larry knew the answer to the question.

_____

4. Sam washed the car and Lola repaired the roof.

_____

5. The tall dark slender horse won the race.

_____

6. Grizzly bears can run fast although they look slow and clumsy.

_____

7. The children laughed joked and played at the birthday party.

_____

8. Last April we moved to 72 Seton Drive Memphis Tennessee.

_____

9. We gave a farewell party for our librarian Ms. Lopez.

_____

10. The train ground to a stop backed up a few feet and stopped again.

_____

11. José I suppose asked for a raise.

_____

12. After running all day Dan was exhausted.

Check your answers on pages 25 and 26 in the Answer Key for Book Three. If you correctly added commas to 10 of 12 sentences, go to Subskill 4C. If not, ask your instructor for help.

Subskill 4C: Using Apostrophes

When you complete this subskill, you will understand the two main functions of apostrophes.

Showing Possession

Possession is generally expressed by adding an apostrophe and s ('s) to a singular noun.

The woman's coat   Milton's chair

When the noun is a **proper noun**—the name of a person or place—and it ends in s, as in Jones, it is made into a possessive according to the same rule:

Jones's car

Paris's suburbs

The only exceptions to this rule are short names that already have two s sounds, such as Moses and Jesus, and certain Greek names that end in es. These names are made into possessives by adding only the apostrophe:

Moses' laws   Aristophanes' plays

Jesus' birth   Sophocles' wisdom

When the noun is plural and ends in s, an apostrophe alone indicates possession:

The three boys' skates were stolen.

The witches' brew contained frogs and spiders.

Plural nouns such as boys and witches are pronounced exactly the same way whether or not they have an apostrophe. Therefore, when the words are spoken, only the context tells the listener when they are possessives. But when they are written, the apostrophe serves this purpose.

When a plural noun does not end in s, the possessive is formed by adding 's:

children's book   geese's flight

No apostrophes are needed with possessive pronouns. The following chart shows the possessives for pronouns:

	Possessive Pronouns	
Pronouns	that modify nouns	that act as nouns
I	my	mine
you	your	yours
he	his	his
she	her	hers
it	its	its
we	our	ours
they	their	theirs

Showing Omission

Apostrophes are used in **contractions** to show where an omission has been made. When you contract your muscles, you pull them together. Similarly, words are pulled together to form contractions. The apostrophe shows where letters have been omitted:

can not	=	can't	they are	=	they're
is not	=	isn't	it is	=	it's
there is	=	there's	you are	=	you're
are not	=	aren't	they have	=	they've
I am	=	I'm	will not	=	won't

There are no regular rules for forming contractions. However, the apostrophe is always placed where one or more letters have been omitted.

Be sure you understand the difference between the possessive pronoun its and the contraction it's. Remember, possessive pronouns do not need apostrophes, while contractions always have apostrophes. In the following sentence, both its and it's are used correctly:

It's a shame that the program lost its funding.

To test whether an apostrophe is needed, ask yourself which word you are using: the contraction of it is, or the possessive pronoun its. No apostrophe is needed with the possessive pronoun.

Because the following word pairs are pronounced the same, they are often confused in writing:

its   it's (it + is)

whose   who's (who + is)

your	you're (you + are)
their	they're (they + are)

The words on the left are possessive pronouns. The words on the right are contractions that may be used in place of the words in parentheses.

In the following exercise, test your understanding of the uses of apostrophes.

Exercise for Subskill 4C

Part A. Write the possessive form for each of the following words:

EXAMPLE: day ____day's____

1. king _____

2. who _____

3. Brahms _____

4. it _____

5. streets _____

6. women _____

7. he _____

Part B. Write the contractions of the following pairs of words in the spaces provided.

EXAMPLE: they have ____they've____

8. does not _____

9. we are _____

10. we will _____

11. I would _____

12. it is _____

13. let us _____

Part C. In some of the following sentences, apostrophes are missing. Rewrite the sentences in the spaces provided, adding apostrophes where they belong. For sentences that are correct, write a C in the space.

EXAMPLE: Theyre giving away Thomass old clothes.

____They're giving away Thomas's old clothes.____

14. He put theirs in the house.

_____

15. Martins house was next to ours.

_____

16. Its all right.

_____

17. The mens tournament will be in July.

_____

18. Its value is in its flexibility.

_____

19. Marys recipe is easier than yours.

_____

Part D. In each of the following sentences, underline the word in each pair that correctly completes the sentence.

EXAMPLE: (Who's, <u>Whose</u>) ball is that?

20. Howie missed (you're, your) call.

21. The bird broke (it's, its) wing.

22. (They're, Their) going to win the game.

23. (Who's, Whose) coming for dinner tonight?

24. (It's, Its) time for us to leave.

25. (There's, Theirs) someone in the kitchen.

Check your answers on page 21 in the Answer Key for Book Three. If you correctly answered at least 20 of the 25 items, go to Subskill 4D. If not, do the Supplemental Exercise for Subskill 4C.

Supplemental Exercise for Subskill 4C

Apostrophes are used to show possession or to show where letters are omitted in a contraction.

· To show possession add an apostrophe and an <u>s</u> to most singular nouns and proper nouns:

your girlfriend's aunt

· When a plural noun ends in <u>s</u>, add only an apostrophe to show possession:

my sons' jackets

· When a plural noun does not end in <u>s</u>, the possessive is formed by adding an apostrophe and an <u>s</u>:

The oxen's yoke

· The possessive pronouns <u>yours</u>, <u>his</u>, <u>hers</u>, <u>its</u>, <u>theirs</u>, and <u>whose</u> do not need apostrophes.

· Apostrophes are also used in contractions, a single word formed from two words, to show where letters were omitted:

do + not = don't   it + is = it's

we + have = we've   they + are = they're

Do the following exercises to test your knowledge of the uses of apostrophes.

Part A. Using the space provided, form the possessive for each of the following:

EXAMPLE: daughter   __daughter's__

1. it   _____   2. country   _____

3. Engels   _____   4. geese   _____

5. teachers   _____   6. Indianapolis   _____

7. men   _____

Part B. Write the contractions of the following pairs of words in the space provided.

EXAMPLE: he had   __he'd__

8. there is   _____   9. will not   _____

10. have not   _____   11. I have   _____

12. who is   _____   13. they will   _____

Part C. In some of the following sentences, apostrophes are missing. Rewrite the sentences in the spaces provided, adding apostrophes where they belong. For sentences that are correct, write a C in the space.

EXAMPLE: My houses roof needs to be repaired.

My house's roof needs to be repaired.

14. The lone maples leaves were turning yellow.

_____

15. Whose suit do you like better?

_____

16. Sandys television gets more stations than ours.

_____

17. His sisters boyfriends took them out for dinner.

_____

18. The womens movement has changed the lives of many men and women.

_____

19. Where have all their bookcases been stored?

Part D. In each of the following sentences underline the word in each pair that correctly completes the sentence.

EXAMPLE: (They're, Their) just in time.

20. (Who's, Whose) going to be there?

21. (You're, Your) book should be returned to the library.

22. When (it's, its) my turn, I'll be ready.

23. The cat bit (it's, its) tongue.

24. (You're, Your) the speaker at the next meeting.

25. (Who's, Whose) story did you believe?

Check your answers on pages 21 and 22 in the Answer Key for Book Three. If you correctly answered at least 20 of 25 items, go to Subskill 4D. If not, ask your instructor for help.

Subskill 4D: Punctuating Quotations

When you complete this subskill, you will be able to punctuate quotations in sentences correctly.

A quotation states exactly what someone said. When you repeat word for word what a person said, you are making a **direct quotation.**

Bill answered, "It's too late for me to go."

In the example given, "It's too late for me to go" is repeated as Bill said it. It is a direct quotation. If a sentence reports what Bill said in somewhat different words, they would be an **indirect quotation.**

Bill answered that it was too late for him to go.

The quotation marks in the direct quotation tell the reader where Bill's actual words begin and end. In the indirect quotation, the words that Bill said are not specifically quoted. For this reason, no quotation marks are needed.

Direct quotations usually include words that tell who is speaking, and may also contain adverbs that describe how the person says the quoted words. These parts of a sentence can be placed before, after, or in the middle of the quotation. For example:

The supervisor said joyfully, "Henry, your work has improved."

"Henry, your work has improved," said the supervisor joyfully.

"Henry," the supervisor said joyfully, "your work has improved."

Commas are always used to separate the direct quotation from the rest of the sentence. Where there are quotation marks, the comma is always placed before the quotation marks. A period used to end a direct quotation is always placed before the last quotation mark. For examples, look at the use of commas in the sentences above.

Any direct quotation that is a complete sentence should begin with a capital letter:

My father remarked, "She needs a good lecture."

If the direct quotation is not a complete sentence, it should begin with a lower case letter. In the following example, the direct quotation is only part of what the person said.

My father said that she needs "a good lecture."

The period still comes within the quotation marks, or before the last quotation mark.

Question marks and exclamation points may be used in direct quotations. For example:

"Have the horses been fed?" asked Janet anxiously.

Ray exclaimed, "You look fantastic!"

Notice that the question mark and exclamation point are placed inside the quotation marks. They tell the reader that what is being quoted is a question or an exclamation. Also notice in the first example that there is no need for a comma after the question mark, and that the entire sentence ends with a period.

As with quotations that are statements, quotations that are questions may be divided into two parts by inserting the words telling who is speaking:

"What in the world," asked Faith, "are they doing?"

When the sentence itself is a question, the question mark is placed after the quotation marks:

Did Mrs. Mason say, "I will not be responsible for my husband's debts"?

The quoted portion is a statement, not a question.

In the following example, the sentence itself is an exclamation, so the exclamation point goes outside the quotation marks:

Then the suspect said, "I'm not really a police officer"!

The placement of the punctuation makes it clear that the quotation itself is a statement, while the entire sentence is an exclamation. There is no need for any punctuation inside the quotation marks when they are followed by an exclamation point or a question mark to end the sentence.

Direct quotations may be longer than one sentence. The next example shows how a two-sentence quotation is punctuated:

"I think Brad is Marie's brother," said Chris. "They look alike."

The new sentence, "They look alike," must begin with a capital letter. In the following example, the words telling who is speaking are at the beginning:

Chris said, "I think Brad is Marie's brother. They look alike."

Complete the following exercise to test your understanding of the punctuation used with quotations.

Exercise for Subskill 4D

Rewrite each of the following sentences in the spaces provided, using commas, periods, quotation marks, exclamation points, and capital letters where they belong.

EXAMPLE: the child said here is a good place to play

The child said, "Here is a good place to play."

1. watch out for the poison ivy the man exclaimed

    _____

2. patrick henry said give me liberty or give me death

    _____

3. you need a new alternator said the mechanic I'll have to order it for you

    _____

    _____

4. her boss said that she could take the day off

    _____

5. where is my coat asked carlos

    _____

6. my new helicopter the boy said sadly is broken

    _____

7. what should we do now whispered sam impatiently

    _____

    _____

8. what a beautiful day exclaimed melinda

_____

9. are you going home for the holidays asked david

_____

10. he said my music was too square for words

_____

11. did he ever say I'm sorry

_____

12. then the landlord asked when do you intend to move out

_____

Check your answers on page 22 in the Answer Key for Book Three. If you punctuated at least 9 of 12 sentences correctly, go to the Self-Check. If not, do the Supplemental Exercise for Subskill 4D.

Supplemental Exercise for Subskill 4D

· Quotation marks are used to show exactly what someone said. While a direct quotation gives the exact words that a person said, an indirect quotation does not. No quotation marks are used with indirect quotations. The direct quotation is always surrounded by quotation marks. Use a comma before the second quotation mark to separate the quotation from the words that tell who is speaking:

"I quit," said Bill.

· Words that are about the speaker can be placed before or after the quotation, or they can interrupt the quotation. Commas are used to separate the interrupting words from the quotation. For example:

"After you left," explained the new employee
sheepishly, "things got out of control."

· Periods and commas are always placed inside (before) the quotation marks. Question marks and exclamation points are placed inside the quotation marks if they are part of the quotation and outside if they are not.

"Have you done your homework?" asked Cindy.

When did he say "I quit"?

The letter from my bank said, "Your account is
overdrawn by $239.45"!

Part A.   The following sentences are all indirect quotations. Rewrite them in the spaces provided as direct quotations.

EXAMPLE: Eddie said he found another job.

_____Eddie said, "I found another job."_____

1.   Juanita asked what time it was.

   _____   _____

2.   Miguel whined that he didn't want to go to bed.

   _____

3.   Did Miguel say good night?

   _____

4.   You've got a lot of nerve to say you quit!

   _____   _____

5.   Harry said that Martha knew the answer.

   _____

Part B.   Punctuation can change the meaning of a sentence. Each of the following sentences is punctuated correctly. By changing the punctuation, however, you can change who said what about whom. Rewrite each sentence in the space provided, changing the punctuation to change the meaning.

EXAMPLE: Maria said, "Robert is late."

   _____"Maria," said Robert, "is late."_____

6.   The police officer stated, "Ms. Anderson is at fault."

   _____

7.   Brian said, "Alfred may go now."

   _____

8.   The instructor stated, "The student is well prepared."

   _____

9.   "Evelyn," said Mr. Marshall, "is the most creative person I know."

   _____

10.   Pedro said, "Gina drove Martha's car."

   _____

   Check your answers on page 22 in the Answer Key for Book Three. If you answered 8 of the 10 items correctly, go to the Self-Check. If not, ask your instructor for help.

SELF-CHECK: SKILL UNIT 4

Rewrite each of the following sentences, adding end punctuation, commas, apostrophes, and quotation marks where they are needed.

EXAMPLE: Every time I visit my home town she sighed Im sorry I ever moved away

"Every time I visit my home town," she sighed,

"I'm sorry I ever moved away."

1. The garbage must be burned buried or disposed of in some way˙

2. Your purse is gone

3. After practicing all day George was tired

4. Wont you look this over before tomorrow morning Caroline asked handing her father a ten-page report

5. To request a catalogue write the company at 201 Brookline Avenue Boston Massachusetts 00215

6. The swallows nests contain a secretion that is used in a delicious soup

7. That thoughtless customer cried the grocer disgustedly has ruined these tomatoes

8. Whose coat is on the floor asked the teacher

9. The price of a cup of coffee needless to say has gone up

_____

_____

10. Its a relief that you found its cause

_____

11. The childrens clothes are soaked

_____

12. How did you feel when you said I do

_____

13. Mr. Chu please have the contract ready by noon

_____

14. See you in Detroit Roberto exclaimed

_____

15. While I was having dinner Judy called me

_____

16. Mr. Dominguez the man I met in the park has a good sense of humor

_____

_____

17. Your feet are bigger than hers

_____

18. Taxes if you ask me are too high

_____

19. Martin pulled off the highway closed the car windows and went to sleep

_____

_____

20. Ill look it up said the librarian and the next time you call me Ill have the answer for you

_____

_____

Check your answers on page 23 in the Answer Key for Book Three. If you answered 16 of 20 items correctly, you have shown that you have mastered these skills. If not, ask your instructor for help.

Skill Unit 5
USING MORE SENTENCE PUNCTUATION

What Skills You Need to Begin: You need to understand subject–verb agreement (Skill Unit 1), be able to recognize compound and complex sentences (Skill Units 2 and 3), and be able to use end punctuation, commas, apostrophes, and quotation marks correctly (Skill Unit 4).

What Skills You Will Learn: When you complete this skill unit, you will be able to use semicolons, colons, parentheses, and dashes correctly.

Why You Need These Skills: You learned in the last skill unit how end punctuation, commas, apostrophes, and quotation marks are useful for clarifying what you want to express in writing. Semicolons, colons, parentheses, and dashes provide more ways to make your writing clearer.

How You Will Show What You Have Learned: You will do the Self-Check at the end of this unit on page 152. The Self-Check consists of 12 sentences. You will rewrite the sentences, adding semicolons, colons, parentheses, and dashes where they are needed. You will have 30 minutes to complete the Self-Check. If you correctly punctuate 10 of 12 sentences, you will have shown that you have mastered these skills.

If you feel that you have already mastered these skills, turn to the end of this unit and complete the Self-Check on page 152.

Subskill 5A: Using Semicolons

When you complete this subskill, you will be able to use semicolons correctly in sentences.

The **semicolon** is easily misused. Inexperienced writers often use semicolons too often and in the wrong ways. When the semicolon is used correctly, it can be an effective way to clarify what you are trying to say.

There are three main uses of the semicolon. The first use is to separate two main clauses that are not joined by a conjunction such as and, but, for, or, or nor. The two clauses should be short in length and closely related in thought. For example:

I like Mrs. Henderson; she is never sarcastic.

You could put a period where the semicolon is and start a new sentence with she. Instead, the semicolon helps show that the second clause is closely related in thought to the first.

A second way to use semicolons is together with **conjunctive adverbs.** Words such as however, moreover, consequently, nevertheless, and therefore are called conjunctive adverbs. When they are used to join two main clauses together, they are preceded by a semicolon:

> He was ill and desperately in need of money;
> nevertheless, he would not ask his father for help.

Note the comma after the conjunctive adverb nevertheless. The order of this sentence is a common order for a sentence with a semicolon: main clause + semicolon + conjunctive adverb + comma + main clause. If you take away the semicolon, the conjunctive adverb, and the comma, you can make two sentences by adding a period and capitalizing the h in he:

> He was ill and desperately in need of money. He would
> not ask his father for help.

The third way to use a semicolon is to replace a comma in a long compound sentence. In a long compound sentence there are usually prepositional phrases or other word groups separated by commas from the independent clauses:

> Because the cat was hungry, we fed it, and after that, it
> would not leave.

In the above compound sentence, the independent clauses are we fed it and it would not leave. Each independent clause is preceded by a prepositional phrase: Because the cat was hungry and after that. A comma and the conjunction and come between the two independent clause phrase combinations. A semicolon used to replace , and will prevent confusion:

> Because the cat was hungry, we fed it; after that, it
> would not leave.

For style reasons, you might want to replace the comma with a semicolon but keep the conjunction:

> Because the cat was hungry, we fed it; and after that, it
> would not leave.

Semicolons must be used to separate the items of a series if the items already contain commas:

> We visited Philadelphia, Pennsylvania, New York, New
> York, and Boston, Massachusetts, this summer.

See how much clearer semicolons make the same sentence:

> We visited Philadelphia, Pennsylvania; New York, New
> York; and Boston, Massachusetts, this summer.

Do the following exercise to test your understanding of the uses of semicolons.

Exercise for Subskill 5A

Rewrite the following sentences if necessary, adding any needed semicolons. In some cases, you will change commas to semicolons. If the sentence is correct, write a C in the space provided.

EXAMPLE: The children are grown up now, they do not need me any longer.

<u>The children are grown up now; they do not need me any longer.</u>

1. You can walk to the park, however, I think you will prefer to take a bus.

   _____

   _____

2. Lily, who is a dreamer, was sitting alone on the porch and Maria, who hates sitting still, was out playing ball.

   _____

   _____

3. Give me a piece of your string mine is all gone.

   _____

   _____

4. Martha was over her flu however she still felt sick.

   _____

   _____

5. The group included Ms. Hernandez, the banker in town, Mr. Rosenthal, a retired farmer, and Dr. Huang, the dentist.

   _____

   _____

6. Three men and a boy sailed away, four men came back.

   _____

   _____

7. I have lived in Miami for only a month, hence I am not well acquainted with the city.

---

8. At the end of the month, however, the work became easier.

---

9. Someone yanked off his beard, soon there was no Santa Claus.

---

10. Some people prepared meals, others looked after the shelters, equipment, and children.

Check your answers on page 23 in the Answer Key for Book Three. If you correctly answered 8 of 10 items, go to Subskill 5B. If not, do the Supplemental Exercise for Subskill 5A.

Supplemental Exercise for Subskill 5A

When semicolons are used correctly, they give useful information to the reader about how ideas are related to each other. But be careful not to overuse semicolons.

· There are three main ways to use semicolons. The first way is to separate short clauses that are not joined by a conjunction such as and, but, for, or, or nor. For example:

> They did not want to go to a movie; they went bowling instead.

· The second way to use semicolons is to join the two main clauses in long compound sentences that use conjunctive adverbs such as however, consequently, nevertheless, indeed, instead, thus, and therefore. After the first clause in the compound sentence, put a semicolon, then the conjunctive adverb, then a comma, and finally the rest of the sentence. For example:

> The gas gauge was not working; consequently, we ran out of gas.

· The third way to use the semicolon is to separate independent clauses that already have commas in them. For example:

Marion, who had studied word processing, wanted to apply for a job; but she realized that she first needed to apply for a social security number.

· In the same way, items in a series should be separated by semicolons if there are commas within the items. For example:

My children take care of Terry, their pet turtle; JD, their dog; Nibbles, their rabbit; and Mittens, their new kitten.

Add semicolons where needed in the following sentences. In some cases, you will change commas to semicolons.

EXAMPLE: He tried to explain I was too tired to listen.

<u>He tried to explain; I was too tired to listen.</u>

1. My sister Janet was good-looking, intelligent, and popular and to tell the truth, I was a little jealous of her.

2. Our car broke down therefore, we were late for the show.

3. Because we were forced to cancel our trip we were unhappy however, we knew we would be going next month.

4. Our trip took us to Denver, Colorado, Las Vegas, Nevada, and San Francisco, California.

5. Ted was elected president Mark was elected vice-president.

6. Your papers are in order, therefore, you may leave.

7. After a long day, Carol was in no mood to talk, she needed to rest.

   _____

   _____

8. Jennifer did not have time to visit her uncle she did, however, give him a call.

   _____

   _____

9. It was colder than we expected indeed, we had to wear sweaters.

   _____

   _____

10. Henry went left, Martha went straight ahead.

    _____

Check your answers on pages 23 and 24 in the Answer Key for Book Three. If you used semicolons correctly in 8 of 10 items, go to Subskill 5B. If not, ask your instructor for help.

Subskill 5B: Using Colons

When you complete this subskill, you will be able to use colons correctly.

Introducing Lists

You have probably noticed that, throughout this book, **colons** have been used to introduce example sentences, following words such as For example. The colon is also used to direct attention to lists of things or people. When the colon is used in this way, it should be placed after a grammatically complete sentence:

> These are my favorite relatives: Uncle Edgar, Grandpa Tipton, and Cousin Henry.

> Use the following ingredients to make guacamole: avocados, onions, tomatoes, lemon juice, oil, salt, and chili peppers.

Phrases such as these are, the following, or as follows are good clues that a colon will be necessary to separate a statement from a list of items. The following is an example of a sentence that does not require a colon because the list of items is not introduced by a complete sentence:

> The only people I recognized at the party were Martha, Carlos, and Emily.

The only people I recognized at the party were is not a complete sentence, so no colon is needed.

In the next example, a list of instructions is preceded by a complete sentence and a colon:

I want you to do as follows: put away your clothes, brush your teeth, and go to bed.

A colon may also be used to introduce a single item:

Jess had one ambition: to win a basketball scholarship.

As with the earlier examples, in this example the item is introduced by a complete sentence and a colon.

Introducing a Long Direct Quotation

Colons are also used to introduce a long direct quotation. For example:

Martin Luther King said:

I say to you today, my friends, that in spite of difficulties and frustrations of the moment I still have a dream. It is a dream that one day this nation will rise up and live out the true meaning of its creed: "We hold these truths to be self-evident; that all men are created equal."

This type of quotation, instead of being set off by quotation marks, is often set off from the rest of the text by being indented.

Separating Elements

The colon is used after the greeting in a business letter to separate the greeting from the body of the letter. Following are three examples:

Dear Mr. Albertini:

Ladies and Gentlemen:

To Whom It May Concern:

In personal letters, a comma is usually used after the greeting:

Dear José,

Another way in which the colon is used to separate elements is when a word or words are used to label important information. For example:

Warning: Testing in progress.

Please note: Prices are subject to change.

In these examples, the elements after the colon begin with capital letters.

In general, the colon tells the reader to watch for what is coming next. What follows the colon should satisfy the expectation that is set up with the words that come before the colon.

Check your ability to use colons correctly by doing the following exercise.

Exercise for Subskill 5B

In some of the following sentences the colon is used correctly and in some it is used incorrectly. Put a C after each sentence that is correctly punctuated. Put an I after each sentence that is incorrectly punctuated.

EXAMPLE: The four seasons are: winter, spring, summer, and fall.
          I

There were four Beatles: John Lennon, Ringo Starr, Paul McCartney, and George Harrison.   C

1. The three clues to the murderer were: stains on the car, the glove on the seat, and the footprint in the mud. _____

2. Invitations have been sent to the following people: Jorge, Louise, Helen, and Martin. _____

3. Watch out: for the step. _____

4. These are the things I enjoy most: soccer, swimming, and hiking. _____

5. Dear Mr. Nelson:
   I am writing to inform you . . . . _____

6. The rental fee includes: gas, electricity, and water. _____

7. One thing stood out: her willingness to learn. _____

8. I was annoyed by Larry's attitude: his lack of self-discipline, his indifference to fellow workers, and his carelessness. _____

9. I would like you to: photocopy the report, send one copy to each committee member, and file the original. _____

10. Warning: Bridge freezes before roadway. _____

Check your answers on page 24 in the Answer Key for Book Three. If you correctly answered 8 of 10 items, go to Subskill 5C. If not, do the Supplemental Exercise for Subskill 5B.

Supplemental Exercise for Subskill 5B

· The colon introduces a list of items after a complete sentence:

> The menu includes several unusual items: rattlesnake stew, seaweed soup, and broiled octopus.

> In the same way, the colon may introduce a single item:

> The coach emphasized one point to the team: to keep up their confidence.

· The colon also introduces a lengthy quotation:

> William Shakespeare wrote in <u>Macbeth</u>:
> Life's but a walking shadow, a poor player
> That struts and frets his hour upon the stage
> And then is heard no more: it is a tale
> Told by an idiot, full of sound and fury,
> Signifying nothing.

· Finally, the colon may separate a greeting from the body of a letter, or it may be used to call attention to an important idea:

> Dear Ms. McIntyre:
> I am writing to ask your assistance with a new project.

> Note: prices are subject to change.

Check your understanding of these three main uses of the colon in the following exercise.

In some of the following sentences, the colon is used correctly and in some it is used incorrectly. Put a C after each sentence that is correctly punctuated. Put an I after each sentence that is incorrectly punctuated.

EXAMPLE: Reminder: Fasten your seat belts before starting the car.

   __C__

   The citizens came from: all over the state.   __I__

1. Brady brought the following to the picnic: hotdogs, salad, and dessert. ____

2. Our monthly bill covers: water, electricity, and gas. ____

3. Janet took the following courses: French, math, and science. ____

4. Pancakes consist of: milk, flour, and eggs. ____

5. Jake was fearless: he could not be intimidated. ____

6. Nathan Hale stated humbly:
   I only regret that I have but one life to lose for my country.
   ___

7. Promise me: you won't forget to write. ___

8. All of his thoughts were centered on one idea: liberation. ___

9. Churchill promised the British citizens three things: blood, sweat, and tears. ___

10. To Whom It May Concern:
    The bearer of this document is authorized to sign invoices for the purchasing department. ___

Check your answers on page 24 in the Answer Key for Book Three. If you correctly answered 8 of 10 items, go to Subskill 5C. If not, ask your instructor for help.

Subskill 5C: Using Parentheses and Dashes

When you complete this subskill, you will be able to use parentheses and dashes in sentences correctly.

As with semicolons, parentheses and dashes can be overused. At the same time, they are useful for getting across certain kinds of information. Therefore, it is important to learn how to use them correctly.

Parentheses

Parentheses set off information that is incidental to a sentence. In fact, this kind of information is often referred to as **parenthetical** information. The information within the parentheses may provide a detail, as in the following example:

The airport is only 15 miles (about a half-hour drive) from the center of town.

You may also use parentheses to qualify or clarify your main point. For example:

During the summer, we took a walk every morning (unless it rained).

Here, unless it rained is a minor qualification to the main point expressed in During the summer, we took a walk every morning. In the next example, the information in parentheses helps clarify the main point:

Only 53 people showed up, so we could not vote on anything (the policy states that two-thirds of the membership, or 62 people, are required for voting).

Note that even when the parenthetical material is a complete sentence, you do not capitalize the first letter or put a period at the end. However, the above sentence could be rewritten as follows:

> Only 53 people showed up, so we could not vote on anything. (The policy states that two-thirds of the membership, or 62 people, are required for voting.)

In this case, since the parenthetical statement is standing on its own, it is treated like a complete sentence, beginning with a capital letter and ending with a period before the second parenthesis.

Parentheses may be used to provide examples that are secondary to the main point of a sentence. A reader can easily understand the following sentence without reading the words in parentheses:

> The coach picked the best players (like Kim, Mitchell, and Abraham) for the big game.

Parentheses are also useful for setting off numbers or letters that enumerate items in lists, as in the following examples:

> The board voted to (1) approve the budget, (2) appoint an election committee, and (3) adopt several resolutions.

> Your choices are to (a) go to the picnic with Margaret, (b) come with me, or (c) stay home with Nicholas.

Another use for parentheses is to set off an exclamation point to express surprise or a question mark to express uncertainty, as in the following examples:

> At the party were the Martins, Henry and his three sisters (!), and Margaret's family.

> Ever since the emergency in 1978(?), a relief system has been in place.

Dashes

Like parentheses, dashes can be used too much. Dashes are used to convey a shade of meaning that cannot be conveyed by any other punctuation mark. Dashes are like commas, but they are stronger because they interrupt a sentence more completely. Compare the following two sentences.

> The dog, nervous as always, rushed to the front gate and started barking.

> The dog—nervous as always—rushed to the front gate and started barking.

The dashes cause the reader to pause longer with the idea that the dog is always nervous. Thus the dashes interrupt the main message. In the following examples, the dashes help emphasize or dramatize a point:

> There were at least 50 flies—and I'm not exaggerating—on the watermelon.

> None of this would be possible without one special person—my mother.

Dashes indicate an abrupt change in the thought or structure of a sentence:

> Let's go for a walk—unless you have something else to do.

The dash is also used to introduce a phrase that summarizes or further explains what is said in the first part of a sentence:

> A good beat, catchy lyrics, excellent musical background, a star singer—all these can make a hit record.

> Love, honor, respect—Arnold wanted them all.

In both of the above examples, what comes after the dash summarizes the main point of the sentence.

Dashes may also be used to set off appositives when the appositives contain commas:

> Those three students—Joseph, Carlos, and Maria—will represent the school.

As with parentheses, the information within dashes gives more detail about a subject that has been introduced—in this case, the three students.

Do the following exercise to check your understanding of the uses of parentheses and dashes.

Exercise for Subskill 5C

Rewrite each of the following sentences in the spaces provided, using dashes or parentheses where needed.

EXAMPLE: What one learns from a grammar book must be immediately applied to reading and writing, that is, if it is ever to be mastered.

> What one learns from a grammar book must be immediately applied to reading and writing—that is, if it is ever to be mastered.

1. Only one employee knew where the safe was the one who was out of town.

_____

_____

2. His three children Frank, Christina, and Robert are in the real estate business together.

_____

_____

3. After considerable effort five tries, the team gave up.

_____

_____

4. Maxwell that's our dog noticed the flames first.

_____

_____

5. Feed a cold and starve a fever or is it starve a cold and feed a fever?

_____

_____

6. You are going to need office supplies such as a stapler, paper clips, and tape at the meeting.

_____

_____

7. The fastest way to get there I think is to take the subway.

_____

_____

8. It's not the heat it's the humidity.

_____

9. I kept him on the phone after all, he was paying for it for half an hour.

_____

_____

10. Entomology the study of insects is a fascinating field.

_____

_____

Check your answers on page 24 in the Answer Key to Book Three. If you correctly punctuated 8 of 10 sentences, go to the Self-Check. If not, do the Supplemental Exercise for Subskill 5C.

Supplemental Exercise for Subskill 5C

You should use parentheses and dashes sparingly. When you use these punctuation marks correctly, they help you clarify or qualify your message.

Parentheses are used to provide minor details, as in the following examples:

The track was 5 miles (8 kilometers) long.

Mr. Ackerman (a friend of ours) was driving the station wagon.

The next example shows how parentheses are used to set off examples:

The halls were decorated with crepe paper the colors of Italy's flag (green, white, and red).

Parentheses are also used to clarify the main point:

Margaret was very careful about locking the door (she had recently been robbed).

Like parentheses, dashes are used to give examples and to clarify main points. Dashes, however, interrupt the main point:

He put the money—all of it—in his mattress.

The dash may also be used to show an abrupt change of thought or sentence structure, as in the following example:

The supplies arrived in the morning, and—wouldn't you know it?—we didn't need them any more.

The dash is also used to set off a summary comment about items named in the main sentence:

Her quick wit, her kind spirit, her common sense, her keen intellect—these qualities represent my best friend.

I got a tie for my birthday—just what I wanted.

Finally, dashes are used to set off appositives:

Some classic movies—*Gone with the Wind, Bambi, National Velvet*—are still popular with audiences.

When dashes are used instead of commas (or parentheses), they can dramatize an appositive:

No other popular musician has influenced Americans as much as Elvis Presley—the king of rock 'n' roll.

Rewrite each of the following sentences, using parentheses or dashes where they are needed.

EXAMPLE: Shortly after I arrived at about 5:30, the phones started ringing.

Shortly after I arrived (at about 5:30),
the phones started ringing.

1. Each of its huge rooms there were no private rooms in this hospital housed about eight patients.

2. The shortest player was still pretty tall 6′3″.

3. The swimmers if they are lucky enough to pass the qualifying trials will have the honor of attending the Junior Olympics.

4. The late television offerings seem to be mostly horror films, science fiction thrillers, and movies about monsters from the deep all of them the kind of entertainment I can do without.

5. Michel comes from Lyons a city in France.

6. The Simmonsville newspaper there is only one paper published there addressed the issue in an editorial.

7. Minor problems for example, a lost key are best handled by the front desk.

8. Behind his seemingly elegant manners, his care for others, his talk about the general welfare, one thing stood out his desire for power over people.

_____

_____

_____

9. She knows him better than you think they went to high school together.

_____

_____

10. Mark Twain actually a pseudonym for Samuel Clemens wrote *Huckleberry Finn.*

_____

_____

Check your answers on page 24 in the Answer Key for Book Three. If you correctly answered 8 of 10 items, go to the Self-Check. If not, ask your instructor for help.

SELF-CHECK: SKILL UNIT 5

Rewrite the following sentences in the spaces provided, adding semicolons, colons, parentheses, and dashes to make correct and effective sentences.

EXAMPLE: The boy was having trouble with his math therefore his sister started helping him with his homework.

The boy was having trouble with his

math; therefore, his sister started helping

with his homework.

1. Her chocolate cream pie well, I just can't find the words to describe it.

_____

_____

2. All of the campers were expected to supply the following sheets, blankets, towels, and pillowcases.

_____

_____

3. Eric had eaten all his vegetables therefore he was allowed to go to the show with his friends.

_____

_____

4. I learned one thing from my last job never volunteer for anything!

_____

_____

5. Make sure to call me when you arrive my phone number is 564-7932.

_____

_____

6. The club selected these people as the new officers Tara Blankenship, president, Peter Roper, vice-president, Elmore Jackman, secretary, and Phyllis Webster, treasurer.

_____

_____

7. Somebody maybe it was Jenny let the cat out of the house.

_____

_____

8. Have the receptionist or whoever answers the phone give you the new address.

_____

_____

9. These are the only foods our cat likes liver, salmon, and tuna fish.

_____

_____

10. Drivers should remember these three rules be alert, be courteous, and obey the traffic rules.

_____

_____

11. He fell in the starting position consequently he lost the race.

_____

_____

12. The letter of application should state major facts about your employability for example, your education and your experience.

_____

_____

_____

Check your answers on page 25 in the Answer Key for Book Three. If you answered 10 of 12 items correctly, you have shown that you have mastered these skills. If not, ask your instructor for help.

Skill Unit 6
USING MODIFIERS IN SENTENCES

What Skills You Need to Begin: You need to be able to recognize simple sentences (Skill Unit 1), compound sentences (Skill Unit 2), and complex sentences (Skill Unit 3).

What Skills You Will Learn: When you complete this skill unit, you will be able to use modifiers correctly. You will be able to position different kinds of modifiers so that they clearly express the meaning of a sentence. You will also be able to recognize and correct sentences with misplaced or dangling modifiers.

Why You Need These Skills: Modifiers help to make sentences interesting for the reader. They also make sentences more informative. Without modifiers, sentences would be boring and unclear. If you write, "The man talked with the woman," you provide much less information than you would by adding modifiers to describe the man and woman and how they talked. For example, different modifiers are added to the same basic words in the following sentences: "The strange man talked in low tones with the troubled woman," and, "The delighted man talked excitedly with the young woman." Modifiers add drama and important detail to your sentences.

Modifiers can be used incorrectly. When they are misplaced or dangling; they can confuse your reader. For this reason, it is important to know how to place modifiers correctly and how to avoid dangling modifiers.

How You Will Show What You Have Learned: You will take the Self-Check at the end of this unit on page 177. The Self-Check consists of two parts. In the first part, you will identify misplaced and dangling modifiers in 10 sentences and rewrite the sentences correctly. In the second part, 10 sets of 4 sentences are presented. You will decide which sentence in each set contains a misplaced or dangling modifier and rewrite the incorrect sentence to eliminate the error. If you correctly answer 17 of 20 items, you will have shown that you have mastered these skills.

If you feel that you have already mastered these skills, turn to the end of this unit and complete the Self-Check on page 177.

Subskill 6A: Positioning Single-Word Modifiers

When you complete this subskill, you will be able to position single-word modifiers effectively in relation to the words or phrases they modify.

You have learned how to recognize various kinds of modifiers and what they modify. Remember that a **modifier** is a word or phrase that describes or changes the meaning of another word or phrase.

The boy left.   (No modifier)

The boy almost left. (The modifier <u>almost</u> changes the meaning.)

The tall boy left quietly. (The modifiers <u>tall</u> and <u>quietly</u> make the description more accurate.)

The three main kinds of modifiers are single-word modifiers, phrase modifiers, and clause modifiers. You will learn how to position single-word modifiers in this subskill.

Positioning Adjectives and Participles

Single-word modifiers, or modifiers that consist of only one word, are the easiest to recognize. Adjectives, participles, and adverbs are single-word modifiers. You have learned that adjectives modify nouns and pronouns, and that participles are verb forms that serve as adjectives. The adjectives and participles in the following sentences answer questions such as "Which one?", "Whose?", "What kind?", or "How many?"

The chair is broken.

We need two chairs.

These chairs cost too much money.

We will buy Henry's chairs.

Adjectives and participles are usually placed directly before the words they modify.

The long, boring movie was a total flop at the box office.

Did you see that awful movie?

Tamara's cat can play for hours with shredded paper.

Adjectives and participles that modify the subject of a sentence are sometimes placed after a linking verb, such as <u>be</u>, <u>seem</u>, or <u>become</u>. These modifiers are known as **predicate adjectives.** In questions, the subject-verb combination is inverted, and the predicate adjective is placed after the subject.

LV
Enrique soon became angry and irritable.

LV
You seem anxious.

LV
Are you tired?

In these sentences, angry, irritable, anxious, and tired are predicate adjectives.

Positioning Adverbs

You remember that adverbs modify verbs, adjectives, or other adverbs. The adverbs in the following sentences answer questions such as "How?", "When?", "Where?", "How much?" or "How often?", and "To what extent?"

Adv
The children played quietly.

Adv
Was the ride very expensive?

Adv Adv
We meet quite often.

Adv
He is usually prompt.

Adverbs That Modify Verbs

An adverb that modifies a verb is usually positioned directly after the verb. If the verb is followed by a direct object, however, the adverb is placed after the object.

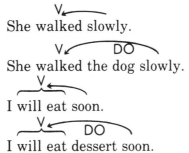

V
She walked slowly.

V   DO
She walked the dog slowly.

V
I will eat soon.

V   DO
I will eat dessert soon.

Adverbs that modify verbs may be placed in other positions in a sentence. A writer can change the emphasis of a sentence by changing the position of the adverb. For example, to emphasize how an action is performed, an adverb is often placed before the verb. In a sentence with a verb phrase, the adverb is positioned directly before the main verb:

Grace carefully put the money away.

I will probably give you an answer next week.

The roof had been badly damaged by the storm.

Adverbs may also be placed at the beginning of a sentence. Adverbs that answer the question "When?" are often found in this position. A comma is used after an adverb that is placed at the beginning of a sentence.

Tomorrow, will you take my cat to the veterinarian?

Suddenly, the door opened.

Some words, such as almost, always, never, just, and only, may be adjectives or adverbs. When they are adverbs, they must be placed directly before the words they modify. If these adverbs are positioned elsewhere, they will modify other words, and the meaning of the sentence will change. The following example shows how the meaning of a sentence changes when the word only is placed in different positions in the same sentence:

(1) Only Frieda told me about the meeting.
(No one else told me.)

(2) Frieda only told me about the meeting.
(She did not show me.)

(3) Frieda told only me about the meeting.
(She told no one else.)

(4) Frieda told me only about the meeting.
(She told me about nothing else.)

Only must be placed before the verb in order to modify it. In sentences 1 and 3, only is an adjective modifying Frieda and me. In sentence 4, only is an adverb modifying the prepositional phrase about the meeting. The verb told is modified only in sentence 2.

In a sentence that contains more than one verb, an adverb must be positioned carefully in order to avoid confusion. Look at this complex sentence:

People who lose their tempers embarrass themselves.

This sentence contains two verbs: the verb lose is part of the adjective clause who lose their tempers, and the verb embarrass is part of the independent clause people embarrass themselves.

The adverb frequently can be added to the sentence to modify either lose or embarrass. If <u>frequently</u> is supposed to modify <u>lose</u>, it should be positioned in the adjective clause <u>who lose their tempers</u>:

People who frequently lose their tempers embarrass themselves.

If <u>frequently</u> is supposed to modify <u>embarrass</u>, it should be positioned in the independent clause <u>people embarrass themselves</u>:

People who lose their tempers embarrass themselves frequently.

OR: Frequently, people who lose their tempers embarrass themselves.

<u>Frequently</u> should not be placed in the following position:

INCORRECT: People who lose their tempers frequently embarrass themselves.

Here, the placement of the adverb makes the sentence confusing. It is unclear whether <u>frequently</u> modifies <u>lose</u> or <u>embarrass</u>. Be careful not to place adverbs in confusing positions in sentences that contain two or more verbs.

Adverbs That Modify Adjectives or Adverbs

An adverb that modifies an adjective or another adverb is always positioned directly before the adjective or adverb:

That's a very good question.

Miguel left too soon to see the movie.

Check your ability to position single-word modifiers effectively by doing the following exercise.

Exercise for Subskill 6A

Rewrite the following sentences so that the words in parentheses clearly modify the underlined words. Remember that some adverbs may be correctly placed in more than one position.

EXAMPLE: The thief <u>entered</u> the room.   (silently)

<u>Silently, the thief entered the room.</u>

OR: <u>The thief entered the room silently.</u>

OR: <u>The thief silently entered the room.</u>

1. Virginia <u>rented</u> the red bicycle.   (only)

2. People who run for exercise <u>get</u> blisters. (frequently)

_____

3. <u>Yogurt</u> is Hope's favorite food. (frozen)

_____

4. Joan's grandfather <u>gave</u> her a nice gift. (yesterday)

_____

5. Christine <u>talks</u> in her sleep. (loudly)

_____

6. Terry built some <u>shelves</u> for the apartment. (new)

_____

_____

7. The dog that <u>howls</u> at night lives next door to me. (usually)

_____

_____

8. Bake the pastries at 350°F. until they are <u>brown</u>. (slightly)

_____

_____

9. Do you <u>sing</u> in the shower? (always)

_____

10. He <u>has finished</u> the job. (finally)

_____

Check your answers on page 25 in the Answer Key for Book Three. If you correctly placed the single-word modifiers in all 10 sentences, go to Subskill 6B. If not, do the Supplemental Exercise for Subskill 6A.

Supplemental Exercise for Subskill 6A

Adjectives and participles are usually positioned directly before the words they modify:

a long meeting   a fried egg

an exhausting day   Gwen's books

Predicate adjectives modify the subject of a sentence. They are placed after linking verbs such as <u>be</u>, <u>seem</u>, and <u>become</u>, as in the following examples:

The cost of the train fare is reasonable. [LV]

George became irritable. [LV]

You seem pleased. [LV]

An adverb that modifies a verb is usually positioned after the verb. If an object follows the verb, the adverb is positioned after the object. However, an adverb may also be placed directly before the verb or at the beginning of a sentence. Changing the position of an adverb changes the emphasis of a sentence.

Bert ran quickly from door to door.

Bert quickly ran from door to door.

Quickly, Bert ran from door to door.

Bert ran from door to door quickly.

When words such as <u>almost</u>, <u>always</u>, <u>never</u>, <u>just</u>, and <u>only</u> are adverbs, they are always placed directly before the verbs they modify:

Tani just won a thousand dollars.

Although I enter many contents, I never win any of them.

In a sentence with two or more verbs, place the adverb so that it clearly modifies the appropriate verb.

The woman whose house was recently robbed called the police.

(<u>Recently</u> clearly modifies <u>was robbed</u>.)

The woman whose house was robbed called the police recently.

(<u>Recently</u> clearly modifies <u>called</u>.)

Adverbs that modify adjectives or other adverbs are always positioned directly before the words they modify.

The test was fairly easy. [Adj]

Gail almost always visits her grandparents on the weekend. [Adv]

Rewrite the sentences on page 162 so that the words in parentheses clearly modify the underlined words. Remember that some adverbs may be correctly placed in more than one position.

EXAMPLE: Pedro left the party. (suddenly)

Pedro left the party suddenly.

OR: Suddenly, Pedro left the party.

OR: Pedro suddenly left the party.

1. Ants ran out of the <u>log</u>. (burning)

2. I <u>have seen</u> that movie. (never)

3. Mel <u>told</u> us that he was going to a Mexican restaurant for lunch. (just)

4. Mel took one taste of Anita's chili and <u>sneezed</u>. (violently)

5. After working all day, Tom and Julia are <u>tired</u>. (usually)

6. I <u>will visit</u> my sister in Vancouver. (soon)

7. That <u>boy</u> is my son. (tall)

8. The tree that grows outside my bedroom <u>brushes</u> against my window. (sometimes)

9. After five o'clock, Louise stops drinking coffee and drinks <u>tea</u>. (only)

10. We <u>felt</u> our way through the dark room. (carefully)

Check your answers on pages 25 and 26 in the Answer Key for Book Three. If you correctly placed the single-word modifiers in 8 of 10 sentences, go to Subskill 6B. If not, ask your instructor for help.

Subskill 6B: Positioning Phrase Modifiers

When you complete this subskill, you will be able to position phrase modifiers correctly in a sentence.

A **phrase** is a group of words that doesn't have a subject or a verb, and that functions as a part of speech. Phrases often serve as modifiers. We will discuss two kinds of **phrase modifiers:** prepositional phrases and participial phrases.

Prepositional Phrase Modifiers

Prepositional phrases begin with a preposition such as <u>at</u>, <u>in</u>, <u>on</u>, <u>around</u>, <u>over</u>, <u>about</u>, <u>for</u>, or <u>of</u>. The prepositional phrase may function in a sentence as either an adjective or an adverb. An adjective prepositional phrase is usually positioned directly after the word or words it modifies:

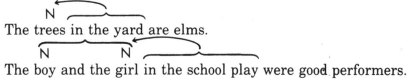

The boy and the girl in the school play were good performers.

Sometimes a prepositional phrase is used as an adverb to modify a verb. An adverb prepositional phrase is usually positioned directly after the verb it modifies. If the verb has a direct object, the adverb prepositional phrase should follow the direct object.

Gina and Maggie left at six o'clock.

Gina and Maggie left school at six o'clock.

You can change the emphasis of a sentence by positioning the adverb prepositional phrase differently. Notice how the emphasis of each of the following sentences is affected by the placement of the adverb prepositional phrase:

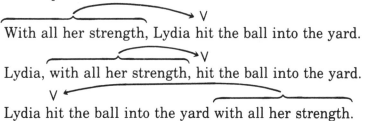

With all her strength, Lydia hit the ball into the yard.

Lydia, with all her strength, hit the ball into the yard.

Lydia hit the ball into the yard with all her strength.

However, an adverb prepositional phrase should not be placed between a verb and its direct object:

V   DO

INCORRECT: Lydia hit with all her strength the ball into the yard.

If a prepositional phrase is not positioned correctly, the sentence may not say what you want it to say.

The two men saw a couple of dogs on their way to work.

In this sentence, the position of the prepositional phrase <u>on their way to work</u> makes it sound as though the dogs were on their way to work! You should relocate the phrase to make the sentence clear:

On their way to work, the two men saw a couple of dogs.

The two men on their way to work saw a couple of dogs.

Be careful to position prepositional phrases in places that will make your sentences clear. Can you see why the following sentence is confusing?

INCORRECT: John paid the waiter with a tired expression on his face.

In this sentence, it is not clear who had the tired expression on his face, John or the waiter. To make the sentence clear, relocate the prepositional phrase. For example, if you meant to say that John had the tired expression, you might write:

With a tired expression on his face, John paid the waiter.

If you meant to modify <u>waiter</u>, you should probably rewrite the sentence:

John paid the waiter who had a tired expression on his face.

Keep your sentences clear and easy to understand by placing prepositional phrase modifiers carefully.

When a sentence begins with a prepositional phrase modifier, the phrase modifier should be followed by a comma:

On her last day at work, Mary said goodbye to her co-workers.

In my own good time, I will get the job done.

Participial Phrases

In Skill Unit 1, you learned that a participle is a verb form that can act as an adjective. A participial phrase is a group of words introduced by a participle. Participial phrases function as adjectives or adverbs. They may modify different parts of a sentence, appearing in different positions:

Excited about the trip, Maggie could not get to sleep.

Whistling softly to himself, Pablo fixed the radio.

At the skating rink, we saw many people slipping and sliding on the ice.

You must place participial phrase modifiers carefully, making sure they modify the appropriate words. Otherwise, your sentences will be confusing:

> INCORRECT: Liza took the steak out of the freezer and gave it to Brian, frozen stiff as a board.

Unless Brian has also been in the freezer, the phrase modifier in this sentence has been misplaced! The participial phrase frozen stiff as a board seems to modify Brian. Positioning the phrase modifier next to the word steak makes the sentence clear:

> Liza took the steak, frozen stiff as a board, out of the freezer and gave it to Brian.

Now the phrase clearly modifies steak.

How would you correct the following sentences?

> INCORRECT: David found the wrench reaching high into the cupboard.

> INCORRECT: Cooked with onions, I will eat potatoes, but not served plain.

In the first sentence, the participial phrase reaching high into the cupboard seems to modify wrench. To make the sentence clear, we have to relocate the phrase:

> Reaching high into the cupboard, David found the wrench.

In the second sentence, the participial phrase cooked with onions seems to modify I. To show that the phrase modifies potatoes, we must position it closer to the word it modifies:

> I will eat potatoes cooked with onions, but not served plain.

Now the sentence is clear.

When a sentence begins with a participial phrase modifier, the phrase should be followed by a comma:

> Looking carefully at the blueprint, Linda began to operate the machine.

> Riding on a huge white stallion, the cowboy galloped into town.

Exercise for Subskill 6B

The following 10 sentences are confusing or unclear due to misplaced phrase modifiers. Rewrite each sentence to make it clear. There may be more than one way to rewrite a sentence correctly.

EXAMPLES: The dog growled at the mailman running out of the house. (The dog was running out of the house.)

Running out of the house, the dog growled at the mailman.

The umpire approached the ball player with a bat in his hands. (The ball player had a bat in his hands.)

The umpire approached the ball player who had a bat in his hands.

1. The lion tamer entered the cage of the lion without a whip.

_____

_____

2. Scratching on her neighbor's door, Susan finally found her cat.

_____

_____

3. I waved to Carlos driving down the street. (Carlos is driving down the street.)

_____

_____

4. Did José get to see Mr. Barton on his way to California? (Mr. Barton is on his way to California.)

_____

_____

5. Jennie stopped to talk to the ticket-taker going into the concert. (Jennie is going into the concert.)

_____

_____

6. Baked with lots of cheese and pepperoni, I like to eat pizza.

_____

_____

7. Maria gave her order to the waitress with a friendly smile. (Maria has a friendly smile.)

_____

_____

8. The dog saved the drowning child swimming against the current. (The dog is swimming against the current.)

_____

_____

9. I baked cookies for our picnic in a hot, crowded kitchen.

_____

_____

10. In the blender, Rachel mixed the strawberries, rum, and ice.

_____

_____

Check your answers on page 26 in the Answer Key for Book Three. If you correctly rewrote all 10 sentences, go to Subskill 6C. If not, do the Supplemental Exercise for Subskill 6B.

Supplemental Exercise for Subskill 6B

A phrase is a group of words that doesn't have a subject or verb and functions as a part of speech. Phrase modifiers may act as adjectives or adverbs. Two kinds of phrase modifiers are prepositional phrases and participial phrases.

A prepositional phrase begins with a preposition. When a prepositional phrase acts as an adjective, it usually follows the words it modifies. When a prepositional phrase acts as an adverb, it may be placed in many different positions in the sentence.

A participial phrase is a group of words introduced by a participle (a verb form that serves as an adjective). A participial phrase may also appear in many different positions in a sentence.

Both participial and prepositional phrases must be positioned carefully, so that it is clear which words they modify. If a sentence is confusing or unclear, you may need to relocate its participial or prepositional phrase.

The 10 sentences on page 168 are confusing or unclear due to misplaced modifiers. Rewrite each sentence to make it clear. There may be more than one way to rewrite a sentence correctly.

EXAMPLE: Served with mustard and sauerkraut, I was eating hot dogs.

I was eating hot dogs served with mustard and sauerkraut.

1. Diane noticed the building superintendent standing at the foot of the stairs.   (Diane was standing at the foot of the stairs.)

   _____

   _____

2. Martha swam after the girl without a life preserver.   (The girl had no life preserver.)

   _____

   _____

3. Hanging from a tree, we found the tangled kite.

   _____

   _____

4. Frank and Rita decided to have children on their wedding day.

   _____

   _____

5. Moth-eaten after so many years, he still loved his old sweater.

   _____

   _____

6. They told me about their party on Saturday.   (They told me on Saturday.)

   _____

   _____

7. I gave a cake to my father freshly baked.

   _____

   _____

8. In the refrigerator, Charlie looked for the milk.

   _____

   _____

9. I read the book you recommended with pleasure.   (I read with pleasure.)

   _____

   _____

10. Drifting over the park, the children saw hundreds of red balloons.

_____

_____

Check your answers on page 26 in the Answer Key for Book Three. If you correctly rewrote 8 of 10 sentences, go to Subskill 6C. If not, ask your instructor for help.

Subskill 6C: Positioning Clause Modifiers

When you complete this subskill, you will be able to correctly position clause modifiers in a sentence.

A **clause** is a group of words that contains a subject and a verb. **Independent clauses** can stand alone and make sense. **Dependent clauses** must be used with independent clauses; they do not make sense when they stand alone.

Two kinds of dependent clauses are used to modify words in an independent clause: adjective clauses and adverb clauses.

Adjective Clauses

An adjective clause begins with a relative pronoun such as who, whom, whose, which, that, or where. In the following sentence, the adjective clause modifies a noun:

Farmers who lived in the flood area were forced to move.

An adjective clause always follows the noun or pronoun that it modifies. You must place adjective clauses correctly in order to make your sentences clear. Look at the following sentence, in which the adjective clause has been misplaced:

INCORRECT: Charles gave a new album to his sister, which he bought in the record store downtown.

Because the modifier which he bought in the record store downtown is misplaced, the sentence sounds as though Charles bought his sister in the record store! The clause modifier must be placed directly after the word it modifies in order to make the sentence clear.

Charles gave a new album, which he bought in the record store downtown, to his sister.

Now, the clause modifier clearly modifies <u>album</u> and not <u>sister</u>. You can also rewrite the sentence to make it less awkward:

> Charles gave his sister a new album, which he bought in the record store downtown.

How would you correct the following sentence?

> INCORRECT: I saw a book on the top shelf that looked like a good mystery.

The clause modifier in this sentence is misplaced. The clause <u>that looked like a good mystery</u> seems to modify <u>shelf</u>. Relocating the clause makes it clear that the clause modifies <u>book</u>:

> I saw a book that looked like a good mystery on the top shelf.

Adverb Clauses

Adverb clauses may be used to modify verbs. Remember that an adverb clause begins with a subordinating conjunction, such as <u>when</u>, <u>since</u>, <u>because</u>, <u>if</u>, or <u>although</u>.

> Carlos gave Maggie the message when she returned.

The verb <u>gave</u> in the independent clause <u>Carlos gave Maggie the message</u> is modified by the dependent adverb clause <u>when she returned</u>.

Unlike adjective clauses, adverb clauses may be placed in several different positions in a sentence without causing confusion:

> Although the sun was in her eyes, Emily hit a home run.
>
> Emily hit a home run, although the sun was in her eyes.
>
> Emily, although the sun was in her eyes, hit a home run.

Notice, however, that when the adverb clause is placed in the middle of the sentence, the sentence sounds awkward. In a short sentence, it is generally wise to position the clause modifier at the beginning or end of the sentence rather than in the middle. And you should generally try to avoid positioning adverb clauses between verbs and their direct objects.

REMEMBER: When an adverb clause begins a sentence, it should always be followed by a comma.

Check your understanding of how to position clause modifiers by doing the following exercise. This exercise does not contain any adverb clauses.

Exercise for Subskill 6C

The following 5 sentences are unclear due to misplaced adjective clauses. Rewrite the sentences so that they are clear. There may be more than one way to rewrite a sentence.

EXAMPLE: Hyacinth couldn't find the car in the lot that her daughter had parked.

<u>Hyacinth couldn't find the car that her daughter had parked in the lot.</u>

1.   Desmond described the haircut to the barber that he wanted.

_____

_____

2.   She wore a wool hat on her head that was too small.

_____

_____

3.   I saw the woman walking with Francine whose name I don't know.

_____

_____

4.   My brother wants to speak to you, whom you met yesterday.

_____

_____

5.   Roberto proposed his new schedule to the committee, which he had just revised.

_____

_____

Check your answers on page 26 in the Answer Key for Book Three. If you correctly rewrote all 5 sentences, go to Subskill 6D. If not, do the Supplemental Exercise for Subskill 6C.

Supplemental Exercise for Subskill 6C

There are two kinds of dependent clause modifiers: adjective clauses and adverb clauses. Adjective clauses always follow the words they modify. You must position adjective clauses correctly in order to make your meaning clear. Adverb clauses, on the other hand, may be placed in many different positions in a sentence. In a short sentence, however, you should position an adverb clause at the beginning or end of the sentence so that it sounds less awkward.

The following 5 sentences are unclear due to misplaced adjective clauses. Rewrite the sentences so that they are clear. There may be more than one way to rewrite a sentence.

EXAMPLE: The car needed a tune-up that I borrowed.

The car that I borrowed needed a tune-up.

1. Josie talked about her work at our party, which is difficult but pays well.

_____

_____

2. The tenants have complained to the housing committee who have no heat.   (The tenants have no heat.)

_____

_____

3. Mario spilled the drink on the waiter that he had just ordered.

_____

_____

4. Leonie saw the woman walking her dog whose purse I found.

_____

_____

5. I returned the record to the store that I had bought.

_____

_____

Check your answers on page 26 in the Answer Key for Book Three. If you correctly rewrote 4 of 5 sentences, go to Subskill 6D. If not, ask your instructor for help.

Subskill 6D: Correcting Dangling Modifiers

When you complete this subskill, you will be able to recognize and correct dangling modifiers.

Sometimes a writer doesn't provide the word or words that a phrase or clause modifier is supposed to modify. When this happens, the phrase or clause is called a **dangling modifier.** Like misplaced modifiers, dangling modifiers are confusing. Look at this sentence:

INCORRECT: After taking a secretarial course, my typing improved.

The phrase modifier in this sentence is after taking a secretarial course. But what word is this phrase modifying? As the sentence is written, the phrase seems to modify typing. But it was not typing that took the course! The author has left out the word that the phrase is supposed to modify. In order to make the sentence clear, you must add words that will show what the modifier is modifying. You may rewrite either the modifier or the independent clause. In the following corrected sentence, the phrase modifier has been rewritten:

CORRECT: After I took a secretarial course, my typing improved.

Here, the phrase modifier has been changed to a dependent clause with the subject I. Now it is clear that I took the secretarial course. To correct the dangling modifier in this sentence, the independent clause can also be rewritten:

CORRECT: After taking a secretarial course, I found that my typing improved.

Now the phrase modifier clearly refers to the word I in the independent clause.

To correct a dangling modifier, you cannot simply place it in another position in the sentence. In both of the corrected sentences above, you had to add the word that the modifier was supposed to be modifying.

The prepositional phrase in the following sentence is a dangling modifier:

INCORRECT: In doubt, a dictionary was consulted.

Who was in doubt? This sentence suggests that the dictionary was in doubt! The word that in doubt is supposed to modify has been left out. There are two ways to correct this sentence. You can rewrite the independent clause a dictionary was consulted and add the word that the phrase is supposed to modify:

In doubt, they consulted a dictionary.

You can also rewrite the phrase modifier as a dependent clause with they as the subject:

Because they were in doubt, a dictionary was consulted.

Both methods of correcting the dangling modifier add words that make it clear who was in doubt.

How would you rewrite the following sentence?

INCORRECT: Driving to Toronto, the highway was crowded.

The participial phrase <u>driving to Toronto</u> seems to modify the word <u>highway</u>. Since the highway is not driving, you must rewrite the sentence:

> As we were driving to Toronto, the highway was crowded.

> Driving to Toronto, we saw that the highway was crowded.

Both of these rewritten sentences make it clear that <u>we</u> are driving and not the highway.

A dangling modifier may be corrected only by rewriting the sentence in which it appears. In order to write clear sentences, you must avoid dangling modifiers.

Check your understanding of how to correct dangling modifiers by doing the following exercise.

Exercise for Subskill 6D

Some of the following 10 sentences on this page and page 175 contain dangling modifiers. If a sentence contains a dangling modifier, rewrite the sentence correctly in the space provided. If a sentence is correct as written, write <u>Correct</u> in the space provided.

EXAMPLE: Driving home, the dog started barking loudly.

<u>When I was driving home, the dog started barking loudly.</u>

1.   Hurrying to work, my head began to ache.

_____

_____

2.   Soaked by the sudden downpour, the bus was a welcome sight.

_____

_____

3.   Tired and angry, his book flew across the room.

_____

_____

4.   Singing Christmas carols, the children walked through the neighborhood.

_____

_____

5. Coming from a rural community, Chicago seemed crowded and noisy.

_____

_____

6. While enjoying lunch, a terrible scream pierced the air.

_____

_____

7. Once in town, you should look up Mr. Ackerman.

_____

_____

8. At the age of five, my family moved to Edmonton.

_____

_____

9. To be sure of a good grade, the material must be studied carefully.

_____

_____

10. After lying in the sun for four hours, my tan turned into a burn.

_____

_____

Check your answers on page 27 in the Answer Key for Book Three. If you correctly answered all 10 items, go to the Self-Check. If not, do the Supplemental Exercise for Subskill 6D.

Supplemental Exercise for Subskill 6D

Modifiers in a sentence must modify something. If a sentence is missing the word or words that are supposed to be modified, the sentence contains a dangling modifier. The following sentence contains a dangling modifier:

INCORRECT: After visiting the dentist, my teeth were clean.

This sentence is missing the word that the modifier is supposed to modify. My teeth did not visit the dentist! To correct this sentence, you must add the missing word or words to either the modifier or the independent clause:

> After I visited the dentist, my teeth were clean.

> After visiting the dentist, I had clean teeth.

Both of these rewritten sentences make it clear who visited the dentist.

Some of the following sentences contain dangling modifiers. If a sentence contains a dangling modifier, rewrite the sentence correctly in the space provided. If a sentence is correct as written, write <u>Correct</u> in the space provided.

EXAMPLE: Waiting for a train, it began to snow.

<u>While I was waiting for a train, it began to snow.</u>

1.   Just before ringing this morning, I turned off the alarm clock.

_____

_____

2.   Having done all we could to help the accident victims, we called the hospital.

_____

_____

3.   While concentrating on the hockey game, my hot chocolate got cold.

_____

_____

4.   Without his keys, the door wouldn't open.

_____

_____

5.   Being an only child, Hector's parents spoiled him.

_____

_____

6.   Driving home from work, a fallen tree blocked the way.

_____

_____

7. To be certain of the sale price, the newspaper was checked.

_____

_____

8. Having forgotten the money at home, the groceries couldn't be bought.

_____

_____

9. Taking a deep breath, Joy walked into the office for her interview.

_____

_____

10. After working all day, his bed was a welcome sight.

_____

_____

Check your answers on page 27 in the Answer Key for Book Three. If you correctly answered 8 of 10 items, go to the Self-Check. If not, ask your instructor for help.

SELF-CHECK: SKILL UNIT 6

Part A. Each of the following sentences contains a misplaced or dangling modifier. Underline the modifier in each sentence and write whether it is misplaced or dangling in the blank after the sentence. Then, correct and rewrite the sentence in the space provided. There may be more than one way to correct some sentences.

EXAMPLES: Going to work, the highway was a traffic nightmare. _dangling_

When I was going to work, the highway was a traffic nightmare.

Kurt reached for a handkerchief sneezing like mad. _misplaced_

Sneezing like mad, Kurt reached for a handkerchief.

1. Wondering what to do next, the phone rang. _____

_____

_____

2.   Gary gave a lecture to his daughter that was formal and stern.

   _____

   _____

   _____

3.   On the right track, the mystery would soon be solved.

   _____

   _____

   _____

4.   They made plans to launch the rocket in the conference room.

   _____

   _____

   _____

5.   Peter dropped his hat almost down the sewer.   _____

   _____

   _____

6.   To finish the puzzle, the solution is in the back of the magazine.

   _____

   _____

   _____

7.   Larry mentioned a new restaurant to his friend with carry-out service and reasonable prices.   _____

   _____

   _____

8.   I brushed the hair on the child's head, which was long and curly.

   _____

   _____

   _____

9.   While waiting for the bus, a fire broke out across the street.

   _____

   _____

   _____

10. Add an onion to the sauce that has been finely chopped.

_____

_____

_____

Part B. In each set of 4 sentences, 3 sentences are correct, and 1 sentence is incorrect due to a misplaced or dangling modifier. Circle the letter of the incorrect sentence in each set. Then, correct and rewrite the sentence in the space provided.

EXAMPLE: **(a)** The car, going about eighty miles per hour, hit a telephone pole.
(b) After we had assembled the toy, we examined it to make sure that we had made no mistakes.
(c) Being chilly, extra blankets were put on the bed.
(d) Wanting the job, Myra practiced for her interview.

Being chilly, we put extra blankets on the bed.

11. (a) For several years, Miguel had my present job.
(b) Left alone in the house, Rita always locked the door.
(c) Seeing clouds overhead, we decided to postpone our fishing trip.
(d) To get a high school equivalency diploma in most states, passing the GED test is important.

_____

_____

12. (a) Carrying a large plant up the stairs, Phil could not see where he was going.
(b) Exhausted, I wanted only to climb into bed.
(c) After Henry met Karina, he could not stop thinking about her.
(d) He sold the watch to the young lady with hands that glowed in the dark.

_____

_____

13. (a) While shopping, my car was stolen from the parking lot.
(b) You need a good strategy and perseverance to win the game.
(c) The police accused the young man of stealing a painting worth several thousand dollars.
(d) The man sat in his favorite chair beside the fireplace.

_____

_____

14. (a) The team, beaten and exhausted, returned to the locker room.
    (b) The player was disqualified by the official who started the fight.
    (c) Getting on the bus, I dropped my wallet.
    (d) From the balcony, we could see most of the city.

15. (a) After spending several days at home, my strength returned.
    (b) After Jorge fished all day, his face and arms were quite sunburned.
    (c) Being a little nervous, he made several mistakes.
    (d) Pass the salt, which is on the top shelf, to Leroy.

16. (a) Driving carefully, the bus driver avoided the two children who darted into the street.
    (b) The committee was very disappointed when Dionne resigned after having been a member for fourteen years.
    (c) Phyllis gave her cat to her niece whose name is Whiskers.
    (d) A strange man with red suspenders knocked on the door.

17. (a) To get a good seat, you will have to pay ten dollars.
    (b) Did you read that horrible story about the child who was kidnapped in the newspaper?
    (c) The baby promptly drank the glass of beer that she found on the table.
    (d) Until the store reopens, we will have to be patient.

18. (a) The man who just waved is my brother.
    (b) Frustrated by the crowds, the shopping trip was unpleasant.
    (c) The detective found the necessary evidence buried deep in the ground.
    (d) At the age of sixteen, Tina got her driver's license.

19. (a) Trudy gave a quartz watch, which she really couldn't afford, to her husband for his birthday.
    (b) Ken read in the newspaper about the new community center.

(c)   When fully extended, our kitchen table will seat twelve people.

(d)   The people who moved next door to us recently made a lot of noise.

_____

_____

20. (a)   Preferred by most athletes, this headband comes in several sizes.

(b)   After paying the bill, we were ready to leave.

(c)   Charlie gave two dollars to the woman out of his pocket.

(d)   When Nancy was ready, she left to see her mother.

_____

_____

Check your answers on pages 27–29 in the Answer Key for Book Three. If you correctly answered 17 of 20 items, you have shown that you have mastered these skills. If not, ask your instructor for help.

Skill Unit 7
WRITING EFFECTIVE SENTENCES

What Skills You Need to Begin: You need to be able to identify and write simple sentences (Skill Unit 1), compound sentences (Skill Unit 2), complex sentences (Skill Unit 3), and sentences with modifiers (Skill Unit 6).

What Skills You Will Learn: When you complete this skill unit, you will be able to use parallel structures in sentences. You will be able to use verb tenses correctly in a sentence that contains more than one verb. You will be able to use the active or the passive voice consistently in a sentence that contains more than one verb. You will be able to write sentences using pronouns that clearly refer to and match their antecedents. You will also be able to avoid sentence fragments.

Why You Need These Skills: To communicate effectively in standard English, you need to write sentences that are complete, logical, and easy to understand.. What you will learn in this unit will help you write complete sentences that are clear and logical.

How You Will Show What You Have Learned: You will take the Self-Check at the end of this unit on page 207. The Self-Check consists of 25 items. If you answer 20 of 25 items correctly, you will have shown that you have mastered these skills.

If you feel that you have already mastered these skills, turn to the end of this unit and complete the Self-Check on page 207.

Subskill 7A: Using Parallel Structure

When you complete this subskill, you will be able to use parallel sentence structures with conjunctions and in comparisons.

Using Parallel Structures With Conjunctions

The way in which a sentence is put together is called **sentence structure.** For a sentence to have a clear meaning, its parts must fit together in the right way. Look at the sentences at the top of the next page. One of them has a problem in its structure.

Her new boyfriend is handsome, talented, and has patience.

Her new boyfriend is handsome, talented, and patient.

The structure problem is in the first sentence. Look at the words that described boyfriend. The words handsome, talented, and has patience are listed together but do not have the same form. Handsome and talented are adjectives; has patience consists of a verb followed by a noun.

The second sentence is correct. Handsome, talented, and patient are all adjectives. They are parallel in structure. **Parallel structure** means that terms (words or groups of words) that are listed together in a sentence are written in the same form.

Does this sentence have parallel structure?

Her new boyfriend has good looks, talent, and patience.

The sentence contains three nouns joined by commas and by the conjunction and. Its structure is parallel because the words in the list are all nouns. This sentence illustrates another way in which incorrect sentence structure can be corrected.

Problems in parallel structure may come up in sentences in which words are connected by coordinating conjunctions (and, or, nor, but) or by paired correlative conjunctions (either . . . or, neither . . . nor, both . . . and, not only . . . but also). Look at this sentence:

Her new boyfriend is friendly but a shy person.

The conjunction but joins an adjective (friendly) and a noun and adjective (shy person). The faulty sentence structure can be corrected by making both terms adjectives:

Her new boyfriend is friendly but shy.

In this sentence, but joins two adjectives. The sentences can also be corrected by making both terms adjective-noun combinations. In the following sentence, but joins two adjective-noun combinations:

Her new boyfriend is a friendly person but a shy one.

In the following sentences, conjunctions join verbal phrases. Which sentence does not have parallel structure?

To paint the room and redecorating it are my goals for the summer.

To paint the room and to redecorate it are my goals for the summer.

In the first sentence, the conjunction and joins an infinitive phrase (to paint the room) and a gerund phrase (redecorating it). This sentence has a structure problem because the phrases are not in the same form.

In the second sentence, <u>and</u> connects two infinitive phrases (<u>to paint the room</u> and <u>to redecorate it</u>). This sentence is parallel in structure.

Here are other correct structures:

> Painting the room and redecorating it are my goals for the summer.

Now <u>and</u> joins two gerund phrases (<u>painting the room</u> and <u>redecorating it</u>).

> To paint the room and redecorate it are my goals for the summer.

In this sentence, <u>to</u> is written only in the first infinitive phrase. In a sentence with a series of infinitives or infinitive phrases, the word <u>to</u> may introduce the first infinitive and be shared by all that follow. For example:

> I like to knit, to sew, and to embroider.

may be written as:

> I like to knit, sew, and embroider.

The word <u>to</u>, which introduces <u>to knit</u>, is shared by <u>sew</u> and <u>embroider</u>.

Look at this sentence:

> INCORRECT: Neither anger nor being stubborn will solve the problem.

The correlative conjunctions <u>neither</u> and <u>nor</u> are followed by a noun (<u>anger</u>) and a gerund phrase (<u>being stubborn</u>). This sentence is not parallel in structure. You could rewrite this sentence as:

> Neither anger nor stubbornness will solve the problem.

Now each correlative conjunction is followed by a noun: <u>anger</u> and <u>stubbornness</u>. You could rewrite the sentence in another way:

> Neither getting angry nor being stubborn will solve the problem.

Now each correlative conjunction is followed by a gerund phrase: <u>getting angry</u> and <u>being stubborn</u>.

Here is another example:

> INCORRECT: Jorge is not only a kind man but also talented.

The correlative conjunctions are <u>not only . . . but also</u>. The words following them are not in the same form. <u>Not only</u> is followed by two modifiers and a noun: <u>a kind man</u>. <u>But also</u> is followed only by one modifier: <u>talented</u>. This sentence is not parallel in structure. You could rewrite the sentence in the following ways:

Jorge is not only a kind man but also a talented one.

Each correlative conjunction is followed by two modifiers and a noun or pronoun.

Jorge is not only kind but also talented.

Each correlative conjunction is followed by one modifier and no nouns.
No other words in the sentence should come between correlative conjunctions and the words they join. The following sentence is written incorrectly:

INCORRECT: Charles not only is a man of great pride but also a person of great importance.

The conjunctions join <u>a man of great pride</u> and <u>a person of great importance</u>. <u>Not only</u> should appear immediately before the first phrase; <u>but also</u> should appear immediately before the second phrase. The sentence should be written this way:

Charles is not only a man of great pride but also a person of great importance.

Are the correlative conjunctions properly placed in this sentence?

It seems either you are tired or sick.

The conjunctions join <u>tired</u> and <u>sick</u>. One conjunction should appear immediately before <u>tired</u> and the other should appear immediately before <u>sick</u>. Here is the correct form of the sentence:

It seems you are either tired or sick.

Using Parallel Structures in Comparisons

For a comparison to be parallel in structure, the words being compared must be in the same form. Comparisons are often indicated by the words <u>as . . . as</u> or <u>than</u>. The following sentence is not parallel in structure:

INCORRECT: Making your own sandwiches is less expensive than to buy them.

In this sentence, <u>making your own sandwiches</u> (a gerund phrase) and <u>to buy them</u> (an infinitive phrase) are compared. The two phrases are not parallel in structure because they do not have the same form. To make the phrases parallel, you could rewrite the sentence in the following ways:

> Making your own sandwiches is less expensive than buying them.

Now two gerund phrases are compared: <u>making your own sandwiches</u> and <u>buying them</u>.

> To make your own sandwiches is less expensive than to buy them.

Now two infinitive phrases are compared: <u>to make your own sandwiches</u> and <u>to buy them</u>.

Here is another example of a sentence that is not parallel in structure:

> INCORRECT: Hard work is as valuable as being determined.

<u>Hard work</u> (a noun and its modifier) is being compared to <u>being determined</u> (a gerund phrase). The comparison is not parallel. You could rewrite the sentence in either of two ways:

> Hard work is as valuable as determination.

Now the comparison consists of two nouns: <u>work</u> and <u>determination</u>.

> Working hard is as valuable as being determined.

Now the comparison consists of two gerund phrases: <u>working hard</u> and <u>being determined</u>.

Recognizing Non-Parallel Structures in Compound Sentences

In compound sentences, the independent clauses do not have to be parallel in structure. Look at the following sentence:

> Her new boyfriend is talented and he is also very patient.

The clauses in this sentence are parallel; both consist of a subject, a linking verb, and a predicate adjective. However, it is also correct to write a compound sentence in which the independent clauses have different sentence structures:

> Her new boyfriend is talented and he also has a great deal of patience.

In this sentence, the writer has decided to vary the structure of each independent clause; the first independent clause has a linking verb followed by a predicate adjective (<u>is talented</u>) and the second independent clause has an action verb followed by a direct object and prepositional phrase (has a great deal of patience). Be sure not to confuse a compound sentence (independent clauses joined by a conjunction) with a sentence that contains a compound element (parts of a sentence joined by a conjunction).

Summary of Parallel Structure

Parallel structure should be used in sentences in which:

· words are connected by coordinating conjunctions: and, or, nor, but;

· words are connected by correlative conjunctions: either . . . or, neither . . . nor, both . . . and, not only . . . but also; and

· comparisons are made by using as . . . as or than.

Here are some steps to follow to make sure that you are using parallel structure in a sentence:

Step 1: Look for the key words mentioned above that show connection or comparison.

Step 2: Find all the terms (words or groups of words) being joined or compared.

Step 3: Determine whether the same form is used for each term.

Step 4: If the terms are not parallel in structure, revise one or more of them so that all are expressed in the same form.

Check your skill at using parallel structure by doing the following exercise.

Exercise for Subskill 7A

Some of the following sentences contain terms that are not parallel. Rewrite these sentences in the space provided to make them parallel in structure. If a sentence contains no errors, write Correct in the space provided.

EXAMPLE: He is praised as much for his dedication as for being talented.

He is praised as much for being dedicated as for being talented.

OR: He is praised as much for his dedication as for his talent.

1. To do a brake job is as difficult as doing a front-end alignment.

_____

_____

2. It is important both to study the various issues and to vote on those issues.

   _____

   _____

3. Neither what she said nor doing as she did changed the judge's mind.

   _____

   _____

4. Swimming is not only enjoyable but a healthy sport.

   _____

   _____

5. Students learn to read, to write, and adding.

   _____

   _____

6. We can soon expect to make journeys to Mars and taking trips to other planets as well.

   _____

   _____

7. It would be smarter to begin our journey now than to postpone it.

   _____

   _____

8. Martha is intelligent, curious, and has ambition.

   _____

   _____

9. To watch a ball game is less exciting than actually playing in one.

   _____

   _____

10. Carl had charm, poise, and was good-looking.

    _____

    _____

Check your answers on page 29 in the Answer Key for Book Three. If you identified the parallel structures or corrected the sentences that were not parallel in structure in all 10 items, go to Subskill 7B. If not, do the Supplemental Exercise for Subskill 7A.

Supplemental Exercise for Subskill 7A

Parts of a sentence must fit together so that the meaning of the sentence is clear. When terms in a sentence are listed together, they should be in the same form, or be parallel in structure. Parallel structure is needed in sentences in which words are connected by coordinating or correlative conjunctions, and in sentences that make comparisons. In order to be sure that the terms in a sentence are parallel, locate the terms that are listed or are being compared and determine whether or not they have the same form. If all these terms are not expressed in the same form, rewrite one or more of them to make them parallel in structure.

Some of the following sentences contain terms that are not parallel. Rewrite these sentences in the space provided to make them parallel in structure. If a sentence contains no errors, write Correct in the space provided.

EXAMPLE: This summer I would like to learn how to swim and roller-skating.

> This summer I would like to learn how to swim and (to) roller-skate.

OR: This summer I would like to learn swimming and roller-skating.

1. Mark is kind, thoughtful, and shows respect.

_____

2. Two qualities that I admire in people are courtesy and being dependable.

_____

_____

3. The children were busy doing the dishes, sweeping the floor, and putting away the food.

_____

_____

4. He was dull, lazy, and a person who was not honest.

_____

_____

5. He loves playing soccer, football, and to go fishing.

_____

_____

6. We enjoyed neither going out to eat nor the shopping mall.

   _____

   _____

7. The women—tired, hungry, and being thoroughly discouraged—returned to the office.

   _____

   _____

8. Diane is both dynamic and a success.

   _____

   _____

9. To drive in the city is much worse than the traffic in the suburbs.

   _____

   _____

10. To read the original story was as exciting as seeing the movie.

    _____

    _____

Check your answers on pages 29 and 30 in the Answer Key for Book Three. If you identified the parallel structures or corrected the sentences that were not parallel in structure in 9 of 10 items, go to Subskill 7B. If not, ask your instructor for help.

Subskill 7B: Using Verb Tenses and Voices Correctly

When you complete this subskill, you will be able to use verb tenses logically. You will be able to use appropriate verb tenses in <u>if</u> clauses. You will also be able to avoid shifting from the active to the passive voice.

Using Verb Tenses Logically

When a sentence tells about two or more actions that happen in the same time period, all of the verbs describing those actions must be in the same tense.

CORRECT: I went downtown and bought a television set.

INCORRECT: I go downtown and bought a television set.

In the first sentence, the verbs <u>went</u> and <u>bought</u> are both in the past tense. In the second sentence, <u>go</u> is in the present tense, but <u>bought</u> is in the past tense. Mixing tenses this way makes the sentence confusing. When tenses are mixed, the reader can't tell when the actions in the sentence took place.

CORRECT: I asked her what she thought.

INCORRECT: I asked her what she thinks.

In the first sentence, the verbs <u>asked</u> and <u>thought</u> are both in the past tense. In the second sentence, <u>asked</u> is in the past tense, but <u>thinks</u> is in the present tense. That makes the second sentence confusing.

When a sentence that has helping verbs tells about two or more actions that happen in the same time period, make sure that the helping verbs are in the same tense as the other verbs. Here are two sentences. Do you see which one has a helping verb in a different tense from the other verb?

She thought she can sing.

She thought she could sing.

In the first sentence, the verb <u>thought</u> is in the past tense, but the helping verb <u>can</u> is in the present tense. The first sentence is incorrect. In the second sentence, the helping verb <u>could</u> is in the past tense. Both verbs—<u>thought</u> and <u>could sing</u>—are written in the same tense. Therefore, the second sentence is correct.

Here is another way in which verb tenses are used incorrectly:

INCORRECT: I got the raise because I worked hard for it.

In this sentence, there are two actions, but each action takes place in a different time period. First the writer <u>worked hard</u>, then he or she <u>got the raise</u>. Because the sentence is written incorrectly, it is hard to tell that the actions take place in two different periods. Both actions are written in the same tense, so they both seem to take place at the same time.

How can you show that one past action took place before the other? You can use the past perfect tense (formed by using <u>had</u> plus the past participle of the main verb). The past perfect tense shows that an action took place further back in time than an action in the past tense. Look at this sentence to see how using the past perfect tense—<u>had worked</u>—makes the two different time periods clear.

CORRECT: I got the raise because I had worked hard for it.

Can you see which one of these two sentences is correct?

Juana wanted to go out that night because she stayed home alone all day.

Juana wanted to go out that night because she had stayed home alone all day.

The verbs in the first sentence are both in the same tense. That is incorrect, because the two actions in the sentence did not happen at the same time. First Juana stayed home alone, then she wanted to go out. The second sentence is correct because it uses two different verb tenses to show two different time periods in the past.

Using Verb Tenses in If Clauses

There are special rules for sentences with dependent clauses introduced by if (if clauses). The tense of the verb in the if clause always determines the tenses of the other verbs in the sentence. This is because the if clause gives a condition that must occur before another action can take place. Look at this sentence:

If you follow my directions, you will find my apartment easily.

Do you see that there are two tenses in this sentence? The verb in the if clause—follow—is in the present tense. The verb in the independent clause—will find—is in the future tense. Whenever you use a present tense verb in an if clause, you must use a future tense verb in the independent clause. That's because the action in the if clause must happen before the second action can take place. Because the verb in the if clause expresses an action that must take place earlier, it can never be in the future tense.

Is the following sentence correct?

If the store will have chocolate cookies, we will buy some.

This sentence is not correct. Both verbs are in the future tense. That makes it sound as though both actions were happening at the same time. But the store must have chocolate cookies before we can buy them. The correct way to write this sentence is:

If the store has chocolate cookies, we will buy some.

Now the verb in the if clause—has—is in the present tense. The verb in the independent clause remains in the future tense. This shows that the action in the if clause has to take place before the action in the independent clause. The verb in the if clause can never be written in the future tense, because there would be no way of showing that the action in the independent clause took place after it.

Which of these sentences is correct?

If you come to my party, I will introduce you to Leroy.

If you will come to my party, I will introduce you to Leroy.

Both verbs in the second sentence are in the future tense. That is not correct. The first sentence is correctly written. The verb in the if clause is in the present tense. This shows that the action in the if clause must happen before the action in the independent clause. You must come to my party before I can introduce you to Leroy.

Notice that this rule applies no matter where the if clause is located in the sentence:

> If you come to my party, I will introduce you to Leroy.

> I will introduce you to Leroy if you come to my party.

No matter how the sentence is written, the two actions must happen in the same sequence. You must first come to my party before I can introduce you to Leroy. The tenses show the sequence of the actions.

Here is another illustration of how the tense of the verb in the if clause determines the tense of the verbs in the independent clause:

> If you had asked, we would have helped.

In this example, the verb in the if clause is in the past perfect tense. Whenever you use a verb in the past perfect tense in an if clause, you must use would have or could have with the verb in the independent clause. This is because the action in the if clause had to take place before the action in the independent clause could happen. You had to ask before we could help.

How would you correct the following sentence?

> INCORRECT: If I would have heard about the party on time, I could have gone.

This sentence is trying to show that one action had to take place before the other action could happen. I had to hear about the party before I could go to it.

> CORRECT: If I had heard about the party on time, I could have gone.

When we put the verb in the if clause into the past perfect tense—had heard—we see that the action in the if clause had to happen first.

Again, it doesn't matter whether the if clause comes before or after the independent clause:

> CORRECT: If I had heard about the party on time, I could have gone.

> CORRECT: I could have gone to the party if I had heard about it on time.

No matter how the sentence is written, the two actions always happen in the same sequence. The tenses keep the sequence of the actions clear.

Using Active and Passive Voices

In the active voice, the subject of the sentence performs the action. In the passive voice, the subject of the sentence receives the action.

ACTIVE VOICE: I cleaned the kitchen yesterday.

PASSIVE VOICE: The kitchen was cleaned yesterday.

In the first sentence, the subject I performed the action cleaned. In the second sentence, the subject kitchen received the action was cleaned.

ACTIVE VOICE: The mail carrier will deliver the package.

PASSIVE VOICE: The package will be delivered by the mail carrier.

In the first sentence, the subject carrier performs the action will deliver. In the second sentence, the subject package receives the action will be delivered.

Do not shift from the active voice to the passive voice within a sentence. Look at these sentences:

INCORRECT: We sat down, drank our coffee, and many important topics were discussed.

CORRECT: We sat down, drank our coffee, and discussed many important topics.

In the first sentence, the subject we performs the actions sat and drank. But the subject topics does not perform an action. It receives the action were discussed. The first sentence is incorrect because it changes voice within the sentence. In the second sentence, the subject we performs all three actions—sat, drank, and discussed. Which of the following sentences is correct?

The gift has been bought, and I also sent a card.

The gift has been bought, and a card has been sent.

In the first sentence, the writer shifts from the passive voice to the active voice. The subject gift receives the action has been bought, but the subject I performs the action sent. This is incorrect. In the second sentence, both subjects—gift and card—receive the actions of has been bought and has been sent. The sentence is correct because both actions are expressed in the passive voice. It is also correct to say:

I bought the gift and also sent a card.

In this sentence, the actions bought and sent are both in the active voice. The sentence is correct because the writer does not shift from one voice to another within the sentence.

Apply what you have learned by doing the following exercise.

Exercise for Subskill 7B

In most of the following sentences, verbs are used incorrectly or inconsistently. Rewrite the incorrect sentences in the space provided. If a sentence contains no errors, write Correct in the space provided.

EXAMPLE: My pulse was taken, and the nurse also checked my blood pressure.

The nurse took my pulse and checked my blood pressure.

OR: My pulse was taken and my blood pressure was checked.

1. If you would have told me about the problem sooner, I would have done something about it.

_____

_____

2. I feel healthier when I jog every morning.

_____

_____

3. The party was a huge success because it was so well planned.

_____

_____

4. I heard she is sick.

_____

_____

5. She designed the dress, and it was sewn by her, too.

_____

_____

6. He says he could not repair the clock.

_____

_____

7. They said they could not afford it.

_____

_____

8. If we wait any longer, we lose our chance.

_____

_____

9. We called her last night, but she could not be reached by us.

_____

_____

10. I could have done better if I studied harder.

_____

_____

Check your answers on page 30 in the Answer Key for Book Three. If you answered all 10 items correctly, go to Subskill 7C. If not, do the Supplemental Exercise for Subskill 7B.

Supplemental Exercise for Subskill 7B

The time periods and the sequence of actions determine the verb tenses used in a sentence. In sentences without if clauses, you must use the same tense for all verbs showing actions that happen during the same time period. Helping verbs must be in the same tense as other verbs if they all show actions in the same time period. When a past action in a sentence takes place before another past action, the action that took place first is in the past perfect tense.

There are special rules for using verb tenses in sentences with dependent if clauses. The present tense is used when the action in the if clause must happen before some future action can take place. The past perfect tense is used when the action in the if clause had to be completed before the action in the independent clause would have or could have taken place.

Use the active voice when the action is performed by the subject of the sentence. Use the passive voice when the action is received by the subject. Do not shift from one voice to another within a sentence.

In most of the following sentences, verbs are used incorrectly or inconsistently. Rewrite the incorrect sentences in the space provided. If a sentence contains no errors, write Correct in the space provided.

EXAMPLE: As we drove away, I wondered whether I forgot to turn off the stove.

As we drove away, I wondered whether I had forgotten to turn off the stove.

1. He says we could not come along.

_____

_____

2.   When they will call me, I will tell them the news.

_____

_____

3.   We scored five runs, but the game was lost by our team.

_____

_____

4.   If it had rained, we would have cancelled the picnic.

_____

_____

5.   She insists that the clerk had made an error.

_____

_____

6.   This job will be a lot easier if Ann will come to help us.

_____

_____

7.   He tells us he helped her out.

_____

_____

8.   If you come over, I'll show you the pictures from my trip.

_____

_____

9.   If she would have tried to tell me the truth, I would have believed her.

_____

_____

10.   He was in good condition because he trains very hard for years.

_____

_____

Check your answers on page 30 in the Answer Key for Book Three. If you answered 8 of 10 items correctly, go to Subskill 7C. If not, ask your instructor for help.

Subskill 7C: Using Correct Pronoun Reference and Pronoun Agreement

When you complete this subskill, you will be able to use pronouns correctly so that it is clear which words they refer to, and so that they agree with the words they refer to in person, number, and gender.

Making Pronoun References Clear

You have learned that pronouns refer to, or take the place of, nouns or other pronouns. The word that a pronoun refers to is called its **antecedent.** When you use a pronoun, you must clearly indicate which word the pronoun is referring to. Look at this sentence:

INCORRECT: Tom told Bill that he had been fired.

Who was fired, Tom or Bill? The antecedent of the pronoun he is unclear. To make the reference clear, you must rewrite the sentence. If Bill is the one who was fired, you can write:

CORRECT: Tom told Bill that Bill had been fired.

Now the meaning of the sentence is clear, but the sentence sounds awkward. A better way to rewrite the sentence might be:

CORRECT: Bill had been fired, and Tom was the one who told him so.

Now it is clear that Bill is the one who was fired, and that the pronoun him plainly refers to Bill. Can you think of other ways to rewrite this sentence so that the pronoun reference is clear?

If Tom is the one who was fired, you can write:

CORRECT: Tom had been fired, and he told Bill what had happened.

Now look at this sentence:

INCORRECT: I saw your touchdown at the game, which was wonderful.

What was wonderful? It is not clear what which refers to. There are at least three ways to rewrite this sentence to clarify its meaning:

CORRECT: Your touchdown, which I saw at the game, was wonderful.

Which clearly refers to touchdown in this version of the sentence. But you might have meant to say something else:

CORRECT: The game at which I saw your touchdown was wonderful.

Now which clearly refers to game. But what if you had meant to say that the experience of seeing the touchdown was wonderful? You might write this version:

CORRECT: Seeing your touchdown at the game was wonderful.

This version shows that the meaning of the sentence is sometimes clearer when the pronoun is left out altogether.

Making Sure That Pronouns and Antecedents Agree

A pronoun must agree with its antecedent in person, gender, and number. Remember that first person pronouns refer to the person(s) speaking (I, me, my, we, us, our, ours); second person pronouns refer to the person(s) spoken to (you, your, yours); and third person pronouns refer to the person(s) or thing(s) spoken about (he, him, his, she, her, hers, it, its, they, them, their, theirs).

A common problem in agreement occurs when a noun is referred to by a second person pronoun. A noun is usually referred to by a third person pronoun. Look at this sentence:

INCORRECT: If an individual eats nutritious foods, you will be healthier.

Using the pronoun you in this sentence is incorrect. The pronoun is intended to refer to individual, a noun. Individual is an antecedent that is being spoken about, so the pronoun that refers to it should be in the third person. Also, individual is singular, so the pronoun that refers to it should be singular. The sentence may be written:

CORRECT: If an individual eats nutritious foods, he will be healthier.

OR

CORRECT: If an individual eats nutritious foods, she will be healthier.

In these sentences, he or she, which are third person singular pronouns, correctly refer to the antecedent individual.

Until recently, a third person masculine singular pronoun (he, him, his) was used when the gender of the antecedent was unknown, or when either gender was being referred to. For example, it was thought to be correct to say "Someone forgot his book" when it was unclear whether someone was male or female. Many people now realize that the exclusive use of the masculine pronoun favors males and ignores females, an attitude known as gender bias. There are several ways to avoid gender bias. Look at these sentences:

> CORRECT: If an individual eats nutritious foods, she or he will be healthier.

Use she or he (or he or she) unless doing so makes the sentence awkward.

Often, the best way to avoid an awkward sentence is to rewrite the sentence using a plural noun and a third person plural pronoun. This is because the plural pronoun they does not express gender.

> CORRECT: If individuals eat nutritious foods, they will be healthier.

The indefinite pronouns everyone, anyone, someone, somebody, no one, and nobody are singular antecedents that also use third person singular pronouns. How would you rewrite this sentence?

> INCORRECT: Everyone received their paycheck.

The plural pronoun their cannot refer to the singular pronoun everyone. You might use the singular pronouns of both genders, his or her (or her or his):

> CORRECT: Everyone received his or her paycheck.

Using both pronouns helps eliminate gender bias. Or you might make the subject plural:

> CORRECT: All employees received their paychecks.

Now the plural pronoun their agrees with the plural antecedent employees, and the problem of gender bias is avoided.

Exercise for Subskill 7C

Each of the following sentences contains an unclear or incorrect use of pronouns. Rewrite each sentence so that each pronoun reference is clear, and so that each pronoun agrees with its antecedent.

EXAMPLE: A person should always do their best.

> A person should always do his or her best.

OR: People should always do their best.

1.   Somebody left their wallet on the counter.

_____

_____

2. Jane told Tina her boyfriend was lying. (It was Jane's boyfriend who was lying.)

_____

_____

3. I bought a dress in that store, which is very fashionable. (The dress is fashionable.)

_____

_____

4. Whenever a consumer shops wisely, you are sure to save money.

_____

_____

5. A parent should respect their child.

_____

_____

Check your answers on page 30 in the Answer Key for Book Three. If you answered all 5 items correctly, go to Subskill 7D. If not, do the Supplemental Exercise for Subskill 7C.

Supplemental Exercise for Subskill 7C

An antecedent is a word that a pronoun refers to. Pronouns must clearly refer to their antecedents and agree with their noun antecedents in person, gender, and number. Gender bias occurs when only the masculine pronoun is used for both genders in a sentence.

Each of the following sentences contains an unclear or incorrect use of pronouns. Rewrite each sentence so that each pronoun reference is clear and so that each pronoun agrees with its antecedent.

EXAMPLE: They are renting an apartment in that building, which is large. (The apartment is large.)

They are renting a large apartment in that building.

OR: The apartment, which they are renting in that building, is large.

1. We saw Jackson strike out in that game, which was exciting. (The game was exciting.)

_____

_____

2. Helen told Mary that her car needed a new muffler. (It was Mary's car that needed the muffler.)

   _____

   _____

3. Everybody at the table unfolded their napkin.

   _____

   _____

4. When a person is tired, you usually make more mistakes.

   _____

   _____

5. Nobody called to inquire about their tickets.

   _____

   _____

Check your answers on page 31 of the Answer Key for Book Three. If you answered 4 of 5 items correctly, go to Subskill 7D. If not, ask your instructor for help.

Subskill 7D: Avoiding Sentence Fragments

When you complete this subskill, you will be able to recognize sentence fragments, and to construct complete sentences without using fragments.

A sentence is a complete thought that contains a subject and a verb. A sentence fragment is only part of a sentence. In our everyday conversation and casual writing, we may use many sentence fragments or incomplete sentences. For example, you might write the following note to someone in your family:

Went to the store. Will be back by six.

These groups of words are fragments because they do not express complete thoughts. Who went to the store? Who will be back by six? These fragments are missing the subject I.

Sometimes sentence fragments can communicate a message clearly. But often they are unclear. Even the note to your family might be misunderstood—someone might think you were saying that someone else went to the store. To be able to communicate effectively in as many situations as possible, you should be able to recognize and write complete sentences.

A complete sentence must have a subject and a verb. It must also express a complete thought. A group of words that does not express a complete thought cannot stand by itself. Look at these groups of words:

Al plays practical jokes. Making people angry.

The first group of words is a complete sentence expressing a complete thought. It has a subject—Al—and a verb—plays. The participial phrase making people angry has no subject or verb. Since it does not express a complete thought, it is a fragment that cannot stand alone. The fragment has been corrected in the following sentence:

Al plays practical jokes and is always making people angry.

The present participle making has been changed to a complete verb—is making. The subject is clearly Al. The fragment has become part of a complete sentence.

How would you correct these groups of words?

INCORRECT: The restaurant is a mile from here. Across the street from the local movie theater.

The first group of words is a complete sentence with a subject—restaurant—and a verb—is—that express a complete thought. The next group is made up of two prepositional phrases—across the street and from the local movie theater. Neither phrase contains a subject or verb, or expresses a complete thought. To remove the fragment, the sentence may be written:

CORRECT: The restaurant, which is across the street from the local movie theater, is a mile from here.

Now the fragments have been joined to a complete sentence to express a complete thought. Another way to correct a fragment is to form two complete sentences. You can do this by specifying the fragment's subject and verb:

CORRECT: The restaurant is a mile from here. It is across the street from the local movie theater.

By using the pronoun it to repeat the subject, and the verb is to repeat the verb, you make a complete sentence out of the fragment.

Here is another type of fragment that should be avoided:

INCORRECT: Ann did all the repairs on my car. The best mechanic in our town.

The first group of words is a complete sentence with a subject—Ann—and a verb—did—that expresses a complete thought. The second group of words is a phrase that describes Ann. It is a fragment that does not express a complete thought and cannot stand alone. The fragment has been corrected in this sentence:

> CORRECT: Ann, the best mechanic in our town, did all the repair work on my car.

Now the best mechanic in our town follows the noun it describes (Ann). It has been inserted into a complete sentence. Or, again, you can form two complete sentences by specifying the fragment's subject and verb:

> CORRECT: Ann did all the repair work on my car. She is the best mechanic in our town.

The subject-verb combination she is makes the fragment into a **complete** sentence and a complete thought.

Another type of sentence fragment is a subordinate clause. In Skill Unit 3, you learned that a subordinate clause has a subject and a verb but cannot stand by itself. A subordinate clause does not express a complete thought. Can the following group of words stand by itself?

> Because the machine is dangerous to operate.

This group of words has a subject—machine—and a verb—is, but it is not a complete thought. The word because makes this group of words a subordinate clause. It cannot stand by itself because it leaves you with a question about the machine. What should happen because the machine is dangerous to operate? This sentence fragment needs an independent clause to complete its meaning:

> Because the machine is dangerous to operate, it should be placed away from children.

It should be placed away from children is not a fragment. It is an independent clause: it has a subject and a verb, and it expresses a complete thought. It does not need any more words to help it make sense. Here, we corrected the subordinate clause fragment by joining it to the independent clause.

How would you correct the fragment in the following groups of words?

> I told her I would babysit. Since I had no other plans.

I told her I would babysit is an independent clause. It has a subject and a verb, and it expresses a complete thought. Since I had no other plans has a subject and a verb. But it does not express a complete thought because it is a subordinate clause. It cannot stand alone. To correct the fragment, you might connect the two sentences:

> Since I had no other plans, I told her I would babysit.

Joining the subordinate clause to an independent clause makes a complete sentence out of a sentence and a fragment.

Exercise for Subskill 7D

Some of the sentences in the following paragraph contain incomplete sentences, or sentence fragments. Rewrite the paragraph so that it contains only complete sentences. You may have to add your own subjects or predicates to some fragments, or rearrange the order of some words.

When I went on my first job interview, I was very nervous. Because I really wanted the job. I went to bed early the night before the interview so I wouldn't be tired. I got up early. The next day. Maybe because I was nervous. I ate a good breakfast. To give me energy. Eileen called me while I was still eating. The best friend I have. Wanting to wish me luck. She said I would certainly get the job. Always being very cheerful. But it turned out that she was right. As usual. I got the job and I stayed there for two years. Until I found a better one.

EXAMPLE: When I went on my first job interview, I was very nervous. Because I really wanted the job.

When I went on my first job interview, I was very nervous, because I really wanted the job.

_____

_____

_____

_____

_____

_____

_____

_____

_____

_____

Check your answers on page 31 in the Answer Key for Book Three. If you correctly identified and rewrote the sentence fragments and made no more than one error, go to the Self-Check. If not, do the Supplemental Exercise for Subskill 7D.

Supplemental Exercise for Subskill 7D

Sentence fragments are groups of words that do not express a complete thought and cannot stand alone. A fragment may be a phrase that lacks both a subject and a verb. It may be a group of words that explains or identifies a noun. Subordinate clauses cannot stand alone, even though they contain subjects and verbs. They are sentence fragments because they depend on independent clauses to complete their meanings. To correct a fragment, you can make it part of a complete sentence. Phrases may be placed near the word or words they modify, or rewritten as separate sentences with their own subjects and verbs. Subordinate clauses should be joined to an independent clause. You can also correct fragments by rewriting a group of words so that it has a subject and a predicate and expresses a complete thought.

Rewrite the following paragraph so that it contains no sentence fragments. You may have to add your own subjects or verbs to some fragments, or rearrange the order of some words.

We are friends with our neighbors. The Montoyas. Living down the hall. They even feed our cat for us. When we go away. Staying away for a long time. Sometimes I cook something special for the neighbors. To thank them. Being the best neighbors we have ever had. I hope we never have to move. Even to a bigger apartment. I wouldn't want to leave them. Because good neighbors are hard to find.

EXAMPLE: We are friends with our neighbors. The Montoyas. Living down the hall.
<u>We are friends with our neighbors, the Montoyas, who live down the hall.</u>

_____

_____

_____

_____

_____

_____

_____

_____

_____

Check your answers on page 31 in the Answer Key for Book Three. If you correctly identified and rewrote the sentence fragments and made no more than one error, go to the Self-Check. If not, ask your instructor for help.

SELF-CHECK FOR SKILL UNIT 7

Some of the following items contain errors in parallel structure, verb tense or voice, or pronoun reference or pronoun-antecedent agreement. Some of the following items are sentence fragments. Rewrite the incorrect sentences and make each sentence fragment a complete sentence in the space provided. If a sentence contains no errors, write Correct in the space provided.

EXAMPLE: He said you lived there for years.
           He said you had lived there for years.

1. Shopping for a birthday present and to find the right card can be hard work.

    _____

    _____

2. If you will meet me after work, we will go shopping together.

    _____

    _____

3. Bill told Howard that his sister was interesting. (It was Bill's sister who was interesting.)

    _____

    _____

4. If a person makes a promise, you should keep that promise.

    _____

    _____

5. Working hard to bring up their children and to set a good example.

    _____

    _____

6. Nina had never learned concentration or how to study.

    _____

    _____

7. If they would have tried harder, they would have won the game.

    _____

    _____

8. Bert not only is kind and understanding, but also very patient.

_____

_____

9. I think we need either more help or cutting down our work load.

_____

_____

10. After Jan worked hard for months, she finally accomplished her goal.

_____

_____

11. Monday, a freezing day, with many people staying at home.

_____

_____

12. Their baby is happy, lively, and has lots of curiosity.

_____

_____

13. To buy an appliance in a department store is less expensive than purchasing one from a local merchant.

_____

_____

14. Everyone has their own way of doing things.

_____

_____

15. I typed the letters, and the envelopes were also addressed by me.

_____

_____

16. Juan bought the paper and read the sports page.

_____

_____

17. Alissa thinks she could do the job tomorrow.

_____

_____

18. If I were there, I would have done things differently.

    _____

    _____

19. Either you should pay attention or turn off the television set.

    _____

    _____

20. Coach Brown was worshipped by the team, admired by the fans, but her staff disliked her.

    _____

    _____

21. A pleasure seeing you at the game last Sunday.

    _____

    _____

22. If I will see him, I will tell him the news.

    _____

    _____

23. Where a great deal of damage was caused by the storm last month.

    _____

    _____

24. The laundry was done, the books were read, and I cooked for the party.

    _____

    _____

25. That man is carrying an open umbrella. Even though it isn't raining.

    _____

    _____

Check your answers on pages 31 and 32 in the Answer Key for Book Three. If you answered 20 of 25 items correctly, you have shown that you have mastered these skills. If not, ask your instructor for help.

Skill Unit 8
WRITING UNIFIED PARAGRAPHS

What Skills You Need to Begin: You need to understand subject–verb agreement (Skill Unit 1) and to know how to form compound sentences (Skill Unit 2) and complex sentences (Skill Unit 3). You also need to know how to use sentence punctuation (Skill Units 4 and 5), how to use modifiers correctly (Skill Unit 6), and how to write effective sentences (Skill Unit 7).

What Skills You Will Learn: When you complete this unit, you will recognize topic sentences in paragraphs and be able to create effective topic sentences of your own. You will also be able to recognize various methods for developing paragraphs and will know some ways to unify ideas within paragraphs. You will be able to identify and remove sentences that do not belong in a particular paragraph. You will learn to write unified paragraphs of your own.

Why You Need These Skills: The sentence is the basic unit in which writers express their ideas. However, a single sentence can communicate only a small amount of information. To express ideas more fully, writers join groups of sentences together to form paragraphs. A paragraph is based on one central idea. Writers group paragraphs together to form themes, essays, and stories that communicate their ideas about a subject. A well-developed, unified paragraph is the basic building block for the communication of ideas.

How You Will Show What You Have Learned: You will take the Self-Check at the end of this unit on page 242. Using two ideas from a list of topics provided, you will develop two paragraphs of at least 100 words each. You will have demonstrated mastery if you have successfully followed a particular method of development in each paragraph and if each sentence in your paragraph is directly related to and helps develop the topic sentence.

If you feel that you have already mastered these skills, turn to the end of this unit and complete the Self-Check on page 242.

Subskill 8A: Recognizing Topic Sentences

When you complete this subskill, you will be able to recognize topic sentences that are stated or implied in paragraphs.

A paragraph is a group of sentences joined together to develop or expand one topic or idea. Every paragraph is based on a single controlling idea. This controlling idea is usually presented directly in one sentence of the paragraph—the **topic sentence. The topic sentence tells what the paragraph is about.** The other sentences in the paragraph are called **detail sentences. They present details to support or explain the topic.** The topic sentence presents an idea in generalized, or summary, form. The detail sentences present specific information about the topic.

Locating Topic Sentences

The topic sentence is usually, but not always, the first sentence in a paragraph. When writers put the topic sentence first, they are starting off with a general idea. Then they add a series of specific details to support that idea. You can diagram this type of paragraph construction as a triangle with a point on the top:

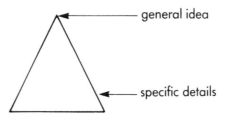

Sometimes writers present a series of specific details first, then sum up the paragraph with a topic sentence that presents a general idea. You might picture an upside-down triangle to describe this type of paragraph construction:

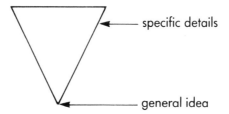

Writers can also present one or two details first, then give the topic sentence, and then add some more details. You might think of an hourglass to express this type of paragraph construction:

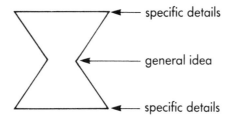

As you read the three short paragraphs below, think about which sentence in each one summarizes what the paragraph is about. That sentence is the topic sentence.

Knowing how to take notes can be a very useful skill in school and on the job. Taking good lecture notes in class can help you remember important information that may be asked for on tests. Taking notes when you are doing research for reports and papers can help you select and organize the information you want to write about. Taking notes on the job can help you remember instructions you need to follow and the order in which those instructions should be carried out.

In the above paragraph, the controlling idea is that taking notes can be a useful skill. That idea is presented in the first sentence of the paragraph. The first sentence is, therefore, the topic sentence. The other sentences present details that explain how note-taking can be useful in school or on the job.

Bells began to ring. People were shouting. Merchants closed up their shops to join the excited throngs on the streets. High up in office buildings, people began to throw paper and ticker tape out of windows. Even the stones of the street seemed to resound with joy. Everybody and everything gave themselves up to a wild celebration.

In this paragraph, the last sentence sums up the details presented in the sentences that have come before. Therefore the last sentence is the topic sentence. Notice how the detail sentences illustrate the main idea presented in the last sentence. Reread the paragraph. Don't you agree that the topic is "a wild celebration"?

There is no more room in my closet for all the dresses, skirts, and blouses that I have. I own more shoes than I can wear. My dresser drawers are overflowing. My clothes are my most valuable and most prized possessions. I probably spend more money on clothes each year than I do on food. People say that I would rather look good than eat well.

In this paragraph, the main idea is presented in the middle of the paragraph. The writer obviously likes clothes and spends a lot of money on them. That idea is summarized in the fourth sentence: "My clothes are my most valuable and most prized possessions." That sentence is the topic sentence. The sentences before and after it support that idea.

Being Sure That You Have Located the Topic Sentence

How can you be sure that you have located the topic sentence of a paragraph? Here's one way to help you decide. Turn your choice into a question beginning with why, how, or what. If the paragraph as a whole answers your question, you can be fairly certain that you did locate the topic sentence.

Look again at the first paragraph on page 212. Turn the first sentence into a question: "How can taking notes be a useful skill in school and on the job?" Do all of the other sentences present answers to this question? They do, so you know that this is the topic sentence.

Suppose you had chosen the last sentence as your topic sentence. Turn that sentence into a question: "How can taking notes on the job help you remember and carry out instructions?" The first three sentences in the paragraph don't answer that question, do they? This tells you, then, that the last sentence cannot be the topic sentence of this paragraph.

Recognizing Implied Topic Sentences

Sometimes writers present a series of details in a paragraph without including a summary sentence. You have to put the details together yourself to decide what the main idea is. In this type of paragraph, the topic sentence is implied or hinted at without actually being stated. A paragraph may be more effective if the reader has to think about the main idea without it being given as a topic sentence. You might diagram this type of paragraph construction as a square, because all of the sentences are equally important in conveying the topic.

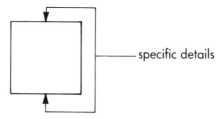

specific details

Writers presenting narrative (storytelling) paragraphs or describing a scene frequently create paragraphs with implied topic sentences such as this one:

> When Rick Ward, a London demolition worker, ripped away a board in a shop, he saw what he thought was a bag made of crocodile skin. He bent down to pick it up. The bag began hissing and spitting. Ward scrambled out of the shop in high gear. The "bag" was a boa constrictor that had escaped from a pet shop next door.

What is the topic sentence in this paragraph? There is no one sentence that sums up everything. The paragraph is held together by an implied idea: "A man had a close call when he mistook a snake for a crocodile-skin bag."

Here's another paragraph with an implied topic sentence. Read the paragraph and decide what the implied idea is.

> For the past week I have been arriving at work before 8:30 every morning. I haven't taken a coffee break, and I have sometimes worked straight through lunch. I have been spending most of my time typing. Tuesday I typed up 22 letters. I didn't get out of the office until 7:30 that night.

Notice that no one sentence in the paragraph presents the topic idea, but that all of the sentences together imply: "I have been working especially hard this week."

Show what you have learned about locating topic sentences by completing the following exercise.

Exercise for Subskill 8A

Read each paragraph below. Locate the topic sentence—the sentence that sums up the details expressed by the other sentences in the paragraph. Underline the entire topic sentence. Remember, the topic sentence is not always the first sentence of a paragraph. If the topic sentence of a paragraph is implied instead of stated, write the idea that is implied on the line below the paragraph.

EXAMPLES: <u>Pet ownership can teach responsibility and caring to a child.</u> Psychologists tell us that pet ownership in the childhood years prepares the child for parenting in adult years. Pets can teach a child about the cycles of life and death. They can teach a child to express fears and emotions. A pet is never too busy to listen. A pet is a special kind of friend. It accepts you even if you didn't get a good grade in your English class.

_____

Owners of discount store chains keep prices down by buying in large quantities and limiting the variety of items they sell. They employ few salesclerks and provide minimal services. This is the opposite of what is done in exclusive and expensive specialty stores. These stores employ many salespeople and offer a broad range of items. Discount stores resemble wholesale warehouses in some respects. They have eliminated costly merchandise displays and expensive advertising. They manage to keep their overhead to a minimum.

<u>Discount store chains use a variety of methods to keep prices low and increase the volume of their sales.</u>

1. Owning a pet can actually improve a person's health. Medical studies have shown that when a person speaks to an animal, the person's blood pressure drops. Since people often pet or stoke an animal when they talk to it, interacting with a pet can help a person relax even more. Simply being in a room with a bubbling fish aquarium can also lessen a person's stress and anxiety levels.

2. The average person will live to be 100. A man of 75 will have the vigor of a man of 45 today. Hearts, lungs, stomachs, and other parts from dead persons will be stored in human banks for transplanting. Artificial parts will also be used. When you go to a doctor, you will sit in a computerized chair that will diagnose your illness. These are just some of the advances medical science may help bring about by the year 2000.

3. Roseanne Murphy of St. Louis, Mo., looked out her kitchen window and saw a driverless car rolling across her lawn. She sprinted out, caught up with the car six houses down the street, and dove into the empty driver's seat. She slammed on the brakes. Roseanne's fast thinking and quick footwork saved the lives of five children. The car stopped just short of hitting the children, three of whom were her own.

4. Thunder and lightning occur more often in summer than in winter for an interesting reason. Electrical storms start when there are quick and definite changes in the temperature of the atmosphere. The upper atmosphere is always cold, and in wintertime the temperature near the earth is also low. Quick changes in temperature are, therefore, less frequent in the wintertime, and fewer electrical storms occur.

5. Some people move out of the city because they want more space or the pleasure of owning their own homes. Others believe that the schools are better. Some people enjoy a small-town atmosphere. Still others are fleeing the noise, crowds, old housing, and dirty air of many cities. In one study, most people questioned gave family and home-life as their reasons for moving. Many described small towns as "healthier for children."

Check your answers on pages 32 and 33 in the Answer Key for Book Three. If you correctly identified the topic sentence in 4 of 5 paragraphs, go to Subskill 8B. If not, do the Supplemental Exercise for Subskill 8A.

Supplemental Exercise for Subskill 8A

A paragraph is a group of sentences joined together to develop or expand one topic or idea. Every paragraph is based on a single controlling idea. This controlling idea is usually presented directly in one sentence of the paragraph—the topic sentence. The topic sentence tells what the paragraph is about. To be sure you have correctly identified the topic sentence, turn the sentence you are considering into a question beginning with why, how, or what. If the paragraph as a whole answers your question, you can be fairly certain that you have correctly identified the topic sentence.

Writers usually, but not always, start a paragraph with the topic sentence. Sometimes writers put the topic sentence at the end of the paragraph to sum up the information presented in the preceding sentences. Sometimes writers place a topic sentence in the middle of a paragraph. Sometimes writers do not actually include a topic sentence in a paragraph. Instead, the detail sentences hint at, or imply, the topic idea. The diagrams below can help you picture these four types of paragraph construction:

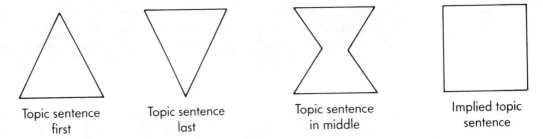

Topic sentence first Topic sentence last Topic sentence in middle Implied topic sentence

Check your ability to identify the topic sentence of a paragraph by completing the following Supplemental Exercise.

Read each paragraph below. Locate the topic sentence, the sentence that sums up the details expressed by the other sentences in the paragraph. Underline the entire topic sentence. Remember, the topic sentence is not always the first sentence of a paragraph. If the topic sentence of a paragraph is implied instead of stated, write the topic idea that is implied on the line below the paragraph.

EXAMPLES:

Over 40 million Americans receive Social Security checks in the mail each month. <u>Under Social Security, assistance is provided to the needy, the aged, and the physically disabled.</u> The program provides pensions for retired workers and their dependents. It also provides disability payments, aid to families of deceased workers, special pensions to certain uninsured elderly people, and Medicare/Medicaid payments.

The foods we eat when we need a snack or a meal in a hurry are likely to contain a high proportion of sugar and fat. At the same time, important minerals, vitamins, and fiber are missing from many of our favorite fast foods. Foods high in sugar and fat but without vitamins and minerals are said to contain "empty calories." If most of our daily diet consists of fast foods, we may not be getting as many nutrients as our bodies need.

<u>Fast foods may not contain important nutrients.</u>

---

1. My friend Michael is a very pleasant person, but he certainly couldn't be called a snappy dresser. His shirt is never tucked in, and one or two buttons always seem to be missing. He usually wears mismatched socks. I remember one day last week when he came to work wearing a pink plaid shirt with a pair of green striped trousers. His shoelaces are usually untied, and the heels of his shoes are always worn down.

---

2. Because adult learners know that further education and training can lead to advance in the workplace, they are usually willing to sacrifice time, energy, and money to complete their education. Since they usually work at a regular job during the day and attend school and study at night, they must schedule time carefully to make every minute count. This means that there is little time to spend with family or in leisure activities. Financial sacrifices are often shared with the entire family. Vacations may be postponed or eliminated altogether. Household purchases may be delayed so that the cost of books and tuition can be met. But all sacrifices will seem worthwhile when the eventual goal is reached.

3. As a child star, she was introduced early to the pressures of the entertainment world. She has faced illness many times and has been near death twice in her life. Her several marriages and divorces have been the focus of media attention. She has had a very public life. Through it all, she remained devoted to her children. Although her weight fluctuated sharply over the years and was often the subject of a popular comic routine, she is still a beautiful woman. She has proven herself a winner in her recent battle with substance abuse. Indeed, Elizabeth Taylor has survived many crises and challenges throughout her long career.

4. Aunt Betty always prepares the turkey and dressing for our family's Thanksgiving celebration. Cousin Bill brings his pecan and pumpkin pies, which are family favorites. My mother usually makes a centerpiece of fall leaves, harvest fruits, and Indian corn as a symbol of fall's plenty. The wonderful aromas of roasting turkey, steaming gravy, and home-baked bread waft from the kitchen to greet the latecomers. Heidi and Bill come from Colorado; Jim, Lucy, and the new baby arrive from Iowa; Carter, Carla, and their three children drive all the way from Kansas.

5. Owning a motorcycle can be fun, convenient, and economical. However, motorcycles can also be very dangerous for the inexperienced driver. Statistics indicate that nearly 20 percent of all persons involved in motorcycle accidents are new cyclists. New cyclists should take precautions to insure their safety. They should take lessons from an experienced cyclist and practice in a protected area before taking to the road. They should purchase and wear the correct protective gear. A protective helmet is a must, and leather gloves and boots are a good idea, too. New cyclists should make sure that their cycles have reflectors and lights because a cycle is much smaller than a car and is not as easy to see on the road. They should drive with the headlight on even in the daytime to increase visibility, and should always be alert to traffic, road, and weather conditions.

Check your answers on pages 33 and 34 in the Answer Key for Book Three. If you correctly identified the topic sentences in 4 of 5 paragraphs, go to Subskill 8B. If not, ask your instructor for help.

Subskill 8B: Writing Effective Topic Sentences

When you complete this subskill, you will be able to write effective topic sentences that present a general subject, limit the subject, and suggest a direction for paragraph development.

Paragraphs are usually fairly short. Most contain from four to ten sentences. In order to cover a topic idea thoroughly in a paragraph, the topic idea should not be too broad. The main job of the topic sentence is to present the general topic and to limit the topic so that it can be covered effectively within the paragraph.

Recognizing Effective Topic Sentences

An effective topic sentence should do three things:
1. It should state the general topic you are writing about.
2. It should limit the general topic to a particular idea or opinion that can be covered in one paragraph.
3. It should suggest a way for developing the topic in the rest of the paragraph.

Compare these two topic sentences:

My old 1976 Ford gets twenty-four miles to the gallon.
My 1976 Ford still gives excellent performance for an old car.

The first sentence presents a subject, the 1976 Ford, but it doesn't suggest a way to develop any ideas about the subject. The second sentence contains the words "excellent performance." This is an idea that can be illustrated in the rest of the paragraph.

Good topic sentences clearly express the main idea and so make the rest of the paragraph easy to develop. They often contain a key word, words, or phrase that leads to details about the main idea. As you read the topic sentences that follow, try to think of details you would use to develop the topic idea:

Knowing how to type is a valuable skill.

The key word is valuable. The detail sentences in the paragraph will prove that typing is a valuable skill. You might write about how many jobs require typing, how typing is necessary in the business world, or how typing can help you communicate and improve your grades in school.

Vitamin E is a miracle drug.

The key word is <u>miracle.</u> The rest of the paragraph should explain the miracles that some people believe Vitamin E can perform. For example, it is claimed to promote healing of skin, prevent wrinkles, and increase energy and resistance to disease.

Rattlesnakes are well adapted to their environment.

The key words are <u>well adapted.</u> The rest of the sentences should show some of the ways in which rattlesnakes are adapted to their environment. For example, their cold blood allows them to survive within great temperature ranges, their coloring lets them blend into their surroundings, and they can burrow quickly into the sand for protection from heat and enemies.

Recognizing Topic Sentences That Are Too Broad

Many topics are too broad, or general, to be covered in one paragraph; there may be just too much information to present in a few sentences. When a topic seems too broad to you, you must narrow it down to make it smaller and more specific. For example, suppose you want to write a paragraph about snakes. You start with the topic sentence:

Snakes are interesting animals.

Can this topic be covered in only four to ten sentences? Entire books have been written about snakes! So you decide to narrow your topic to rattlesnakes. You write the following topic sentence:

Rattlesnakes are beautiful but frightening animals.

But this topic is still too broad to cover successfully in only one paragraph. You decide to narrow the topic down further, and you develop the following topic sentence:

Rattlesnakes are well adapted to their environment.

At last you have a subject that is paragraph size!

As this example shows, you can turn a topic sentence that is too broad into one that is just right. The way to do this is to look at the key words in your topic sentence. The first versions of the snake topic sentence used such key words as <u>interesting</u> and <u>beautiful but frightening.</u> These words don't suggest good detail sentences because they are too general. They don't give you a focus for the detail sentences that must follow. By putting the key idea "well adapted to their environment" into the topic sentence, you started off with a clear focus for the more detailed ideas that might follow.

The first sentence below is another topic sentence that is too broad. Notice how it has been narrowed down to a workable size in the second sentence.

Some people have financial difficulties.
Credit cards can sometimes lead people
into financial difficulties.

Here the broad sentence could lead to any of dozens of paragraphs: There are many kinds of financial difficulties. What kind of difficulty does the writer want to talk about? By deciding to talk about credit card difficulties, the writer has found a focus on which to center the rest of the paragraph.

Recognizing Topic Sentences That Are Too Narrow

You have just learned that a good topic sentence should not be so broad that you can't cover the topic effectively in one paragraph. On the other hand, a topic sentence must not be so narrow that you won't have anything else to develop in the paragraph. The following topic sentence is too narrow:

My old 1976 Ford gets twenty-four miles to the gallon of gas.

What else can be said? The topic sentence is too narrow to lend itself to further development. This kind of sentence should be used in the paragraph as an example. You need to broaden this topic sentence so that it presents a main idea you can prove or explain. Here is an effective revision of this narrow topic sentence:

My 1976 Ford still gives excellent performance for an old car.

Now you can develop this topic sentence with supporting details or examples:

The car still gets twenty-four miles to the gallon of gas. Even though it's 10 years old, it runs smoothly and quietly. Its brakes, clutch, and fuel system are in excellent condition.

You can tell when a topic sentence is too narrow: It is a "dead end" for further ideas. Either you will have nothing more to say on the subject, or every other idea you can think of will also be a dead end. To solve this problem, step back a bit. Ask yourself what kind of sentence might introduce the sentence you have just written. Try to think of some key words that include the information presented in the narrow topic sentence. In the example above, the key words are <u>excellent performance</u> and <u>old car.</u> From these key words you can develop a paragraph by giving the detailed information to show the car's performance qualities and its age.

Show your understanding of how to write an effective topic sentence by completing the following exercise.

Exercise for Subskill 8B

Read each topic sentence on page 221. You may find that some are too broad to be effective topic sentences. You may find that others are too narrow to be effective topic sentences. On the lines following each sentence, rewrite it to make it a more effective topic sentence. Improve the sentences that are too broad by adding detail. Improve the sentences that are too narrow by making them less detailed. Remember that an effective topic sentence must present a general subject, be neither too broad nor too narrow, and suggest a way to develop the subject in the rest of the paragraph.

EXAMPLE: Ponce de Leon searched for the Fountain of Youth. <u>Ponce de Leon's fruitless search for the Fountain of Youth had some positive results.</u>

1. Computers are complex machines.

_____

_____

2. Boston is a large city in New England.

_____

_____

3. Many people enjoy sports.

_____

_____

4. The Thanksgiving Day Parade was viewed by more than one million people.

_____

_____

5. Evan's Boutique is an expensive men's clothing store.

_____

_____

6. I went to Mexico City for my vacation this year.

_____

_____

Ask your instructor to evaluate the topic sentences you have written. If you have written at least 4 effective topic sentences, go to Subskill 8C. If not, do the Supplemental Exercise for Subskill 8B.

Supplemental Exercise for Subskill 8B

An effective topic sentence should limit a general subject to a particular opinion or angle and should suggest a way to develop the subject in the rest of the paragraph. Some topic ideas are too broad to be covered in a single paragraph. You must narrow these topics to a workable size. Some topic ideas are too narrow to be developed further. You should broaden these topic ideas by building in an opinion or an angle that you can develop in the rest of the paragraph.

Check your ability to write effective topic sentences by completing the following Supplemental Exercise.

Read each topic sentence below. You may find that some are too broad to be effective topic sentences. You may find that others are too narrow to be effective topic sentences. On the lines following each sentence, rewrite it to make it a more effective topic sentence. Improve the sentences that are too broad by adding detail. Improve the sentences that are too narrow by making them less detailed. Remember that an effective topic sentence must present a general subject, be neither too broad nor too narrow, and suggest a way to develop the subject in the rest of the paragraph.

EXAMPLE: What you eat can affect your health.
<u>Studies have shown that eating foods high in Vitamin A can help prevent some forms of cancer.</u>

1. John Adams was the first President to live in the White House.

2. Many people own pets.

3. My car broke down on the highway yesterday.

4. I have a job interview tomorrow morning.

5. Many inventions have had an effect on modern life.

6. Some of today's movies are very frightening.

Ask your instructor to evaluate the topic sentences you have written. If you have written at least 4 effective topic sentences, go to Subskill 8C. If not, ask your instructor for help.

Subskill 8C: Identifying Methods of Paragraph Development

When you complete this subskill, you will be able to recognize how transition words and phrases and repetition of words help link the sentences of a paragraph so that ideas flow smoothly from one sentence to the next. You will also be able to identify five basic ways to develop a paragraph.

You have seen that a topic sentence presents a general idea and suggests a way to develop the idea further. The development of the topic sentence is what the rest of a paragraph is all about. The rest of the paragraph consists of detail sentences that add information to support or illustrate the topic. Later in this subskill we will look at some techniques for organizing information into detail sentences. First, though, we will study some ways to make ideas flow smoothly within a paragraph.

Organizing a Paragraph and Linking Its Sentences

It is the topic sentence that starts the ideas in a paragraph flowing. Once you have written an effective topic sentence, ideas for developing it will start to come to mind. Probably you can think of many ideas about the topic sentences you studied in Subskill 8B. Once you have the ideas, the problem is how to use them. This is a problem in **organization.** How should the ideas, or details, in a paragraph be presented to support the topic sentence?

Writers use several methods to organize their ideas effectively. The method used often depends on the subject of the paragraph. Details in a paragraph may be organized **chronologically** (according to time), **spatially** (according to direction), or **in order of importance.** A paragraph describing "a typical day" would probably be organized chronologically. The writer would use words such as first, next, then, and later to indicate the order of the events. **These words are called transitional words.**

A paragraph describing what a room looks like would probably be organized spatially. The writer would probably use transitional words such as on the left, to the right, in the center, and above to indicate where different things are located in the room.

A paragraph giving reasons or presenting an argument or opinion would probably be organized in order of importance. The writer might decide to give the most important details first. Or the writer might decide to give the least important details first and build up to a climax. The lead paragraphs in newspaper articles are examples of giving the most important details first. The transitional words used in such a paragraph would indicate relative importance: foremost, most significant, least important, and of little consequence are some examples.

These and other transitional words help link the ideas in the sentences of a paragraph. There are many ways of writing transitions from one idea to the next; you will see a number of examples in the paragraphs discussed in the rest of this subskill.

Developing a Paragraph

What do you do with the supporting details after you think of them? What is the best way to arrange them in the paragraph? What do you do if you have too many details? How can you come up with additional details if you have too few? In this section we will look at some ways in which writers develop their ideas.

Let's say you have decided on the subject you are going to write about, and you have written an effective topic sentence. Ideas are starting to come to mind. The first thing to do is jot them down so you won't forget any of them. Keep jotting ideas down until you have at least three, and as many as twelve. As you write, you will find that one idea leads to another. Don't worry about the order or sequence in which you jot them down. At this point, don't even worry about making each idea into a complete sentence.

Now that you have your ideas captured so that they won't fly away, you are ready to study the most useful ways of organizing ideas into paragraph sentences. Here are five key ways to use ideas and details in a paragraph:

1. Supply relevant details, such as facts or statistics to support the topic.
2. Supply examples to illustrate or explain the topic.
3. Use details that contrast or compare to illustrate the topic.
4. Give reasons that show cause or effect or explain why the topic sentence is true.
5. Use a combination of the above methods to develop the topic.

The subject of your paragraph and the kind of details or ideas that you want to use will determine which method you choose.

Supply Relevant Details

Sometimes a paragraph can best be developed by supplying relevant facts or statistics to prove or support the topic idea. All of the facts together explain the topic idea. In the paragraph below, note how the different relevant details, facts, and statistics support the idea that Joe DiMaggio was a great baseball player:

> In 1976, baseball writers voted Joe DiMaggio the Greatest Living Player, and with good reason. For one thing, DiMaggio was a lifetime .325 hitter. He also had power, slugging 361 home runs in his career. DiMaggio's record of hitting safely in 56 straight games in 1941 might never be equalled. Three times he was voted the American League's Most Valuable Player. In addition, DiMaggio was an excellent fielder, who used his speed and instincts to make difficult plays look easy.

In this paragraph, the writer lets an accumulation of details prove the topic idea. All of the sentences work together to support the main idea—how Joe DiMaggio was great. This working together makes the paragraph unified. Notice, too, that the paragraph contains a series of transitional words and phrases that keep the information flowing smoothly from sentence to sentence. Reread the paragraph, looking for such transitions as for one thing, also, and in addition.

Supply Examples

An example is a case, situation, or incident used to illustrate or explain a general principle. The examples in a paragraph answer the questions "why?", "how?" or "what kind?" In the paragraph that follows, notice how the supporting information is made up of examples—not facts or statistics—that answer the question "what kind?" Each example can stand alone to prove the topic idea.

> After the Declaration of Independence was adopted, the new United States faced enormous difficulties. It was at war for its life. Its small and untrained armies under General George Washington were opposed to the mighty power of Great Britain. Its little ships stood against the fleets of the Royal Navy. Arms and ammunition were scarce and there was little money for buying supplies. The new country was struggling under odds that seemed too heavy to bear.

In the paragraph above, the topic sentence mentions the enormous difficulties that the United States faced after the adoption of the Declaration of Independence. These are the key words that point a way to develop the paragraph. Notice that those difficulties are then specifically identified and listed in the rest of the paragraph.

The writer of this paragraph does not use transitional words to keep the paragraph unified. Instead, this writer repeats words from one sentence in the next. Notice the use of the word its in several sentences. Its stands for the new United States, which was used in the first sentence. Also notice how the writer repeats the word <u>new</u> in the first and last sentences. The technique of **repetition** is another good way to keep ideas flowing within a paragraph. Repetition is another way to achieve smooth transitions.

Contrast or Compare Ideas

Another way to develop a topic sentence is by showing similarities and differences between two things. Here are two such paragraphs. The first is an example of development by contrast.

Although they were twins, Andy and Arthur were nothing alike, except in size. Both were somewhat small for their age. But Andy had black eyes; Arthur brown. Andy had a round face; Arthur's forehead was very high and his face rather long and thin. Their dispositions were different too. Andy was sociable, friendly, smiling, and playful; Arthur was shy, withdrawn, sensitive, and serious. Andy was good at sports; Arthur played the piano for pleasure or spent hours with his nose in a book. Yet never were two boys more devoted to each other.

This contrast paragraph focuses on differences. Notice how the writer sets this up by saying that the boys <u>were nothing alike</u>. Quickly disposing of the one similarity, the writer goes on to describe the ways in which they were different. First Andy, then Arthur—their appearance and behavior are contrasted at several points.

A contrast paragraph explores differences. In a comparison paragraph, the writer explores similarities between two people, ideas, or objects. Often one side of the comparison will be familiar to a reader, so that the familiar details can help the reader understand the other side of the comparison. Notice how the following comparison paragraph has been developed:

In its activity and structure a modern office building seems to resemble a beehive. The hive is home for thousands of bees and the center for their key "businesses" of honey-making and egg development. Bees race in and out of the hive, creating a sense of constant movement. A cross-section of a hive would reveal several distinct "business" areas and thousands of small compartments in which honey is made or eggs grow. Similarly, a modern office building houses thousands of workers who race in and out, going to and from work. The building is divided into sections—separate wings and floors—and each section contains lots of small offices and work stations. Workers leaving an office building at 5:00 P.M. seem to buzz with relief, and anyone standing in their way is bound to get "stung."

This comparison paragraph focuses on similarities. Notice how the writer sets this up by saying that an <u>office building seems to resemble a beehive.</u> These words tell you that the paragraph will show the ways in which the statement is true. First the writer gives you several details about a beehive. Then you are given the ways in which a modern office building has similar characteristics.

Notice the different ways in which details are arranged in the contrast and in the comparison paragraphs. In the first paragraph, the contrasting details are alternated. For each point, the writer shows first one side, then the other. In the second paragraph, the writer presents all of the information about the beehive in one group of sentences. Then the writer relates the similarities between the office building and the beehive in a second group of sentences. The second group of sentences follows the same order as that of the details presented in the first part.

Either writer could have used the other one's methods. The writer of the paragraph about the twin boys could first have given all the information about Andy. Then, following the same sequence, the information about Arthur could have been presented. Similarly, in the office-beehive paragraph, each point could have been compared before moving on to the next point. It is up to you to decide whether to alternate details or present them in groups when you write contrast or comparison paragraphs. The kinds of details you want to use will usually suggest the method to you. Some writers try both methods in order to decide which works best for a given topic.

Give Reasons to Explain Cause and Effect

"Cause and effect" is another way of saying "reasons and result." A topic sentence that states an outcome or result calls for detail sentences that explain what happened or why.

A paragraph developed by cause and effect must not only raise the question of why something happens but must also answer the question with specific reasons. The cause or causes described in the paragraph must explain the result:

> Sugar has long been criticized because it can lead to tooth decay and obesity. However, a more serious argument can be made for limiting sugar intake: Excess sugar consumption has been linked to disease. A diet high in sugar is likely to contain too little of many essential nutrients. In particular, key vitamins and minerals that the body needs for day-to-day functioning and repair may be in short supply. Continued lack of these nutrients can cause or contribute to the development of a variety of ailments. Eye problems and skin diseases are due directly to vitamin deficiencies. Some types of headaches and allergies may be intensified when key nutrients are missing from the diet. The body's ability to resist illness, and to recover from major illness, is also hampered by the nutrient deficiencies that may result from a high intake of sugar.

The topic sentence states that sugar is linked to disease. The rest of the paragraph explains this statement by showing how eating high-sugar foods can lead to nutrient deficiency and disease. The paragraph begins by stating the effect and then proceeds to explain the causes.

Use a Combination of Methods

Writers also use a combination of these methods within a single paragraph to develop a topic:

> The milk of each type of mammal is species-specific for the needs of that particular mammal. Consider the baby seal. The first struggle of the newborn seal, born in the Arctic, is to keep warm. What it needs is to produce lots of blubber quickly to insulate its tiny body from the cold. The milk from a seal's mother is rich, creamy, and fat-producing—perfect for the baby seal's needs. As another example, consider the baby rabbit. It needs to be able to run quickly to escape predators. The milk of a mother rabbit has almost ten times as much protein as human milk. Like a rabbit, a baby calf also needs to be able to stand and run quickly to evade enemies. Its mother's milk is ideal for developing muscle tissue. Humans, on the other hand, are mental beings. Our survival and success depend on brain power. Studies have shown that the milk of a human mother is unsurpassed for the development of nerves and gray matter.

The topic sentence of this long paragraph is <u>The milk of each type of mammal is species-specific for the needs of that particular mammal</u>. The paragraph uses three different methods of development to support the topic sentence. The predominant method is the use of examples. The needs of four different baby mammals are presented, along with the ways their mothers' milk meets these needs. The different needs are also compared and contrasted throughout the paragraph. In addition, factual details are presented within each example as support.

The writer of this paragraph has employed both transitional words and repetition to keep the sentences flowing smoothly. Reread the paragraph to look for transitions such as <u>as another example</u>, <u>like</u>, and <u>on the other hand</u>. Also notice the repetition of words such as <u>baby</u>, <u>mother</u>, <u>milk</u>, and <u>it</u>. Can you see how these repetitions help you move comfortably from one sentence to another?

You are likely to use a combination of methods when you have many details to support the topic. When you do use more than one method of paragraph development, it's important to be clear about which is the predominant method. If the predominant method is cause and effect, you might use factual detail and example to explain and describe the causes and effect(s).

Check your ability to identify different types of paragraph development by completing the following exercise.

Exercise for Subskill 8C

Read each paragraph on pages 229 and 230. In the space provided, identify the method or methods used to develop the topic idea. Look for the five basic ways of developing paragraphs: supplying relevant details, examples, contrasts or comparisons, reasons showing cause and effect, and combinations of two or more of these.

EXAMPLE: Over 250,000 paper cranes were presented to officials in Moscow in 1985. They were the first shipment of a grass-roots peace project that aims to send almost two million origami cranes—one for every child living in Moscow. Over 600 religious and secular groups, in 41 states, Puerto Rico, and Canada, whose members range from kindergarten students to senior citizens, participated in the project. Each colorful bird, which takes 28 steps to make, represents a prayer for the full life and health of a child and for peace.

METHOD(S) OF PARAGRAPH DEVELOPMENT: relevant detail, examples

1. In most countries, money consists of coins and paper currency; however, in some places, people use various objects as money. In the Nicobar Islands, off the coast of India, coconuts have been used as money for hundreds of years. Residents of these islands purchase items ranging from boxes of matches to racing canoes with "money" they pick from trees. In the Santa Cruz Islands, the red feathers of a small, rare bird are very valuable and can be used to purchase supplies. On the island of Yap, in the Philippines, people use huge round stones, some up to 12 feet high, as money. They don't give or take the stones when something is sold. Instead, they write the transaction down on the face of the stone "coin" and a seller expects to receive something of equal value in return at a later time.

METHOD(S) OF PARAGRAPH DEVELOPMENT: _____

2. Mrs. Roundy's name seemed aptly chosen, for she was a roly-poly little lady composed all of curves and circles. Her little round nose, between oval eyes accented by arching brows, was centered in her face and set off by a round chin. Her face was encircled by a halo of white hair, inperceptibly joined behind small round ears to a series of double chins rippling and multiplying when she laughed. The pink blouse she wore described a larger circle, an ampler world, to which her short curved arms, ending in pudgy fingers, formed a perfect orbit. There was not a straight line in her figure. She was just one jolly oval, and her little round-toed shoes seemed to propel her along like casters under a solid piece of furniture.

METHOD(S) OF PARAGRAPH DEVELOPMENT: _____

3. The payroll deduction plan for buying government bonds is a systematic, profitable, safe, and patriotic way to save money. Once you decide how much of your salary you can afford to put by, your savings are made automatically. The money you want to save is deducted, or taken out of, your paycheck. You can go ahead and budget your whole salary check, knowing that your provision for a rainy day is accumulating regularly without your missing it. Your money is not

only accumulating, it is earning interest. And the interest rate is good, better than some banks pay on savings. There can be no safer investment than United States bonds. They are as safe as the government itself. When you buy them, you have the fine feeling that your money is working for Uncle Sam even while it is increasing for you.

METHOD(S) OF PARAGRAPH DEVELOPMENT: _____

4. Baseball and football appeal to different types of people. Those who enjoy baseball like to live at a slower pace than do football fans. Baseball games have no time limit, while football games are closely regulated by a game clock. Baseball games also include lots of brief intermissions, while football games include only one halftime break. In addition, baseball fans appreciate finesse more than football fans, who generally come out to see players attack each other with brute force. Finally, baseball fans are statistics "nuts." They can recall the lifetime batting averages of even obscure players. The actions of many football players, particularly offensive linemen, are never measured in a statistical way. Therefore, statistics are not as meaningful to a football fan.

METHOD(S) OF PARAGRAPH DEVELOPMENT: _____

5. The room we entered was clean but very untidy. The freshly scrubbed floor was littered with papers. All the furniture was newly polished, but it had been shoved over in front of the window. Not one of the pictures on the walls was hanging straight. Clean ruffled curtains hung at the window, but one was tied up properly and the other dragged on the floor. Chair cushions were piled in one corner, and the drawers of the desk and the table hung open. A highly polished brass candlestick lay on the floor, and another propped the door open. No single movable thing in the room seemed in place.

METHOD(S) OF PARAGRAPH DEVELOPMENT: _____

Check your answers on page 34 in the Answer Key for Book Three. If you correctly identified the method(s) of development in 4 of 5 paragraphs, go to Subskill 8D. If not, do the Supplemental Exercise for Subskill 8C.

Supplemental Exercise for Subskill 8C

Every paragraph contains a topic idea, usually stated directly in a topic sentence, and a series of detail sentences that explain or support the topic. The five basic ways to develop a topic sentence in an expository paragraph are to supply relevant details, examples, contrasts or comparisons, reasons for cause and effect, and to use a combination of two or more of these methods.

Check your ability to identify the different method(s) of paragraph development by completing the following exercise.

Read each paragraph below. In the space provided, identify the primary method(s) of paragraph development that the writer has used.

EXAMPLE: The southeastern corner of Missouri is called the "Boot Heel." It juts down between Arkansas and Tennessee, below the rest of the southern border, like the high heel of a cowboy's boot. The Mississippi River, flowing down to mark the western boundary of Tennessee, forms the back of the heel. The front of the heel is the St. Francis river, flowing down into Arkansas. A straight line between the two rivers at the thirty-sixth parallel, marking the northern border of Mississippi County, Arkansas, forms the base of the boot heel. The whole area amounts to nearly three thousand square miles.

METHOD(S) OF PARAGRAPH DEVELOPMENT: <u>relevant detail, example, comparison</u>

1. The modern football game has been likened to the games of ancient Rome. Several similarities can be pointed out. Observe the wildly excited crowds sitting in a bowl-shaped coliseum and cheering loudly for their favorite competitors. The crowd sometimes expresses approval or disapproval in a thumbs-up or thumbs-down gesture. Examine the struggling arm locks and clashing hand-to-hand combat on the field. Could this be what it was like to observe the competition in an arena in ancient Rome?

METHOD(S) OF PARAGRAPH DEVELOPMENT: _____

2. If you haven't already begun a personal exercise program, perhaps it is time you considered one. Exercise can help you control your weight. It can increase your energy and stamina. Exercise can help you build stronger muscles and bones. It can increase your heart and lung capacity. Exercise can even help you reduce the effects of stress. The results of a regular and safe exercise program are well worth the effort and time involved.

METHOD(S) OF PARAGRAPH DEVELOPMENT: _____

3. Computers are changing every aspect of modern life. Automatic data processing, word processing, electronic mail, and computerized robots are revolutionizing the workplace. Automatic teller machines have changed the way we do our banking, and the increased use of electronic funds may eventually turn us into a cashless society. In many homes, the personal computer is already serving as electronic file cabinet, personal tutor, game arcade, reference library, at-home shopping service, and word processing tool. It is possible that in the future we may do much of our work at home, communicating with

the office electronically, or studying from a computer monitor instead of from a blackboard or traditional textbook. The changes to come may be dramatic or subtle, but each of us has already been affected by the computer revolution.

METHOD(S) OF PARAGRAPH DEVELOPMENT: _____

4. In considering the advantages and disadvantages of moving our business to a new location, we should take several factors into account. While our present location offers our customers easy access from the expressway, the proposed new location is located on a less traveled secondary street. We are now located near our suppliers and transportation contractors. This would not be the case in the proposed location. The rent at our proposed location would be lower than at our present location. However, it remains to be seen if savings due to the lower rent expenditure would offset the anticipated increase in supply and transportation costs and the possible loss of income due to reduced customer accessibility.

METHOD(S) OF PARAGRAPH DEVELOPMENT: _____

5. Blood loaded with fat carries oxygen less efficiently than does blood with low fat. Experiments have proven that the heart has to work almost twice as hard during exercise after a high-fat meal as after a high-starch meal. Blood with high fat content takes longer to reach and nourish tissues. Fat also requires twice as much oxygen for conversion into energy as protein or carbohydrates. It makes sense, therefore, to avoid eating unnecessary fat.

METHOD(S) OF PARAGRAPH DEVELOPMENT: _____

Check your answers on page 34 in the Answer Key for Book Three. If you correctly identified the method(s) of development for 4 of 5 paragraphs, go to Subskill 8D. If not, ask your instructor for help.

Subskill 8D: Recognizing Irrelevant Details

When you complete this subskill, you will be able to recognize sentences in a paragraph that present details that do not support the topic sentence of the paragraph. You will also be able to unify paragraphs by removing these irrelevant details.

You have already learned that the topic sentence presents a controlling idea that all other sentences in the paragraph should support or explain. In a **unified paragraph,** all of the detail sentences work together to support the topic sentence.

Writers must be careful not to put into a paragraph any stray sentences that do not belong there. Every sentence must contribute something to the topic of the paragraph. Irrelevant details do not have a clear relationship to the topic sentence or the purpose of the paragraph.

Look at the following paragraph. Identify the topic sentence. Do you think every sentence in this paragraph really belongs there?

> I love to travel. I love to visit all sorts of places. So far, I have been in every state in the United States and have visited two foreign countries. I have ridden the waves at Coney Island and dipped my feet into Puget Sound. I have crossed the Appalachian Mountains and have seen Pikes Peak, the Grand Canyon, and Mt. Rainier. My brother has never traveled at all. I was in New Orleans for Mardi Gras and in St. Louis for the Veiled Prophet's Ball. I spent a week in Bermuda and six weeks in Germany. I think I shall always spend my vacations in some sort of travel.

Obviously, the sentence about the writer's brother is off the topic. All the other sentences are about "my travels." The brother's lack of travel experience seems to interrupt. It takes away from the unity of the paragraph.

Read the following paragraph and identify the topic sentence. See if you can locate any irrelevant details in the paragraph.

> Working as a salesclerk is as good as taking a course in business administration. As a salesperson, one learns such terms as "net worth," and "gross profit and loss." Markups and markdowns are indicators of how well the merchandise moves. Cranky customers are a pain. Inventories are a system for counting the merchandise on hand. This helps project future sales and determines quantities to reorder. I despise the endless counting of men's ties on Aisle 7, Table 3. Counting sales receipts of the day, week, month, quarter, and year enables the merchant to analyze and plan the store's future operations and sales. I always talk to Ms. Shaw, the manager. I have learned a great deal in on-the-job training as a salesperson.

Did you spot the following sentences as irrelevant details?: <u>Cranky customers are a pain. I despise the endless counting of men's ties on Aisle 7, Table 3.</u> and <u>I always talk to Ms. Shaw, the manager</u>. If you thought these sentences were irrelevant, you were right, because those three sentences don't fit in with the topic sentence: <u>Working as a salesclerk is as good as taking a course in business administration</u>. The three irrelevant sentences interrupt this main idea. Remember, paragraph unity exists when all the sentences in the paragraph develop and expand the main idea expressed in the topic sentence.

Check your ability to recognize irrelevant details by completing the following exercise.

Exercise for Subskill 8D

Part A. Read each of the following short paragraphs. Underline the paragraph's topic sentence. Then cross out each sentence that does not belong.

EXAMPLE: <u>Larry was a good mechanic</u>. No mechanical job was a problem for him. He knew how to handle tools, and he took good care of them, too. If anything went wrong with an appliance, at home or at the shop, Larry was the man who fixed it. ~~I never could put a nut on a bolt properly myself~~. If the kids' toys got broken, Larry mended them. He was always rigging up gadgets for his wife. I think he was a born mechanic.

1. Our course consists of four main divisions: mathematics, general science, English, and social studies. Mathematics gives us a good review of number operations, fractions, decimals, and word problems. General science includes the basic elements of several sciences. I really have too little time to study properly. English consists of reading and grammar. And social studies combines history, geography, and civics.

2. The city of Chicago made elaborate preparations to receive the Queen. They brought out the red carpet and shined up the golden plates. They studied protocol. Chicago ladies went on shopping sprees to get new hats and dresses for the royal occasion. The Queen is a very gracious, charming monarch. Stores decorated their windows with their most attractive wares. Buildings were painted and flowers were planted all along the route of the royal procession. The mayor planned a splendid banquet. Nothing was left undone to show Her Majesty the hospitality of the Windy City.

Part B. The item below consists of a topic sentence followed by an outline of details for a paragraph. Most of the details pertain to the main idea of the topic sentence. However, some are irrelevant. Mark an X beside any irrelevant detail.

EXAMPLE:
TOPIC SENTENCE: My son's kindergarten teacher is an outstanding teacher of young children.

_____	a.	incredible patience
_____	b.	untiring enthusiasm
_____	c.	endless energy
X	d.	never married
X	e.	wears jeans to work
_____	f.	creative in her teaching methods
_____	g.	builds each child's self-esteem
_____	h.	genuinely likes children and relates well to them.
X	i.	manages her money well.

3. The doctor made diet the most important part of curing the disease.

_____ a. fresh vegetables

_____ b. methods of cooking

_____ c. nursing care during recovery

_____ d. kinds of seasonings

_____ e. snacks between meals

_____ f. exercise out of doors

_____ g. vacation in dry climate

_____ h. freshly-squeezed juices

_____ i. medication at regular times

Check your answers on page 34 in the Answer Key for Book Three. If you correctly completed all 3 items, go to Subskill 8E. If not, do the Supplemental Exercise for Subskill 8D.

Supplemental Exercise for Subskill 8D

Unity means oneness. When we refer to paragraph unity, we are describing the quality of a paragraph where all the sentences develop and expand one main idea. A unified paragraph should not contain any sentences that do not support or explain the main idea. Irrelevant details do not support or explain the idea stated in the topic sentence. Sentences containing irrelevant details will spoil paragraph unity, and should be removed.

Part A. Read each of the following short paragraphs. Underline the paragraph's topic sentence. Then cross out each sentence that does not belong.

EXAMPLE: If you want to study efficiently, have a pleasant, quiet place to work with good light and a good desk. The temperature should not be warm enough to make you drowsy; and if possible, there should be no bed in the room to tempt you. A good education is important in our modern world. Have your pencils, paper, books, and exercises all ready before you start. And do not have a radio turned on or children playing nearby.

1. The scientific name of the Black Oak tree consists of two Latin words. One means "beautiful tree." I also give my wife flowers on her birthday. She really appreciates it. The other means "fleece" and refers to the surfaces of the leaves. They are velvety when young. The winter buds are downy. The Black Oak varies in form in different areas of the world.

2. People disagree about fluoride, a natural substance that goes into the water we drink along with other minerals. A lot of people don't have time to read the newspapers. Some people want to raise the level of fluoride in the water. They say that it helps fight cavities in teeth. I dread the dentist myself. Others disagree. They say that it's bad for the kidneys and that you shouldn't put a medication in the water. Scientists say fluoride isn't medication, but an element that occurs in nature and can improve our health.

Part B.   The item below consists of a topic sentence followed by an outline of details for a paragraph. Most of the details pertain to the main idea of the topic sentence. However, some are irrelevant. Mark an X beside any irrelevant detail.

EXAMPLE:

Topic Sentence: Rome is a city of contrasts.

_____ a.   the old and the modern

_____ b.   the rich and the poor

_____ c.   the elegant restaurants and the tiny coffee shops

__X__ d.   August temperatures of 103

_____ e.   asphalt and atriums

_____ f.   monuments and parks

__X__ g.   fire trucks and fires

_____ h.   office skyscrapers and original town hall

__X__ i.   children in uniform

3.   Building a true friendship requires that we open ourselves to another person.

_____ a.   trust with personal information

_____ b.   shoes that are run-down at heels

_____ c.   ideas to exchange

_____ d.   feelings to share

_____ e.   arguments about politics

_____ f.   doesn't use napkins when eating

_____ g.   asking questions all the time

_____ h.   jealousy

_____ i.   asks for help

Check your answers on page 35 in the Answer Key for Book Three. If you correctly completed 2 of 3 items, go to Subskill 8E. If not, ask your instructor for help.

Subskill 8E: Writing Unified Paragraphs

When you complete this subskill, you will be able to write unified paragraphs that start with a topic sentence and follow a particular method of development. You will also be able to use a Writer's Checklist to evaluate your paragraphs.

You are about to begin writing your own paragraphs. How do you decide what to write about? How do you decide what to say? This is a problem faced by professional writers as well as people who write only occasionally. Even professional writers often find themselves staring at a sheet of paper, unable to think of anything to write.

Usually the situation in which you have to write gives you clues for starting off. In an exam, you are usually given a topic. At work, you might be asked to explain something, to list the steps in a process, or to report on decisions made at a meeting. In writing a letter you usually have a specific purpose (such as complaining about an appliance that doesn't work properly, or asking for information so you can plan a trip). In writing to a friend you will want to tell about personal events. Whatever the occasion for writing, you will be comfortable about the task if you follow these steps:

1. Identify the purpose of the writing.

2. Jot down a list of points you want to make relating to that purpose. A simple word or phrase will do for each idea. Don't worry about the logical order of ideas at this stage. Let one idea lead to another.

3. Check over the list you just made. Are there any other points you should add?

4. Think of the points you want to make in the topic sentence of the paragraph. The list of ideas can help you. Is there one idea on it that seems to include several other ideas? One that is more important than the others? One which several other ideas are part of? The "big idea" on your list can give you the key word(s) for your topic sentence.

5. If you don't find a "big idea" for a topic sentence in your idea list, think again about the purpose of the writing. Use that as the basis for your topic sentence. ("I need information for a trip to South Carolina.")

6. Write the topic sentence. Make sure that it is neither too broad nor too narrow. Does it contain key words that will lead into the development of the rest of the paragraph?

7. Now think about the other ideas on your list. Are there any irrelevant details that don't belong in your paragraph? Remove them from (cross them off) your list. Are there too many ideas on the list? Place a check next to the most important ones, the ones you want to be sure to cover. There should be from three to six important ideas on the list.

8. Decide on the order in which you will write about the ideas. You may want to write the number 1 next to the idea you will write about first, the number 2 next to the idea that will follow, and so on.

9. Think about how you can best use those ideas to develop the "big idea" in your topic sentence. Will you compare or contrast? Will you describe something spatially or chronologically? Will you start from a small detail and work up to a climax? Will you start from a large generalized concept and narrow down to a specific point? Let the ideas themselves suggest to you the method of development you should try.

10. Now start writing. Take one idea and shape it into a sentence. Remember that you need a subject and verb. Remember that

modifiers help make your meaning clear. Take another idea and shape it into the next sentence. Use transitional words and repetition to lead from one sentence to the next.

11. Keep writing until you have one sentence for each important idea on your list. Then reread your paragraph. Be sure there are no irrelevant details in it. Did you cover all the information you wanted in the paragraph? Do the ideas flow smoothly from one sentence to the next? Do all the sentences in the paragraph support or explain the topic sentence? This is the time to add or remove sentences from your paragraph.

12. Check the sentences themselves. Do all subjects and verbs agree? Are all verb tenses the same or in the correct relationship? Are the modifiers in the correct position? Now is the time to fix any sentence details that need repairing.

13. Read your paragraph again. Does it need a windup sentence? A windup sentence can be a restatement of the important part of the topic sentence. It can also be the final detail that completes the information needed to support or explain the topic sentence.

There are two ways to learn to write. The first is by doing it yourself. The second is by reading what other people write, and trying to see how good writers build their paragraphs. You need to do both of these to improve your writing. You will find that the more you write and analyze your writing, the easier writing will be for you and the better your writing will become.

The following exercise will give you practice in writing paragraphs. Use the suggestions in this section to develop and write your paragraphs. Then review your paragraphs before you ask your instructor to evaluate them. Ask yourself the questions on the following checklist to help you decide if your paragraphs are unified and correctly presented. Put a check beside each question to which you feel you can answer "yes."

Paragraph Writer's Checklist

_____ Have I presented a clear topic sentence that is neither too broad nor too narrow?

_____ Have I used a logical method of paragraph development? Which method(s) have I used? _____

_____ Are my sentences arranged in a logical order appropriate to that (those) method(s)?

_____ Have I used transitional words or repetition to help my sentences flow smoothly?

_____ Is every sentence related to the topic sentence? Have I omitted all irrelevant details?

_____ Have I indented the first sentence of my paragraph to show where the paragraph begins?

_____ Have I capitalized the first word of each sentence?

_____ Have I checked my spelling, punctuation, and verb tenses?

Exercise for Subskill 8E

Choose any two of the topics listed below. Write a unified, well-developed paragraph about each of the topic sentences you have chosen. Identify your method of paragraph development.

- How I hate to get up in the morning!
- My job has several main duties.
- I think education is worth the effort it takes to gain it.
- Most of my days follow a regular routine.
- Everybody should learn to swim.
- Some of the advertisements on television are as entertaining as some programs.
- A person's clothing expresses his or her personality.
- Sometimes an argument helps a friendship grow; other times it marks the end.
- You can get lost in a good movie.

1. METHOD OF DEVELOPMENT: _____

TOPIC SENTENCE: _____

_____

_____

_____

_____

_____

_____

_____

_____

_____

_____

2. METHOD OF DEVELOPMENT: _____

TOPIC SENTENCE: _____

_____

_____

_____

_____

_____

_____

_____

_____

_____

_____

_____

After writing each paragraph, check it against the Writer's Checklist on page 238. Now give your paragraphs to your instructor, who will help you analyze them to see how they can be improved. If your instructor says you have correctly completed the exercise for Subskill 8E, go to the Self-Check. If not, or if you want more practice in writing paragraphs, complete the following Supplemental Exercise for Subskill 8E.

Supplemental Exercise for Subskill 8E

Review the suggestions for writing paragraphs in this subskill.

Choose any two of the topic sentences below. Write a unified paragraph that develops each topic sentence. Identify your method of development for each paragraph.

- _____ is a person who has influenced my life.
- The gasoline shortage forced drivers to change their habits.
- Children should learn to do math computations without the help of a calculator.
- The English language is more difficult to learn than _____ .
- The quarterback in football and the general of an army are alike in many ways.
- Foods high in salt (or sugar) can be bad for your health.
- A good book (or movie) should possess three major qualities.
- _____ is my favorite kind of music for the following reasons.
- My car is an absolute mess.

1. METHOD OF DEVELOPMENT: _____

TOPIC SENTENCE: _____

_____

2. METHOD OF DEVELOPMENT: _____

TOPIC SENTENCE: _____

After writing each paragraph, check it against the Writer's Check-list on page 238. Now give your paragraphs to your instructor, who will help you analyze them to see how they can be improved. If your instructor says you have correctly completed the Supplemental Exercise for Subskill 8E, go to the Self-Check. If not, ask your instructor for additional help.

SELF-CHECK FOR SKILL UNIT 8

For any two of the topic sentences in the following list, and using any method of development that seems appropriate, write a unified, well-developed paragraph. Note these guidelines:

EVALUATION:

1. Each paragraph will be at least one hundred words in length.
2. Each sentence in the paragraph will directly relate to and help develop the topic sentence.
3. The paragraph will contain no irrelevant details.
4. Even though your paragraphs meet the first three criteria, you may be asked to revise and correct your paragraphs according to your instructor's suggestions on paragraph unity, paragraph development, grammar, spelling, and mechanics.

List of Topics

· Prior planning and auto maintenance could have prevented the problems on our recent trip.
· There are certain things you should always remember when you go fishing.
· I am continuing my education for several good reasons.
· American-made cars have some advantages over foreign imports.
· I'd rather play ball myself than watch a professional game.
· My brother (sister) and I are alike (different) in many ways.
· I believe (or I don't believe) in early marriages.
· I prefer city life to country life.
· I prefer country life to city life.
· I like best to live in a small town.

1. METHOD OF DEVELOPMENT: _____

TOPIC SENTENCE: _____

_____

_____

_____

_____

_____

_____

_____

_____

_____

_____

_____

2. METHOD OF DEVELOPMENT: _____

TOPIC SENTENCE: _____

_____

_____

_____

_____

_____

_____

_____

_____

_____

_____

Give your paragraphs to your instructor for evaluation. If you successfully composed two unified paragraphs, you have shown that you have mastered these skills. If not, ask your instructor for help.

Skill Unit 9
USING THE DICTIONARY

What Skills You Need to Begin: You need to be able to put words in alphabetical order by their first letter.

What Skills You Will Learn: When you complete this skill unit, you will be able to alphabetize words that begin with the same letter by using the other letters in the words. You will be able to use guide words to locate words in a dictionary. You will also be able to use the dictionary to find the correct spelling, syllable division, pronunciation, part of speech, form of different parts of speech, meaning, and origin of a word.

Why You Need These Skills: You know how to write sentences and put sentences together into unified paragraphs. But if you misspell a word, if you use a word incorrectly because you are not sure of its meaning, or if you divide a word incorrectly on a line, you will confuse your reader and distract your reader's attention from the meaning of what you have written. The dictionary will help you spell correctly and use words correctly when you speak and write. When you know how to use the dictionary, you will be able to say and write exactly what you mean.

How You Will Show What You Have Learned: You will take the Self-Check at the end of this unit on page 264. The Self-Check contains 10 words. You will use a dictionary to find the end-of-line division, phonetic entry, part of speech, definition, and origin of those words. If you get at least 8 of 10 words correct, you will have shown that you have mastered these skills.

If you believe you have already mastered these skills, turn to the end of this unit and complete the Self-Check on page 264.

Subskill 9A: Finding Words in the Dictionary by Using Alphabetical Order and Guide Words

When you complete this subskill, you will be able to use alphabetical order and guide words to locate words in the dictionary.

The sample dictionary page below is from *Webster's New World Dictionary, Compact School and Office Edition*. Refer to this dictionary page often as you read about how to use the dictionary. You will need to use a dictionary to complete some of the activities in this unit.

abstracted

ab(s)-, from + *trahere,* to draw] **1.** thought of apart from material objects **2.** expressing a quality so thought of **3.** theoretical **4.** *Art* not representing things realistically —*n.* (ab'strakt) a summary —*vt.* **1.** (ab strakt') to take away **2.** (ab'strakt) to summarize —**in the abstract** in theory as apart from practice —**ab·stract'ly** *adv.*

ab·stract'ed *adj.* absent-minded

ab·strac'tion *n.* **1.** an abstracting **2.** an abstract idea **3.** mental withdrawal **4.** an abstract painting, sculpture, etc.

ab·struse (ab strōōs') *adj.* [< L. *ab(s)-,* away · + *trudere,* to thrust] hard to understand

ab·surd (ab surd') *adj.* [< Fr. < L. *absurdus,* not to be heard of] so unreasonable as to be ridiculous —**ab·surd'i·ty** *n., pl.* **-ties** —**ab·surd'ly** *adv.*

a·bun·dance (ə bun'dəns) *n.* [see ABOUND] a great supply; more than enough —**a·bun'dant** *adj.* —**a·bun'dant·ly** *adv.*

a·buse (ə byōōz') *vt.* **a·bused', a·bus'ing** [< L. *ab-,* away + *uti,* to use] **1.** to use wrongly **2.** to mistreat **3.** to insult; revile —*n.* (ə byōōs') **1.** wrong use **2.** mistreatment **3.** a corrupt practice **4.** insulting language —**a·bu'sive** (-byōōs'iv) *adj.* —**a·bu'sive·ly** *adv.*

a·but (ə but') *vi.* **a·but'ted, a·but'ting** [< OFr. *a-,* to + *bout,* end] to border (*on*) —*vt.* to border on

a·but'ment *n.* **1.** an abutting **2.** a part supporting an arch, bridge, etc.

a·bys·mal (ə biz'm'l) *adj.* **1.** of or like an abyss **2.** very bad —**a·bys'mal·ly** *adv.*

a·byss (ə bis') *n.* [< Gr. *a-,* without + *byssos,* bottom] **1.** a bottomless gulf **2.** anything too deep for measurement

-ac [< Fr. < Gr.] *a suffix meaning:* **1.** relating to [*cardiac*] **2.** affected by [*maniac*]

Ac *Chem.* actinium

AC, A.C., a.c. alternating current

a·ca·cia (ə kā'shə) *n.* [< Gr. *akakia,* thorny tree] **1.** a tree or shrub with yellow or white flower clusters **2.** the locust tree

ac·a·dem·ic (ak'ə dem'ik) *adj.* **1.** of academies or colleges **2.** having to do with liberal arts rather than technical education **3.** formal **4.** merely theoretical —**ac'a·dem'i·cal·ly** *adv.*

a·cad·e·mi·cian (ə kad'ə mish'ən, ak'ə də-) *n.* a member of an academy (sense 3)

a·cad·e·my (ə kad'ə mē) *n., pl.* **-mies** [< Gr. *akadēmeia,* place where Plato taught] **1.** a private secondary school **2.** a school offering training in a special field **3.** an association of scholars, writers, etc. for advancing an art or science

a·can·thus (ə kan'thəs) *n., pl.* **-thus·es, -thi** (-thī) [< Gr. *akē,* a point] **1.** a plant with lobed, often spiny leaves **2.** *Archit.* a representation of these leaves

a cap·pel·la (ä' kə pel'ə) [It., in chapel style] unaccompanied: said of choral singing

ac·cede (ak sēd') *vi.* **-ced'ed, -ced'ing** [< L. *ad-,* to + *cedere,* to yield] **1.** to enter upon the duties (of an office) **2.** to assent; agree (*to*) —**ac·ced'ence** *n.*

ac·cel·er·an·do (ak sel'ə ran'dō, -rän'-) *adv., adj.* [It.] *Music* with gradually quickening tempo

ac·cel·er·ate (ak sel'ə rāt', ak-) *vt.* **-at'ed, -at'ing** [< L. *ad-,* to + *celerare,* hasten] **1.** to increase the speed of **2.** to cause to happen sooner —*vi.* to go faster —**ac·cel'er·a'tion** *n.* —**ac·cel'er·a'tor** *n.*

ac·cent (ak'sent) *n.* [Fr. < L. *ad-,* to + *canere,* sing] **1.** the emphasis given a spoken syllable or word **2.** a mark showing such emphasis or

accomplish

indicating pronunciation **3.** a distinguishing manner of pronouncing [an Irish *accent*] **4.** *Music & Verse* rhythmic stress —*vt.* (*also* ak sent') **1.** to emphasize; stress **2.** to mark with an accent

ac·cen·tu·ate (ak sen'choo wāt') *vt.* **-at'ed, -at'ing** to accent; esp., to emphasize —**ac·cen'·tu·a'tion** *n.*

ac·cept (ək sept') *vt.* [< L. *ad-,* to + *capere,* take] **1.** to receive willingly **2.** to approve **3.** to agree to **4.** to believe in **5.** to say "yes" to **6.** to agree to pay —**ac·cept'er** *n.*

ac·cept'a·ble *adj.* satisfactory —**ac·cept'a·bil'·i·ty** *n.* —**ac·cept'a·bly** *adv.*

ac·cept'ance *n.* **1.** an accepting **2.** approval **3.** assent **4.** a promise to pay

ac·cept·ed (ək sep'tid) *adj.* generally regarded as true, proper, etc.; conventional

ac·cess (ak'ses) *n.* [see ACCEDE] **1.** approach or means of approach **2.** the right to enter, use, etc. **3.** an outburst

ac·ces'si·ble *adj.* **1.** easy to approach or enter **2.** obtainable **3.** open to the influence of (with *to*) —**ac·ces'si·bil'i·ty** *n.*

ac·ces·sion (ak sesh'ən) *n.* **1.** an attaining (a throne, power, etc.) **2.** assent **3.** *a)* increase by addition *b)* an item added

ac·ces·so·ry (ək ses'ər ē, ak-) *adj.* [see ACCEDE] **1.** extra; additional **2.** helping in an unlawful act —*n., pl.* **-ries 1.** something extra or complementary **2.** one who, though absent, helps another to break the law

ac·ci·dent (ak'sə dənt) *n.* [< L. *ad-,* to + *cadere,* to fall] **1.** an unintended happening **2.** a mishap **3.** chance

ac'ci·den'tal (-den't'l) *adj.* happening by chance —**ac'ci·den'tal·ly** *adv.*

ac·claim (ə klām') *vt.* [< L. *ad-,* to + *clamare,* to cry out] to greet or announce with loud approval; hail —*n.* loud approval

ac·cla·ma·tion (ak'lə mā'shən) *n.* **1.** loud applause or strong approval **2.** an approving vote by voice

ac·cli·mate (ak'lə māt', ə klī'mət) *vt., vi.* **-mat'ed, -mat'ing** [see AD- & CLIMATE] to accustom or become accustomed to a different climate or environment: also **ac·cli·ma·tize** (ə klī'mə tīz') **-tized', -tiz'ing** —**ac'cli·ma'tion** *n.*

ac·cliv·i·ty (ə kliv'ə tē) *n., pl.* **-ties** [< L. *ad-,* up + *clivus,* hill] an upward slope

ac·co·lade (ak'ə lād') *n.* [Fr. < It. *accollare,* to embrace] an approving mention; award

ac·com·mo·date (ə käm'ə dāt') *vt.* **-dat'ed, -dat'ing** [< L. *ad-,* to + *com-,* with + *modus,* a measure] **1.** to adjust; adapt **2.** to supply (*with* something) **3.** to do a favor for **4.** to have room for

ac·com·mo·dat·ing *adj.* obliging

ac·com·mo·da'tion *n.* **1.** adjustment **2.** willingness to do favors **3.** a help or convenience **4.** [*pl.*] lodgings or space, as in a hotel, on a ship, etc.

ac·com·pa·ni·ment (ə kump'ni mənt) *n.* **1.** anything that accompanies something else **2.** an instrumental part supporting a solo voice, etc.

ac·com·pa·nist (ə kum'pə nist) *n.* one who plays an accompaniment

ac·com·pa·ny (ə kum'pə nē, ə kump'nē) *vt.* **-nied, -ny·ing** [see AD- & COMPANION] **1.** to go with; attend **2.** to add to; supplement **3.** to play an accompaniment for or to

ac·com·plice (ə käm'plis) *n.* [< *a* (the article) + LL. *complex,* accomplice: see COMPLEX] one who knowingly helps another break a law

ac·com·plish (ə käm'plish) *vt.* [< L. *ad-,* intens. + *complere,* fill up] **2.** an abstract idea

Alphabetical Order

Entries in the dictionary are arranged in **alphabetical order** from
<u>a</u> to <u>z</u>. When words have the same first letter, they are listed alpha-
betically according to the second letter of each word. When the first and
second letters are the same, the words are listed by the third letter of
each word, and so on.

Find the word <u>abuse</u> on the dictionary page and circle it. Now find
the word <u>academy</u> on the same page and circle it. Since <u>abuse</u> and
<u>academy</u> begin with the same letter, you must look at the second letter
of each word to put the two words in alphabetical order. Underline the
second letter of each word. The letter <u>b</u> comes before the letter <u>c</u>, so
<u>abuse</u> is listed before <u>academy</u>.

Now find the word <u>accent</u> and circle it. <u>Accent</u> begins with the same
first and second letters as <u>academy</u>. You must look at the third letter
of each word to put the two words in alphabetical order. Underline the
third letter of each word twice. Since <u>a</u> comes before <u>c</u>, <u>academy</u> is listed
before <u>accent</u>.

The following words all start with <u>se</u>. Are they in alphabetical
order?

> settle
> several
> setup
> setter
> seven

Since each word begins with <u>se</u>, you must look at the third letter of each
word to place it in alphabetical order. In some of the words, the third
and fourth letters are the same, so you must look at the fifth letter.
Now the words are in alphabetical order:

> setter
> settle
> setup
> seven
> several

Guide Words

Words that appear in alphabetical order in the dictionary are called
entry words. They are always printed in dark type called **boldface
type.** Turn back to the sample dictionary page on page 245. Look at the
top of the page. The two words in large, dark type on either side of the
page are the guide words. The guide word on the left side of the page
is the first entry word on the page. The guide word on the right side of
the page is the last entry word on the page. Every entry word on that
page comes in alphabetical order between the two guide words.

Guide words help you find words in the dictionary. They let you
know at a glance if the word you are looking for is on a page.

<u>Abstracted</u> is the first full entry word on the dictionary page. <u>Ab-
stracted</u> is also the guide word that appears at the top left side of the

page. <u>Accomplish</u> is the last entry word on the dictionary page. <u>Accomplish</u> is also the guide word that appears at the top right side of the page. Every word on the page starts with the letters <u>ab</u> or <u>ac</u>. The page contains words that go in alphabetical order from <u>abstra-</u> to <u>accomplis-</u>. Among the entry words on the page are <u>abyss</u>, <u>accelerate</u>, <u>accent</u>, <u>accepted</u>, <u>accessory</u>, <u>acclimate</u>, <u>accommodating</u>, <u>accompany</u>.

Do the following exercise to check your understanding of alphabetical order and guide words.

Exercise for Subskill 9A

Part A. Alphabetize each set of words by placing 1 next to the word which should appear first in each set, 2 next to the second word, and so on.

EXAMPLE:	5	sweater
	6	threaten
	1	breakfast
	2	cleanliness
	3	heaven
	4	instead

1. _____ bullion
   _____ billion
   _____ bunion
   _____ behavior
   _____ blender
   _____ brilliant

2. _____ gentle
   _____ generous
   _____ geranium
   _____ genuine
   _____ gently
   _____ geometry

Part B. Read each pair of guide words and the entry word listed below them. If the entry word would be found on the page with these guide words, write <u>Yes</u> in the space provided. If the entry word would not appear on the same page as the guide words, write <u>No</u>.

EXAMPLE:

begrudge   **belong**

         bent   <u>No</u>

elixir   **embargo**

3. elk _____

cuddle   **culvert**

4. cumber _____

book   bookworm

    5. booklet _____

officer   often

    6. offer _____

formal   forth

    7. format _____

mental   mercurial

    8. Mercury _____

occult   ocean

    9. occupant _____

preceding   prefix

    10. precious _____

Check your answers on page 35 in the Answer Key for Book Three. If you correctly answered all 10 items, go to Subskill 9B. If not, do the Supplemental Exercise for Subskill 9A.

Supplemental Exercise for Subskill 9A

Words in the dictionary are listed in alphabetical order. Words that have the same first letter are listed alphabetically according to the second letter. When their first and second letters are the same, words are listed alphabetically by the third letter of each word, and so on.

The guide words at the top of a dictionary page are the same as the first and last entries on that page. Every word on that page would come alphabetically after the guide word on the left and before the guide word on the right.

Part A. Alphabetize each set of words by placing 1 next to the word which should appear first in each set, 2 next to the second word, and so on.

EXAMPLE: _4_ heavy
           _5_ precaution
           _1_ emergency
           _3_ gallery
           _2_ fear
           _6_ relief

1. _____ harvest   2. _____ livelihood
   _____ handle   _____ likeable
   _____ hanger   _____ locust
   _____ headlong   _____ lonesome
   _____ haul   _____ lightning
   _____ hasty   _____ lime

Part B. Read each pair of guide words and the entry word listed below them. If the entry word would be found on the page with these guide words, write Yes in the space provided. If the entry word would not appear on the same page as the guide words, write No.

EXAMPLE:

geodesist   **geotropism**

                  geography   _Yes_

sawdust   **scar**

              3. saucy _____

infinitude   **inhabit**

              4. infuriate _____

flinch   **flower**

              5. fluke _____

comeuppance   **commander**

              6. commanding _____

debatable   **decane**

              7. decade _____

articulately   **as**

              8. asbestos _____

entrust   **enunciate**

9. entry _____

forced   **forehead**

10. force _____

Check your answers on page 36 in the Answer Key for Book Three. If you correctly answered 8 of 10 items, go to Subskill 9B. If not, ask your instructor for help.

Subskill 9B: Using the Dictionary to Pronounce Words Correctly

When you complete this subskill, you will be able to use the dictionary to find the correct pronunciation of a word.

Every entry word is divided into units of pronunciation or **syllables.** Each syllable usually contains a vowel sound with one or more consonant sounds. The dictionary shows the pronunciation of a word in parentheses or between slant lines after the boldface entry. This is called the **pronunciation entry.**

Look at the dictionary entry for the word <u>pronunciation</u> on this page. Find the pronunciation entry. You will see some letters and other symbols that may not be familiar to you. These are some of the ways in which pronunciation is shown. In this subskill we will look at the meaning of these unfamiliar marks and symbols.

> **pro·nun·ci·a·tion** (prə nun'sē ā'shən) *n.* **1.** the act or way of pronouncing words **2.** *a)* any of the accepted or standard pronunciations of a word *b)* the representation in phonetic symbols of such a pronunciation

Accent Marks

Look at the pronunciation entry for the word <u>pronunciation</u> on this page. Notice that the symbols are arranged in groups, with a space or a slanted line separating groups of symbols. Each group of symbols represents a **syllable.** A syllable consists of one or more sounds pronounced together.

Now consider the two short slanted lines separating some groups of symbols. These lines are **accent marks.** The syllable immediately in front of each accent mark is to be pronounced with extra emphasis or stress.

You can see that one of the accent marks is darker than the other. The syllable before the darker line gets the stronger stress or emphasis when you pronounce the word. But the syllable before the lighter line also gets some stress. In most words you will find only one accent mark: fa′ ther, car′ ry, Christ′ mas, in tend′, con nec′ tion. Say these words aloud, with the emphasis or accent on the syllable indicated.

When there are two accent marks in the pronunciation entry, the heavier mark indicates the **primary emphasis,** and the lighter mark indicates the **secondary emphasis.** Some words with both primary and secondary emphasis are: dic′ tion ar′ y, hor′ ri fy′, di lap′ i dat′ ed, con′ ver sa′ tion. Say these words aloud, with a strong emphasis on the syllable before the primary accent mark and a lighter emphasis on the syllable before the secondary accent mark.

Sometimes a shift in the syllable being accented will change the meaning of a word. Pronounce the words in each of the following pairs:

de′ sert	de sert′	fre′ quent	fre quent′
ob′ ject	ob ject′	con′ vict	con vict′
con′ duct	con duct′	con′ test	con test′

The first word in each pair is a noun or adjective; the second is a verb. The meanings are different but related. The only change to indicate the meaning is the shift in pronunciation of the accented syllable.

Phonetic Spelling and Diacritical Marks

English words are not always pronounced as they are spelled. That's obvious when you say the words know, psychology, and enough. Some letters or letter combinations can be pronounced in more than one way: through, rough. Some sound combinations or pronunciations can be represented by more than one spelling: knee, need, knead. The pronunciation entry in the dictionary uses **phonetic spelling** to indicate the correct pronunciation of a word.

The symbols you saw in the pronunciation entry are **phonetic symbols.** Some are the same as letters in the alphabet. Some are variations on letters in the alphabet. Some phonetic symbols share the same letter, but add above it an additional mark or symbol that indicates pronunciation. These additional symbols are known as **diacritical marks.** They indicate special pronunciation of vowel sounds. Two diacritical marks used with all vowels are the **macron** and the **breve.**

The macron (–) above a vowel indicates that it is a long vowel. A long vowel has the same sound as its name.

$\bar{a}$ is pronounced as in gate

$\bar{e}$ is pronounced as in he

$\bar{i}$ is pronounced as in ice

$\bar{o}$ is pronounced as in go

$\bar{u}$ is pronounced as in use

The breve (˘) above a vowel indicates that it is a short vowel. In some dictionaries, pronunciation of a short vowel sound may be shown with no mark at all.

ă or a is pronounced as in cat
ĕ or e is pronounced as in let
ĭ or i is pronounced as in it
ŏ or o is pronounced as in not
ŭ or u is pronounced as in cut

Other diacritical marks are used with various vowels to indicate special vowel sounds.

ä is pronounced as in father
ōō is pronounced as in boot
u̶ is pronounced as in fur, her, and girl
ô is pronounced as in horn
ou is pronounced as in out
oi is pronounced as in oil

Consonant pronunciations are less likely to vary than vowel pronunciations. There are a few exceptions. The symbol f is used for all pronunciations of the sound this letter usually represents; watch for words containing ph that should be pronounced f: phone (fōn). Because c sounds like an s or k, the letter c alone is not used in the phonetic entry. Instead, an s or k is used. When g sounds like j, as in gym, the letter j is used to show that sound.

It is a good idea always to check the pronunciation key in the dictionary you are using. Some dictionaries use slightly different phonetic symbols. The pronunciation key may be at the bottom of each page, or at the bottom of every other page, in your dictionary. It may be in the introduction at the beginning of the dictionary, or it may be inside the front and/or back covers. The pronunciation key uses common English words to demonstrate all of the phonetic symbols. Here is a sample pronunciation key:

fat	āpe	cär	ten	ēven	is	bīte	gō	tōol	look
oil	out	up	fu̶r	chin	she	thin	then		

ŋ as in ring   ə as in ago   ô as in raw   zh as in leisure

The **schwa (ə),** which looks like an upside-down e, is usually used to indicate the uh sound that you make when you barely pronounce a syllable, or when you pronounce a syllable very quickly. All of the vowels (a, e, i, o, u) can sometimes be barely pronounced, or pronounced as the uh, the schwa sound.

ə is the a in ago (ə gō′)
ə is the e in agent (ā′ j ə nt)
ə is the i in sanity (san′ ə tē)
ə is the o in comply (kəm plī′)
ə is the u in focus (fō′ kəs)

Show your understanding of a dictionary pronunciation entry by doing this exercise.

Exercise for Subskill 9B

Part A. In each item below, two phonetic spellings are shown for the word given. Choose the correct phonetic spelling for each word. Put a check next to your choice. Use the pronunciation key in your dictionary if you need help. Be sure to check the definition of words that are unfamiliar to you.

EXAMPLE: scheme
      a. skēm   √
      b. skeme

  1. shade
      a. shād
      b. shäd

  2. truck
      a. truk
      b. trūk

  3. father
      a. fə′ ther
      b. fä′ thər

  4. censor
      a. cen′ sər
      b. sen′ sər

Part B. Use your dictionary to help you complete the following statements. In each set, make a check next to the correct answer. Be sure to check the definition of words that are unfamiliar to you.

EXAMPLE: The a̱ in table is pronounced like the
      a. a̱ in sad
      b. a̱ in gate   √

  5. The o̱ in matrimony is pronounced like the
      a. o̱ in money
      b. o̱ in cone

  6. The u̱ in fugue is pronounced like the
      a. u̱ in usual
      b. u̱ in cut

  7. The i̱ in dial is pronounced like the
      a. i̱ in fit
      b. i̱ in wine

  8. The o̱u in mound is pronounced like the
      a. o̱o in choose
      b. o̱u in out

Check your answers on page 36 in the Answer Key for Book Three. If you correctly answered all 8 items, go to Subskill 9C. If not, do the Supplemental Exercise for Subskill 9B.

Supplemental Exercise for Subskill 9B

The pronunciation entry in the dictionary gives four aids to pronunciation. 1. The word is divided into syllables. 2. The word is respelled phonetically or the way it sounds. 3. Diacritical marks show the pronunciation of vowel sounds. 4. An accent mark shows which syllable is stressed or emphasized when the word is spoken. Review the phonetic symbols shown in this subskill. Then do the following exercise.

Part A. Choose the correct phonetic spelling for each word. Put a check next to your choice. Use the pronunciation key in your dictionary if you need help.

EXAMPLE: creep
    a. krēp   ___✓___
    b. kreep   _____

1. device
    a. di vīs′ _____
    b. di vīz′ _____

2. ether
    a. ē thēr _____
    b. ē′ thər _____

3. flex
    a. flēx _____
    b. fleks _____

4. hamster
    a. ham′ stər _____
    b. ham′ stēr _____

Part B. Use your dictionary to help you complete the following statements. In each set, make a check next to the correct answer.

EXAMPLE: The o in modest is pronounced like the
    a. a in father   ___✓___
    b. o in Monday _____

5. The c in cello is pronounced like the
    a. s in sour _____
    b. ch in chin _____

6. The e in beast is pronounced like the
    a. e in theme _____
    b. i in dribble _____

7. The e in money is pronounced like the
    a. e in her _____
    b. the e in even _____

8. The o in mom is pronounced like the
    a. a in car _____
    b. a in cat _____

Check your answers on pages 36 and 37 in the Answer Key for Book Three. If you correctly answered 6 of 8 items, go to Subskill 9C. If not, ask your instructor for help.

Subskill 9C: Using Entry Words to Spell and Divide Words Correctly

When you complete this subskill, you will be able to use the dictionary to find the correct spelling of a word. You will be able to divide words correctly when they come at the end of a line.

Finding Correct Spellings

Each entry word is spelled correctly. Therefore, when you need to know how to spell a word, the dictionary will tell you. But, you ask, if I can't spell the word, how will I find it in the dictionary?

The first thing to do is to say the word. If you say the words desk or paper or pen, you will hear the letters and you will spell the words correctly. Many English words are spelled the way they sound, like bring, stamp and cat. Your study of phonetic symbols in Subskill 9B has shown you the pronunciations that various letters and letter combinations can have. With practice, you will be able to think of possible spellings quickly. Then you can use your dictionary to determine which is the correct one.

Suppose you want to find the spelling of the color blue; if you sound the word out, you will know that it begins with bl. Using guide words and your knowledge of alphabetical order, you would go to the section of the dictionary where the words beginning with bl are listed. You know that the next sound is $\overline{oo}$. The sound $\overline{oo}$ can be spelled many ways. So you might spell blue:

bloo, blew, or blue.

To find the correct spelling, you would look up each possible spelling in the dictionary. You will find that:

· there is no listing for bloo
· the definition of blew says it is the past tense of blow and
· the definition of blue says that it is a color.

Therefore, you will know from the definition that blue is the correct spelling for the color.

You should also be aware that the word you are looking for may not appear as an entry word. It may be a variation of an entry word. For example, suppose you are looking for the word collector. Here's the way you may find it in your dictionary:

col·lect (kə lekt') vt. [< L. com-, together + legere, gather] 1. to gather together 2. to gather (stamps, etc.) as a hobby 3. to call for and receive (money) for (bills, rent, etc.) 4. to regain control of (oneself) —vi. to assemble or accumulate —adj., adv. with payment to be made by the receiver [to telephone collect] —n. (käl'ekt) [also C-] a short prayer —col·lec'tor n.

As you can see, the word <u>collector</u> is on the last line of the entry. <u>Collector</u> and <u>collectable</u> are different forms of the entry word. Different forms of a word are often printed in boldface or dark type following the entry word. Sometimes the type is smaller than that of the entry word.

Note too that when a word can be spelled in two different ways, both spellings will be given in the entry in boldface type. The first spelling is generally preferred. In the above entry, <u>collectable</u> and <u>collectible</u> are both correct.

Dividing Words by Syllables

When you are writing, if you need to divide a word at the end of a line, the dictionary will tell you where to do it. Turn back to page 245 and look at the entry words in boldface type. The syllables are divided by dots or accent marks. When you continue a word from one line to another, break it between syllables. Don't forget to place a hyphen after the last syllable on the first line. Never carry a one-letter syllable to a new line.

Is this lesson nec-
essary?   YES!

You could also divide the word by placing a hyphen after the second syllable:

neces-
sary

Test your understanding of the use of the dictionary to spell and divide words by doing the following exercise.

Exercise for Subskill 9C

Each of the words listed below is misspelled. Find each word in the dictionary. See how each should be spelled and divided. Rewrite each word in the space provided, showing correct spelling and syllable division. Use hyphens between syllables as you would for an end-of-line division.

EXAMPLE: buoyent   <u>buoy-ant</u>

1. faverite   _____

2. guerilla   _____

3. paralel   _____

4. goten   _____

5. possable   _____

Check your answers on page 37 in the Answer Key for Book Three. If you correctly answered all 5 items, go to Subskill 9D. If not, do the Supplemental Exercise for Subskill 9C.

Supplemental Exercise for Subskill 9C

Once you find the dictionary entry for the word you are looking up, the boldface type tells you how to spell it correctly. Dots and accent marks indicate the syllable divisions of a word. When you break a word at the end of a line, place a hyphen after the last syllable on the first line. Now do the following exericse.

The words below are all spelled incorrectly. Use your dictionary to find out how they should be spelled. In the space beside each word, write the correct spelling and the syllable divisions. Use hyphens between syllables as you would to indicate an end-of-line division.

EXAMPLE: chivelrus   chiv-al-rous

1. consummed   _____

2. doubleheder   _____

3. guidence   _____

4. jaming   _____

5. lubricetor   _____

Check your answers on page 38 in the Answer Key for Book Three. If you correctly answered 4 of 5 items, go to Subskill 9D. If not, ask your instructor for help.

Subskill 9D: Identifying Parts of Speech and Selecting the Correct Definition

When you complete this subskill, you will be able to find out what part of speech an entry word can be; you will also understand the dictionary abbreviations of parts of speech. You will be able to identify the forms of an entry word used as different parts of speech, and you will be able to find the correct definition of a word from among several in the dictionary entry.

Finding Parts of Speech

You can find the part of speech of an entry word after the phonetic entry and before the definition. The part of speech is usually abbreviated and shown in dark (boldface) type. The chart on the inside front and back covers of this book summarizes the parts of speech you have learned. The chart on page 258 shows the abbreviations used in dictionary entries for each part of speech.

Part of Speech	Abbreviation	Part of Speech	Abbreviation
noun	n.	adverb	adv.
pronoun	pron.	preposition	prep.
verb	v., vt., or vi.	conjunction	conj.
adjective	adj.	interjection	interj.

Look again at the dictionary entry for <u>collect</u> shown on page 255. Find all the abbreviations of the parts of speech.

The abbreviation *vt.* means transitive verb. Remember that a transitive verb must have an object.

Jose collected stamps.

The word <u>collect</u> may also be used as an intransitive verb, shown by the abbreviation *vi.* Remember that an intransitive verb does not have an object.

A crowd collected around the speaker.

When a verb is irregular, the dictionary entry also gives you the past, past participle, and present participle forms, if these are in any way unusual. For example,

fit (fit) *vt.* **fit′ ted** or **fit, fit′ ted, fit′ ting. . . .**

The dictionary will also give you the comparative and superlative forms of adjectives and adverbs, and any other special spellings a word form may have.

Choosing the Correct Definition

Note that four definitions are given for the word <u>collect</u> as a transitive verb, and that additional definitions are given for each of its other parts of speech. You will find several definitions of most words in their dictionary entries. The way in which the word is used in a sentence will help you determine which meaning it has in that sentence. The part of speech and its context are the clues you need.

Find the word <u>accent</u> on the dictionary page shown on page 245 early in this chapter. How may definitions are given for <u>accent</u> used as a noun? How many definitions are given for <u>accent</u> used as a transitive verb? The following examples show the different meanings of the word <u>accent</u>.

Be sure to accent the second syllable of "particular." **vt. 1**
Accent the "tic" in "particular." **vt. 2**
Her German accent was so thick we could hardly understand what she was saying. **n. 3**
In a waltz, the accent is on every third beat. **n. 4**

You may find a word in a sentence and not be sure which of its meanings is the correct one. Look, for example, at this sentence:

He took a <u>dip</u> in the early morning ocean and then <u>dipped</u> into a book that was lying on the table.

Which two definitions are correct in this sentence?

According to the dictionary, the word <u>dip</u> has all of the following meanings:

1. to put into liquid for a moment (vt)
2. to take out as by scooping up (vt)
3. to lower (a flag, etc.) and immediately raise again (vt)
4. to go down into a liquid and quickly come out (vi)
5. to sink suddenly (vi)
6. to slope down (vi)
7. to go (into) so as to dig something out (vi)
8. to look into or study something superficially
9. a brief plunge (n)
10. a liquid, sauce, etc. into which something is being dipped (n)
11. a downward slope (n)

To find the correct meaning, try each definition to see whether the meaning fits into the context of the sentence. Then choose the best definition.

He took <u>a brief plunge</u> in the early morning ocean and then <u>looked superficially into</u> a book that was lying on the table.

Check your understanding of the use of a dictionary to determine the part of speech of a word and its meaning within a sentence by doing this exercise.

Exercise for Subskill 9D

Part A. Use your dictionary to fill in the table below.
In the column headed <u>Parts of Speech</u>, list the part or parts of speech given for each entry word shown. Some entry words may be listed more than once in the dictionary. Write the part of speech for each entry and indicate what form each part of speech is.
In the column headed <u>Different Forms</u>, write any other forms of the word given in the entries and indicate what part of speech that form is.

Entry Word	Part(s) of Speech	Different Forms
EXAMPLE: fine	adj., adv., n., vt.	fined, dining, vt.
1. project		
2. scoop		
3. machine		
4. excuse		
5. southeast		

Part B. The way a word is used in a sentence determines its meaning. Six definitions of the word beam are listed below. Read the sentences below and choose the correct definition for each sentence. Write the number of the definition in the space next to each sentence.

1. a long, thick piece of wood (n.)
2. a steady radio or radar signal   (n.)
3. the width across the hips   (n.)
4. a slender shaft of light   (n.)
5. to smile warmly (vi.)
6. to direct (a radio signal, etc.)   (vt.)

EXAMPLE: 5   Marti was beaming when she received the award.

6._____   The co-pilot realized the radio was broken when he could not hear the beam.

7._____   She used to be broad across the beam, but now she's not.

8._____   The shop teacher told the students to get three beams from the supply room.

9._____   Satellites beam signals to cable stations.

10._____   A beam from the usher's flashlight lit the aisle seats.

Part C.   Look up each of the following words. In the space provided next to each word, write the definition that applies to auto repair.

EXAMPLE: bearing   a part of a machine on which another part revolves, slides etc.

11. transmission   _____

12. wrench   _____

13. muffler   _____

14. exhaust   _____

15. battery   _____

Check your answers on pages 37 and 38 in the Answer Key for Book Three. If you correctly answered 12 of 15 items, go to Subskill 9E. If not, do the Supplemental Exercise for Subskill 9D.

Supplemental Exercise for Subskill 9D

Reread the explanation of how to use a dictionary entry to identify parts of speech and choose the appropriate meaning of a word. Then do this exercise.

Part A. Use your dictionary to fill in the table below.

In the column headed Part(s) of Speech, list the part or parts of speech given for each entry word shown. Some entry words will be listed more than once in the dictionary. Write the part of speech for each entry and indicate what form each part of speech is.

In the column headed Different Forms, write any other forms of the word given in the entries and indicate what part of speech that form is.

Entry Word	Part(s) of Speech	Different Forms
EXAMPLE: bargain 1. orbit	n, vi	bargainer, n
2. catch		
3. define		
4. figure		
5. purchase		

Part B. The way a word is used in a sentence determines its meaning. Below are six definitions of the word negative. Read the sentences below and choose the correct definition for each sentence. Write the letter of the definition in the space next to each sentence.

EXAMPLE: e   He held the negative up to the light to see it better.

a. expressing denial or refusal; saying "no".
b. opposite to or lacking what is positive
c. having an excess of electrons
d. a quantity to be subtracted
e. a film from which positive photographic prints are made
f. a negative word or phrase

6. _____ She was negative about the suggestion and didn't want to talk about it.

7. _____ They answered in the negative.

8. _____ Once you take away the negative sum, you'll have a balanced budget.

9. _____ The battery was negatively charged.

10. _____ The negative had a scratch in it.

Part C. Look up each of the following words. In the space provided next to each word, write the definition that applies to carpentry.

EXAMPLE: horse   a supporting frame with legs.

11. plane   _____

12. board _____

13. level _____

14. saw _____

15. ruler _____

Check your answers on page 38 in the Answer Key for Book Three. If you correctly answered 12 of 15 items, go to Subskill 9F. If not, ask your instructor for help.

Subskill 9E: Locating the Etymology of a Word

When you complete this subskill, you will be able to locate the part of an entry which tells you the etymology of a word. You will also be able to use the symbols of etymology to determine the origin and development of an entry word.

Words in modern English come from many different languages. Many words come from Latin and Greek words. Others have been taken from Arabic, French, German, Spanish, and Hebrew. You will even find a few words of Hindi, Swahili, and various American Indian origins.

If you look up the word inscribe, for example, you will find that it comes from two Latin words, in and scribere. In means "in," and scribere means "to write."

Most dictionaries show the origin, or source, of an entry word by placing this information in brackets before or after the definition. The information usually includes the name of the language from which the word is derived, as well as the meanings of the word in earlier times. This information is called the **etymology,** or origin and development, of the word. By knowing how to read the etymology, you can learn about the history of a word. Knowing the etymology of a word can also help you spell it correctly and understand its meaning. The study of etymology will increase your vocabulary and make your use of words more interesting.

The following chart shows some of the symbols and abbreviations used to show the language source of a word.

< or fr.	is derived from	Heb.	Hebrew
Ar.	Arabic	L.	Latin
Fr.	French	ME.	Middle English
G.	German	OE.	Old English
Gr.	Greek	Sp.	Spanish

There is a complete list of the abbreviations that indicate word origins in the front of your dictionary.

Let's look at the etymology of one entry word.

ab·bre·vi·ate (ə brē′ vē āt) vt. -at -ed, -at ing.
[<L. ad-, to + brevis, short] to make shorter; esp., to shorten (a word) by omitting letters.

The symbol ≤ means "derived from." The L. means the word comes from the Latin language. The symbol + means "plus" or "added to." The etymology, or origin, of abbreviate, then, is:

from the Latin prefix ad, meaning to, plus the Latin root word brevis, meaning short.

The word abbreviate literally means "to shorten." Knowing the history of this word may help you remember its meaning.

Check your understanding of etymology by completing the Exercise for Subskill 9E below.

Exercise for Subskill 9E

Find the following words in your dictionary. Beside each word write its etymology. Refer to your dictionary's list of abbreviations if you come across one that you do not know.

EXAMPLE: transmit   [<L. trans-, over + mittere, send]

1. conscript   [   ]

2. barrow   [   ]

3. apology   [   ]

4. guitar   [   ]

5. butter   [   ]

Check your answers on page 39 in the Answer Key for Book Three. If you correctly answered all 5 items, go to the Self-Check. If not, do the Supplemental Exercise for Subskill 9E.

Supplemental Exercise for Subskill 9E

Etymology is the origin and development of words. In the dictionary, an explanation of a word's origin is given in symbols and abbreviations before or after the definition. A guide to these symbols and abbreviations is usually located in the front of your dictionary. Look at the chart in your dictionary, and then do this Supplemental Exercise.

Find the following words in your dictionary. Beside each word write its etymology. Refer to your dictionary's list of abbreviations if you come across one you do not know.

EXAMPLE: pull   [O.E. pullian, to pluck]

  1. film   [   ]

  2. natural   [   ]

  3. prejudice   [   ]

  4. candy   [   ]

  5. apostle   [   ]

Check your answers on page 39 in the Answer Key for Book Three. If you correctly answered 4 of 5 items, go to the Self-Check. If not, ask your instructor for help.

SELF-CHECK: SKILL UNIT 9

Using a dictionary, complete the chart for each underlined word in the sentences below. Remember to use the list of abbreviations and the pronunciation key in your dictionary when you need them. You will fill in the following information on the chart:

· the division of the word into syllables (Column A)
· the phonetic spelling (Column B)
· the abbreviation for the part of speech of the word as it is used in the sentence (Column C)
· the definition of the word as it is used in the sentence (Column D)
· the etymology of the word (Column E)

EXAMPLE: The solo flight was a test of nerves as well as technical skill.

1. He was a paragon of creativity.

2. The vultures fed on the elephant's carcass.

3. Brown rice and beans combine to form a complete protein.

4. Their cookies won first prize.

5. A successful manager helps the people he or she supervises to become successful.

6. The ramifications of the problems loomed larger every day.

7. Acting in a comedy takes a lot of concentration.

8. Each sister felt that the other had knifed her in the back.

9. The "Hallelujah Chorus" is my favorite section of the piece.

10. She wore flannel pajamas in the wintertime to keep warm.

	A Syllable Division	B Phonetic Spelling	C Part of Speech	D Definition	E Word Origin
EXAMPLE: solo	so·lo	so'lo	adj.	a performance by one person alone	L. solus, alone
1. paragon					
2. carcass					
3. protein					
4. cookies					
5. people					
6. ramify					
7. comedy					
8. knife					
9. Hallelujah					
10. pajamas					

Check your answers on pages 39 and 40 in the Answer Key for Book Three. If you correctly answered 8 of 10 items, you have shown that you have mastered these skills. If not, ask your instructor for help.

Skill Unit 10
SPELLING

What Skills You Need To Begin: You need to be able to look up words in the dictionary to check the spelling of difficult words.

What Skills You Will Learn: When you complete this skill unit, you will be able to spell troublesome words that have ie and ei in them. You will be able to spell words formed by adding prefixes and suffixes to word bases. You will be able to spell plurals. You will be able to pronounce and spell words that are commonly mispronounced and misspelled. You will learn how to use memory aids to spell words correctly.

Why You Need These Skills: A misspelled word can change the meaning of a sentence. It can also distract readers and interfere with their understanding of the meaning. Readers who come upon incorrectly spelled words are forced to stop and try to figure out their correct spelling and meaning. When you write, you want your readers to understand your message. This unit will increase your effectiveness in getting a written message across clearly.

How You Will Show What You Have Learned: You will do the Self-Check at the end of this unit on page 292. The Self-Check consists of 30 items. If you correctly answer 25 of 30 items, you will have shown that you have mastered these skills.

If you feel that you have already mastered these skills, turn to the end of this unit and complete the Self-Check on page 292.

Subskill 10A: Spelling Words With ie and ei

When you complete this subskill, you will be able to spell words with ie and ei.

The following jingle is so helpful, it is worth memorizing:

Place i before e, except after c,

or when sounded like a,

as in neighbor and weigh.

266

"i before e":

believe   piece   niece

achieve   grief   chief

"except after c":

receive   ceiling   deceit

receipt   conceit   perceive

"or when sounded like a, as in neighbor and weigh":

vein   sleigh   reign

neigh   reindeer   eight

Do not be confused by words in which i is followed by er, ent, ence, or ency. In these words, the i gives the letter c the phonetic sounds s or sh. The spelling of these words is not determined by the "i before e, except after c" rule.

financier   conscience   deficiency

efficient   ancient   sufficient

EXCEPTIONS: The spelling ei is often followed by an s or z sound. Other ei words that are exceptions to the rule follow no particular pattern. The words underlined in the following nonsense sentence are some important exceptions to the "i before e" rules in the jingle:

Neither the weird sheik, nor those he seized either, are at leisure.

Exercise for Subskill 10A

Part A. Write each word correctly by filling in the blanks with either ie or ei.

EXAMPLE: height

1. ch___f
2. fr___ght
3. conc___t
4. defic___nt
5. y___ld
6. v___l
7. fr___nd
8. for___gn
9. counterf___t
10. hyg___ne
11. consc___nce
12. rec___ved
13. effic___ncy

Part B. Some of the following words are misspelled. Write them correctly in the space provided. If a word is spelled correctly, write <u>Correct</u> in the space provided.

EXAMPLE: greif ____grief____

14. deciet _____   15. liesure _____

16. field _____   17. wieght _____

18. reciept _____   19. shreik _____

20. releive _____   21. niece _____

22. sieze _____   23. peice _____

24. anceint _____   25. neither _____

Check your answers on page 40 in the Answer Key for Book Three. If you correctly completed all 25 items, go to Subskill 10B. If not, do the Supplemental Exercise for Subskill 10A.

Supplemental Exercise for Subskill 10A

There are ways to avoid confusing <u>ie</u> with <u>ei</u> when you spell words with these letters. Remember these suggestions:

- When the vowel combination sounds like $\bar{e}$ (long $\bar{e}$), the spelling is usually <u>ie</u>:

     fierce   hygiene   siege

- BUT when a <u>c</u> comes before the vowel combination, the spelling is usually <u>ei</u>:

     deceit   perceive   ceiling

- When the vowel combination sounds like $\bar{a}$ (long $\bar{a}$), the spelling is usually <u>ei</u>:

     neighbor   weigh   reign

- There are some exceptions to these rules. Note that in some of the exceptions below, the <u>ei</u> combination is followed by an <u>s</u> or <u>z</u> sound.

     sheik   leisure   height
     seize   neither   forfeit

- Don't get confused by words in which a <u>c</u> is followed by <u>i</u> and <u>er</u>, <u>ent</u>, <u>ence</u>, or <u>ency</u>. The spelling of these words is not determined by the "<u>i</u> before <u>e</u>, except after <u>c</u>" rule. In these words, the <u>i</u> gives the letter <u>c</u> the phonetic sounds <u>s</u> or <u>sh</u>.

It's a good idea to memorize the ei-ie words you use most often in your writing. Pay particular attention to those words that are exceptions to the rule. When in doubt, use the dictionary.

Part A. Write each word correctly by filling in the blanks with either ie or ei.

EXAMPLE: eighth

1. c___ling
2. rec___ver
3. n___ghbor
4. forf___t
5. r___ns
6. pat___nt
7. f___rce
8. n___ther
9. gr___vance
10. w___rd
11. defic___nt
12. for___gn
13. fr___nd

Part B. Some of the following words are misspelled. Write them correctly in the space provided. If a word is spelled correctly, write Correct in the space provided.

EXAMPLE: anceint ___ancient___

14. conscience _____
15. vien _____
16. riegn _____
17. deciet _____
18. sheik _____
19. seive _____
20. beleive _____
21. relief _____
22. concieted _____
23. liesure _____
24. wieght _____
25. sheild _____

Check your answers on page 41 in the Answer Key for Book Three. If you correctly completed 20 of 25 items, go to Subskill 10B. If not, ask your instructor for help.

Subskill 10B: Spelling Words Formed By Adding Prefixes

When you complete this subskill, you will be able to spell words that are formed by adding prefixes to word bases.

Consider the following words:

dismiss

missile

missive

mission

emission

You can see that they all have the letters <u>miss</u> in common. If you look up any one of these words in the dictionary, you will find that it comes from a form of the Latin verb <u>mittere</u>, which means "to send." All of the words on this list are formed by building on the word base <u>miss</u>, and all mean something that has to do with "send." The different words having <u>miss</u> as their base are formed by placing other groups of letters before or after the base and, sometimes, both before and after the base.

It is the **word base** that gives every word its main meaning. In Skill Unit 9 (Using the Dictionary), you learned that many of our English words come from other languages and other periods in history. You can usually find the meaning of a word's base in the etymology part of the word's dictionary entry.

In the list above, two words have letters placed before the base— <u>dismiss</u> and <u>emission</u>. The <u>dis</u> in <u>dismiss</u> and the <u>e</u> in <u>emission</u> are prefixes. **A prefix is one or more syllables attached to the beginning of a word base**. Every prefix has a meaning. Prefix meanings can be found in the dictionary, either as entry words or as part of the etymology of the word starting with the prefix. The meaning of the prefix adds to the meaning of the word base. Thus, <u>dis</u> means "from" or "away," so <u>dismiss</u> means "send away." Some other words with this prefix are:

dispel   disperse   disconnect

The prefix <u>dis</u> has other meanings as well:

<u>dis</u>, meaning "the opposite of"   +   <u>able</u>   =   disable

<u>dis</u>, meaning "not, on the contrary"   +   <u>appear</u>   =   disappear

The other word on the list above that contains a prefix is <u>emission</u>. Here, the prefix <u>e</u> means "out." An <u>emission</u> is something that is sent out, as radioactivity might be sent out during a nuclear reaction. Some other words in which the prefix <u>e</u> has the same meaning are:

edict	educate	erase
eject	elaborate	evacuate
emerge	emotion	event

The prefix e has other meanings as well:

e, meaning "from" + vade = evade
e, meaning "up"   + rect = erect

As these examples show, the same prefix can be used with numerous word bases.

The spelling of a word base does not change in any way when a prefix is added:

dis + agree   = disagree   im + possible = impossible
un + able   = unable   re + turn   = return
sub + marine = submarine   pre + fix   = prefix

When the consonant at the beginning of a word base is the same as the consonant at the end of a prefix, the word they form together keeps both consonants:

un + named   = unnamed   ir + rational = irrational
im + material = immaterial   mis + spell   = misspell

For more information about the spelling and meaning of any new words, word bases, and prefixes, consult a dictionary.

Exercise for Subskill 10B

Combine one of the prefixes in List A with a word base from List B to form the word that best fits the meaning of each sentence. Write the new word in the space provided. Use a dictionary if you need more help with the meanings of prefixes and word bases.

Prefix	Meaning	Word Base
a	not, on, without	shore
ante	before	mobile
anti	against, opposed to	part
auto	self	monthly
bi	two	navigate
circum	around	content
de	down from, away from	precious
inter	among	war
mal	bad, ill	date
semi	half, partly, not fully	national

List A (Prefix, Meaning) and List B (Word Base).

EXAMPLE: An agreement between two countries is <u>binational</u>.

1. A person who opposes violence is probably _____ .

2. A person who is ill-pleased may be a _____ .

3. Meetings held among representatives of several nations are

    _____ .

4. If you get paid twice a month, you get a _____
    paycheck.

5. Columbus thought he could sail around the world. He tried to

    _____ the globe.

6. When his sailors went _____ , they were
    happy to be on land once more.

7. If you put last Monday's date on a letter, you would _____

    _____ the letter.

8. A _____ gem is not as valuable as a dia-
    mond.

9. The visitors will go away next weekend. They are scheduled to

    _____ in the afternoon.

10. Because it appeared to move by itself, an important invention of

     about a century ago came to be called the _____ .

Check your answers on page 41 of the Answer Key for Book Three.
If you correctly completed all 10 items, go to Subskill 10C. If not, do
the Supplemental Exercise for Subskill 10B.

Supplemental Exercise for Subskill 10B

A prefix is a syllable that is added before the main part of a word.
The main part of a word is the word base. When a prefix is added, there
is no change in the spelling of the word base. Prefix meanings can be
found in the dictionary, either as entry words or as part of the etymology
of an entry word.

Combine one of the prefixes from List A with a word base from List B to
form the word that best fits the meaning of each sentence. Write the new
word in the space provided.

List A		List B
Prefix	**Meaning**	**Word Base**
ab	not, away from	legible

dis	taking away, apart from	important
il	not	carriage
in	not	permanent
ir	not	solved
mis	wrong	service
re	again, back	regular
semi	partly, halfway	numerable
un	not	form
uni	single, as one	elect

EXAMPLE: The mystery remained   _unsolved_ .

1. The mayor has served one term and now she expects us to _____ her.

2. She is running a most unusual, _____ campaign.

3. Her _____ campaign workers seem to be on every street in town.

4. Their petition signatures are so _____, the committee is suffering from eyestrain.

5. Her followers are single-minded and _____ in their praise for her.

6. After her interview, the governor took the blame and _____ her of talking out of turn.

7. Everyone agrees the news reports of the event were so unfair, they did her a _____ .

8. It would be a great _____ of justice if people voted for her opponent because of those news items.

9. The opposition says she is away so much, she is only a(n) _____ resident in the city.

10. Remember, every vote counts in this election. No citizen should think his or her vote is _____ .

Check your answers on page 41 in the Answer Key for Book Three. If you correctly completed 8 of 10 items, go to Subskill 10C. If not, ask your instructor for help.

Subskill 10C: Spelling Words Formed By Adding Suffixes

When you complete this subskill, you will be able to spell words that are formed by adding suffixes to word bases.

A suffix is one or more syllables attached to the end of a word base. Like the prefixes you studied in Subskill 10B, every suffix has a meaning. Suffix meanings can be found in the dictionary. Common suffixes, like ly, will appear as entry words. Less common suffixes will be defined in the etymology part of the entry words to which they are attached.

Prefixes change the meaning of a word base. Suffixes generally change the form or the part of speech of the word base. For example, the suffixes ed and ing change the tense of verbs:

    play   played   playing   beg   begged   begging

The suffixes er and or change verbs to nouns that mean "the person who does" something:

    make   maker   sail   sailor

The suffixes ion, tion, sion, and ation change verbs to nouns that mean "the act of" or "the state of being."

Some suffixes change a noun form to another noun form:

    physics   physicist   violin   violinist

    music   musician

The suffixes al, ial, able or ible form adjectives out of various nouns and verbs:

    accident   accidental   president   presidential

    believe   believable   force   forcible

The suffixes ty, ity, and ness change adjectives to nouns:

    active   activity   careless   carelessness

The suffix ly generally changes adjectives to adverbs:

    happy   happily   bad   badly

The suffix er is added to an adjective to tell you that there is more or less of something when two items are being compared. The suffix est is added to an adjective to tell you that there is the most or the least of something when three or more items are being compared:

    small   smaller   smallest

    big   bigger   biggest

Let's consider again the words we examined when we studied prefixes:

dismiss
missile
missive
mission
emission

There are three different suffixes in the words in this list: <u>ile</u> in <u>missile</u>, <u>ive</u> in <u>missive</u>, and <u>ion</u> in <u>mission</u> and <u>emission</u>.

The suffix <u>ile</u> means "having to do with" or "suitable for." You learned in Subskill 10B that the word base <u>miss</u> means "send." A <u>missile</u> would be "something suitable for sending," and thus is the term used for a long-range weapon. Some other words with the suffix <u>ile</u> are:

docile projectile tactile

The suffix <u>ive</u> means "relating to," "belonging to," or "having the quality of." A <u>missive</u> has the quality of being sent; it is a letter. Some other words with the suffix <u>ive</u> are:

active destructive native

The suffix <u>ion</u> comes from a Latin verb form. It is used to create nouns. Thus, <u>mission</u> means "a sending out"; people who go on a <u>mission</u> have been sent out to do a particular thing. Some other words with the suffix <u>ion</u> are:

apparition demonstration interpretation

You learned in Subskill 10B that adding a prefix to a word base never changes the spelling of the word base. Suffixes, however, often change the spelling of a word base. The following rules will help you spell words with suffixes correctly.

Adding the Suffixes <u>ness</u> and <u>ly</u>

When the suffixes <u>ness</u> and <u>ly</u> are added, the spelling of the word base usually remains the same:

complete + ly = completely complete + ness = completeness

truthful + ly = truthfully truthful + ness = truthfulness

dry + ly = dryly dry + ness = dryness

EXCEPTION: When the word base ends in <u>y</u> preceded by a consonant and has more than one syllable, the <u>y</u> usually becomes an <u>i</u> when adding the suffixes <u>ness</u> or <u>ly</u>:

busy + ly = busily busy + ness = business

EXCEPTIONS TO THE EXCEPTION: In a few one-syllable words ending in y, the y becomes an i when ly is added:

gay + ly = gaily   day + ly = daily

Adding a Suffix to Words That End With a Silent e

When the word base ends in a silent e, keep the silent e before a suffix beginning with a consonant:

sincerely	definitely	lovely
advertisement	useless	wasteful

When the word base ends in a silent e, drop the silent e before a suffix beginning with a vowel:

sincerity	definitive	lovable
advertising	usable	wasted

EXCEPTIONS: Some exceptions help to avoid confusion between two similar words:

dyeing (coloring cloth)   dying (near death)

When there is a c or a g before a silent e in the word base, the silent e is often kept before a suffix beginning with a vowel:

courageous   serviceable

Other exceptions help to maintain pronunciation of vowel sounds in the word base:

canoeing	shoeing	herein
lineage	mileage	acreage

Still other exceptions maintain the appearance of the new word:

argument   truly

(To see how much appearance counts in spelling, try writing any of these words incorrectly!)

Adding a Suffix to Words That End with y

When a word base ends in y preceded by a consonant, the y changes to i except before a suffix beginning with i:

shabby	shabbier	shabbiness
marry	marriage	marrying
dignify	dignified	dignifying
glory	gloried	glorified

When a word base ends in y preceded by a vowel, the y does not change:

buy	buyer	buying
betray	betrayed	betrayal
employ	employee	employer
play	player	playful

EXCEPTIONS:

babyhood	paid	gaiety
laid	said	shyness

Adding a Suffix to a Word and Doubling the Final Consonant

When a one-syllable word base ends in a single consonant preceded by a single vowel, the final consonant is doubled when adding a suffix beginning with a vowel:

run	runner	running
big	bigger	biggest
quiz	quizzed	quizzical

When a word base of two or more syllables ends in a single consonant preceded by a single vowel, <u>and</u> the word is pronounced with the stress on the final syllable, the final consonant is usually doubled when adding a suffix beginning with a vowel:

ad mit'	admittance	admitted
be gin'	beginner	beginning
com pel'	compelled	compelling
for get'	forgettable	forgetting

BUT when the newly formed word is pronounced with the stress on its first syllable, the final consonant is not doubled:

pre fer'   preferred   BUT: pre' ference

When a word base of two or more syllables ends in a single consonant preceded by a single vowel, <u>but</u> the word is pronounced with the stress on the first syllable, the final consonant is not doubled before a suffix beginning with a vowel:

tra' vel   traveling   mur' der   murdered

Exercise for Subskill 10C

Part A.   Add the suffixes to the word bases as indicated. You may have to add, drop or change letters before the suffixes can be added.

EXAMPLE: refer + ed _____ referred _____

1. arrive + al   _____

2. study + ous   _____

3. amuse + ing   _____

4. betray + er   _____

5. true + ly   _____

6. happy + ness   _____

7. study + ing   _____

8. remit + ed   _____

9. baby + hood   _____

10. fumble + ing   _____

Part B. Complete the spelling of the words in parentheses, if necessary.

EXAMPLE: The car gets good gas (mil_ea_ge).

11. The (adverti____ment) took up a whole page.

12. Her gown was (lov____ly).

13. The tools were (us____less) without proper lighting.

14. The officer's story was (believ____able).

15. Guess who's (com____ing) for breakfast?

16. The idea (occu____ed) to me in a dream.

17. The tires are (servic____able).

18. The teacher (orde____ed) him to leave the class.

19. The music was beautiful, the lyrics (forge____able).

20. Who (murde____ed) the butler?

Check your answers on page 42 in the Answer Key for Book Three. If you correctly completed all 20 items, go to Subskill 10D. If not, do the Supplemental Exercise for Subskill 10C.

Supplemental Exercise for Subskill 10C

Suffixes are syllables attached to the end of a word base. In order to avoid spelling problems when you add a suffix, remember the following rules:

· When adding <u>ness</u> and <u>ly</u> to a word base ending in <u>y</u> preceded by a consonant, change the <u>y</u> to <u>i</u>.

· When adding a suffix to a word base ending in a silent <u>e</u>, keep the silent <u>e</u> when the suffix begins with a consonant; drop the silent <u>e</u> when the suffix begins with a vowel.

· When adding a suffix to a word base ending in y preceded by a vowel, the y is not changed.

· Double the final consonant when the word base ends in a single consonant preceded by a single vowel and the suffix begins with a vowel if the word base has one syllable, or when a word base of more than one syllable is pronounced with the accent on the syllable before the suffix.

There are exceptions to all these rules. Review Subskill 10C to become familiar with them. Consult your dictionary when a word or suffix is unfamiliar to you.

Part A. Add the suffixes to the word bases as indicated. You may have to add, drop or change letters before the suffixes can be added.

EXAMPLE: hardy + ness <u>hardiness</u>

1. acre + age _____

2. courage + ous _____

3. busy + ness _____

4. love + able _____

5. omit + ed _____

6. model + ing _____

7. grace + ful _____

8. order + ly _____

9. time + less _____

10. style + ish _____

Part B. Complete the spelling of the words in parentheses.

EXAMPLE: The thought of using those animals in a lab experiment was (repe<u>ll</u>ent).

11. Some people have a (prefe____ence) for city life.

12. The first baseman was a better (hi____er) than the shortstop.

13. Harvard was (omi____ed) from the list of colleges that have such programs.

14. Everyone spent the day (stud____ing) before the final exam.

15. We are going (cano____ing) on the Colorado River.

16. She (marr____ed) an older man.

17. Harold is not the (marr____ing) type.

18. He sold the (da____ly) paper.

19. His father was (dignif____ed).

20. Have you heard the saying, "Money can't buy (happ____ness)"?

Check your answers on page 42 in the Answer Key for Book Three. If you correctly completed 16 of 20 items, go to Subskill 10D. If not, ask your instructor for help.

Subskill 10D: Spelling Plurals

When you complete this subskill, you will be able to spell noun plurals correctly.

Most nouns have both singular and plural forms. Singular means referring to one item only. Plural means referring to more than one item. A noun is singular when it refers to one item only:

> flower   tornado   airplane

A noun is plural when it refers to two or more items:

> flowers   tornadoes   airplanes

As the above examples indicate, the plural forms of nouns generally end in s. The following rules apply to noun plurals:

Rule 1: Form the plural of most nouns by adding s to the singular form:

> tent   tents   movie   movies

Rule 2: When a noun ends in s, ch, sh, x, or z, form the plural by adding es:

> bass   basses   torch   torches
>
> crash   crashes   tax   taxes
>
> waltz   waltzes

Rule 3: When a noun ends in y preceded by a consonant, form the plural by changing the y to i and adding es:

> fantasy   fantasies

When a noun ends in y preceded by a vowel, form the plural by adding s:

> valley   valleys

Rule 4: The plurals of most nouns ending in f̲ or f̲e̲ are formed by changing the f̲ to v̲ and adding e̲s̲:

wife	wives	calf	calves
leaf	leaves	wolf	wolves
self	selves	loaf	loaves

However, nouns ending in f̲f̲ or f̲f̲e̲, and certain other nouns, keep the f̲f̲ or f̲f̲e̲ when the plural is formed:

proof	proofs	giraffe	giraffes
chef	chefs	bluff	bluffs

Some nouns in this group may have either plural form:

wharf	wharfs or wharves
scarf	scarfs or scarves
hoof	hoofs or hooves

If you are unsure about the spelling of any of these words, consult a dictionary.

Rule 5: When a noun ends in o̲ preceded by a consonant, form the plural by adding e̲s̲:

hero	heroes

When a noun ends in o̲ preceded by a vowel, form the plural by adding s̲:

video	videos

For most nouns that end in o̲ and refer to music, form the plural by adding s̲:
piano	pianos

Some nouns in this group may have either form in the plural:

zero	zeros or zeroes
mosquito	mosquitos or mosquitoes

Rule 6: The plural forms of some nouns are irregular:

mouse	mice	child	children
man	men	tooth	teeth
woman	women	ox	oxen

Rule 7: The plural forms of some nouns are the same as the singular:

deer	sheep	fish
wheat	traffic	dozen

Note that the names of several animals are in this category.

Rule 8: The plural of a compound noun is generally formed by using the plural form of the noun part of the compound:

mother-in-law   mothers-in-law

looker-on   lookers-on

There are some exceptions:

drive-in   drive-ins

two-year-old   two-year-olds

Exercise for Subskill 10D

Write the correct plural forms of the nouns in the spaces provided.

EXAMPLE: spy   _____ spies _____

1. cave   _____
2. son-in-law   _____
3. hoax   _____
4. battery   _____
5. bee   _____
6. goose   _____
7. shrimp   _____
8. grief   _____
9. tomato   _____
10. deer   _____
11. safe   _____
12. soprano   _____
13. essay   _____
14. glue   _____
15. roof   _____

Check your answers on page 42 in the Answer Key for Book Three. If you correctly completed all 15 items, go to Subskill 10E. If not, do the Supplemental Exercise for Subskill 10D.

Supplemental Exercise for Subskill 10D

The plural form of a noun refers to more than one item. In summary, here are the eight rules for spelling plurals correctly:

(1) To form the plural of most nouns, add <u>s</u> to the singular form: <u>dogs</u>.

(2) To form the plural of nouns ending in <u>s</u>, <u>ch</u>, <u>sh</u>, <u>x</u>, or <u>z</u>, add <u>es</u> to the singular form: <u>churches</u>.

(3) To form the plural of nouns ending in <u>y</u> preceded by a consonant, change the <u>y</u> to <u>i</u> and add <u>es</u>: <u>cherries</u>. To form the plural of nouns ending in <u>y</u> preceded by a vowel, add <u>s</u>: <u>days</u>.

(4) To form the plural of most nouns ending in <u>f</u> or <u>fe</u>, change the <u>f</u> to <u>v</u> and add <u>es</u>: <u>thieves</u>. Other nouns in this group keep the <u>f</u> and add <u>s</u>: <u>roofs</u>. A few noun plurals can be formed either way: <u>hoofs</u> or <u>hooves</u>.

(5) To form the plural of nouns ending in <u>o</u> preceded by a consonant, add <u>es</u>: <u>potatoes</u>. For nouns ending in <u>o</u> preceded by a vowel, add <u>s</u>: <u>radios</u>. For nouns ending in <u>o</u> referring to music, add <u>s</u>: <u>altos</u>.

(6) Some very common nouns have irregular plurals: <u>mice</u>, <u>children</u>, <u>teeth</u>.

(7) Some nouns have the same form in the plural as in the singular: <u>deer</u>.

(8) To form the plural of a compound noun, add <u>s</u> to the noun part of the compound: <u>commanders-in-chief</u>.

Write the correct plural forms of the nouns in the spaces provided.

EXAMPLE: note _____ notes _____

1. board _____
2. buzz _____
3. sash _____
4. courtesy _____
5. potato _____
6. wife _____
7. five-year-old _____
8. trout _____
9. portfolio _____
10. alley _____
11. foot _____
12. ox _____
13. puff _____
14. ax _____
15. church _____

Check your answers on page 42 in the Answer Key for Book Three. If you correctly completed 12 of 15 items, go to Subskill 10E. If not, ask your instructor for help.

Subskill 10E: Pronouncing Words Correctly to Aid Spelling

When you complete this subskill, you will be able to pronounce and spell correctly words that are commonly mispronounced and misspelled.

People often misspell words because they do not pronounce them correctly. A word may be spoken carelessly in conversation but still be understood. This can cause people to spell the word as it is mispronounced. In this subskill, we will look at some common types of mispronunciation that lead to spelling errors.

One common mistake in pronunciation is to add or leave out a syllable. For example, if you pronounce <u>athlete</u> with more than two syllables, you are likely to spell it incorrectly; if you pronounce <u>privilege</u> with fewer than three syllables, you are likely to spell it incorrectly. The following words are often pronounced with an extra syllable. The trouble spots are underlined.

ath<u>l</u>ete   hind<u>r</u>ance   disas<u>tr</u>ous

The following words are often pronounced with too few syllables:

lit<u>e</u>rature	vet<u>e</u>ran	min<u>i</u>ature
aux<u>i</u>liary	med<u>ie</u>val	accompan<u>i</u>ment
main<u>te</u>nance	priv<u>i</u>lege	temp<u>er</u>ature
envir<u>o</u>nment	diff<u>e</u>rent	des<u>pe</u>rate
represent<u>a</u>tive	sep<u>a</u>rate	mem<u>o</u>ry

A second common mistake is to add or leave out a letter. In the following words, the underlined letters are often trouble spots:

arc<u>t</u>ic	Feb<u>r</u>uary	govern<u>m</u>ent
quan<u>t</u>ity	drow<u>ned</u>	candi<u>d</u>ate
lab<u>o</u>ratory	choco<u>l</u>ate	Wed<u>nes</u>day
lib<u>r</u>ary	mischievous	su<u>r</u>prise

A third common mistake is to pronounce letters in the wrong sequence. Carefully pronounce each of these words as you study their spelling:

incidentally   tragedy   prejudice

adolescence   interpret   preliminary

children   relevant

Carefully pronounce each word as you review these three lists. These words are among the words that are most likely to be misspelled. You may want to write the words as you pronounce them to help you remember the spelling. If you are not sure of the correct pronunciation, consult your dictionary. Saying the words correctly will help you remember how to spell them correctly.

Exercise for Subskill 10E

Some of the following words are misspelled. Spell them correctly in the space provided. If the word is spelled correctly, write Correct in the space provided.

EXAMPLE: pervided provided

1. maintance _____
2. envirment _____
3. persentation _____
4. library _____
5. auxilary _____
6. artic _____
7. accompaniment _____
8. athelete _____
9. labratory _____
10. incidently _____
11. tradegy _____
12. relevant _____
13. representive _____
14. hinderance _____
15. choclate _____

Check your answers on page 43 in the Answer Key for Book Three. If you correctly completed all 15 items, go to Subskill 10F. If not, do the Supplemental Exercise for Subskill 10E.

Supplemental Exercise for Subskill 10E

Pronouncing words correctly can be an aid to spelling them correctly. Many errors are made because people leave out or add a syllable or letter. Other spelling mistakes occur when people pronounce letters in the wrong sequence. Being aware of the trouble spots in these words and pronouncing them correctly can help you to avoid these common errors. If you are not sure of how a word should be pronounced or spelled, consult your dictionary. Repeat the correct pronunciation of the word to yourself as you write it.

Some of the following words are misspelled. Spell them correctly in the space provided. If the word is spelled correctly, write Correct in the space provided.

EXAMPLE: Febuary   February

1.   literture   _____

2.   quanity   _____

3.   drownded   _____

4.   diffrent   _____

5.   laboratory   _____

6.   bachlor   _____

7.   vetran   _____

8.   temperture   _____

9.   childern   _____

10. interpert   _____

11. perliminary _____

12. antarctic   _____

13. canidate   _____

14. goverment   _____

15. auxiliary   _____

Check your answers on page 43 in the Answer Key for Book Three. If you correctly completed 12 of 15 items, go to Subskill 10F. If not, ask your instructor for help.

Subskill 10F: Using Memory Aids to Improve Spelling

When you complete this subskill, you will be able to use memory aids to spell words correctly.

Memory aids are techniques or "tricks" we can use to help us remember more accurately. Spelling is a matter of remembering—remembering how words are spelled correctly. One good memory aid for spelling correctly is to pretend your mind is a camera. Use it to take a photograph of the word you want to spell. You can take a photograph of a word with your mind's eye.

Close your eyes and imagine your name written on a board. Now do the same thing with a word that is less familiar to you. You may want to write it down first. Look at it carefully; notice all the letters and how they are shaped.

This "camera trick" can help you remember how to pronounce and spell the problem words you studied in Subskill 10E. It will also help you remember the problem words you will study in this subskill.

Another memory aid is to find hidden words within words, or to think of an idea or phrase that you can associate with the correct spelling of a problem word. Here are some suggestions:

There is iron in our environment.

Know and ledge are in knowledge.

There's a liar in familiar.

There's labor in a laboratory.

How can you believe a lie?

I want a piece of pie!

Which candidate did you vote for?

Do you want an explanation of our plan?

The next time you misspell a word, try to find a memory aid that will help you in the future. Here are one student's problem words, and the techniques she used to spell them correctly:

cemetery	Remember the three e's.
stationary	Means standing; remember the a.
stationery	Used to write letters; remember the e.
exhilarate	There's hi and la in exhilarate.
annihilate	Comes from the Latin word nihil, or nothing.

As the last word on her list shows, the etymology of a word (found in the dictionary) can sometimes suggest a memory aid to spell a word correctly.

Memory Aids for Words With Silent Letters

Many words in English have silent letters. If you think of the letters in these words in groups or patterns, you will be able to recognize the words more easily and spell them correctly. Some common silent letter patterns are:

- final silent e, which usually gives a long sound to the vowel that comes before the final e:

  prīme   whāle   dūne

  scēne   surprīse   brōke

- final silent n or b preceded by m:

  hymn   condemn   solemn

  climb   thumb   limb

  (These mn words often have other forms in which the n is pronounced: hymnal, condemnation, solemnity.)

- silent g after an i that is pronounced ī (long i) or ā (long a):

  resign   weigh   height

  assignment   sleigh   sleight

- silent h after x and before a vowel:

  exhibit   exhaust   exhale

- silent p before s, usually at the beginning of a word:

  psychology   psychic   pseudonym

  psalm

- silent l after a and before k or m:

  psalm   calm   palm

  talk   walk   stalk

- silent h after c, a combination pronounced k (hard k sound):

  psychology   psychotherapy   psychiatry

- silent t after s:

  hasten   fasten   wrestle

- silent w before r at the beginning of a word:

  wreck   wretched   wrist

Memory Aids for Words With Double Letters

The "camera trick" you have learned about in this subskill may be the best help for remembering the spelling of some of these words. Many double-letter words, though, are formed by combining two words into a compound word, in which the last letter of the first word is the same as the first letter of the last word. Look at these compound words:

$$\text{bath} + \text{house} = \text{bat}\underline{\text{hh}}\text{ouse}$$

$$\text{with} + \text{hold} = \text{wit}\underline{\text{hh}}\text{old}$$

For these words, it's simple enough to remember the spelling of the original words themselves.

Often the original words have double letters. The resulting compound word will then have two, or sometimes three, sets of double letters:

$$\text{room} + \text{mate} = \underline{\text{roo}}\text{mmate}$$

$$\text{book} + \text{keeper} = \underline{\text{boo}}\text{kkeeper}$$

As you may imagine, there are a few exceptions:

$$\text{eight} + \text{teen} = \text{eighteen}$$

$$\text{where} + \text{ever} = \text{wherever}$$

Other words have one, two, or three sets of double letters, but they are not compound words. It may help you remember how to spell these words by grouping them according to the number of double-letter sets in them:

1 set of double letters	2 sets of double letters	3 sets of double letters
o<u>cc</u>asional	aggre<u>ss</u>ive	co<u>mmitt</u>ee
para<u>ll</u>el	a<u>cc</u>o<u>mm</u>odate	Mi<u>ss</u>i<u>ss</u>i<u>pp</u>i
disa<u>pp</u>oint	po<u>ss</u>e<u>ss</u>ion	
nece<u>ss</u>ary		

You can use the memory aids suggested in this subskill and invent some new ones of your own. The most important property of a memory aid is its ability to remind you of the correct spelling. Here's a chance for you to practice thinking up memory aids that will help you spell correctly. Write a memory aid for three of the following words. Use the ideas in this subskill or some new ones of your own.

twelfth _____

carburetor _____

yacht _____

awkward _____

amateur _____

license _____

Keep a list of words you misspell. Check the dictionary to be sure you know how to pronounce and spell each word on your list correctly. Then write some technique that will be a memory aid for you next to each word.

Exercise for Subskill 10F

Part A. Each word below has a silent letter. Next to each word, write another word with a silent letter in the same pattern.

EXAMPLE: limb __thumb__

1. wrack _____

2. pseudoscience _____

3. plight _____

4. autumn _____

5. price _____

6. exhilarate _____

7. chalk _____

8. whistle _____

Part B. Look again at the memory aids listed on pages 286–289. For each of the following words, a memory aid has been described in this subskill. Next to each word, write that memory aid or any other one that can help you remember how to spell the word.

EXAMPLE: sleigh __silent g after long vowel group of words__

 9. familiar _____

10. piece _____

11. explanation _____

12. cemetery _____

13. bookkeeper _____

14. solemn _____

15. exhibit _____

Have your instructor check your answers. Some possible answers are shown on page 43 in the Answer Key for Book Three, but other answers may be correct as well. If you correctly answered all 15 items, go to the Self-Check. If not, do the Supplemental Exercise for Subskill 10F.

Supplemental Exercise for Subskill 10F

If you learn how to use your own memory, you will find that it can be your best help in spelling difficult words correctly. Memory aids are ways to use your memory to help spelling. Here are some reliable memory aids you can use to improve your spelling:

- Turn your memory into a camera, and "photograph" the difficult word you want to remember.

- Find hidden words within words, or a way to remember a difficult letter or letters. (<u>Know</u> and <u>ledge</u> are in <u>knowledge</u>.)

- Use word groups or patterns to remember words with silent letters.

- Remember that in compound words, the last letter of the first word and the first letter of the last word may be the same. (<u>bath</u> + <u>house</u> = <u>bathhouse</u>)

- Remember other words with double letters in groups, according to whether they have one (<u>occasional</u>), two (<u>accommodate</u>), or three (<u>Mississippi</u>) sets of double letters.

Part A. Each word below has a silent letter. Next to each word, write another word with a silent letter in the same pattern.

EXAMPLE: sleigh   <u>reign</u>

1. trestle   _____

2. exhibit   _____

3. condemn   _____

4. psychiatrist   _____

5. wring   _____

6. space   _____

7. balm   _____

8. flight   _____

Part B. Look again at the memory aids listed on pages 286–289. For each of the following words, a memory aid has been described in this subskill. Next to each word, write that memory aid or any other one that can help you remember how to spell the word.

EXAMPLE: assign   <u>silent g after long vowel group of words</u>

9. environment   _____

10. knowledge   _____

11. stationary   _____

12. roommate   _____

13. exhale   _____

14. hymn   _____

15. candidate   _____

Have your instructor check your answers. Some possible answers are shown on pages 43 and 44 in the Answer Key for Book Three, but other answers may be correct as well. If you correctly answered 12 of 15 items, go to the Self-Check. If not, ask your instructor for help.

SELF-CHECK: SKILL UNIT 10

In each set of words, find the misspelled word, if there is one, and write it correctly in the space provided. If all words in the set are spelled correctly, write Correct in the space provided. No set has more than one misspelled word.

1. possible
   ocupant
   terrible

   _____

2. acter
   painter
   seller

   _____

3. quantity
   quality
   candidate

   _____

4. merrily
   gradually
   handyly

   _____

5. handkerchief
   height
   seive

   _____

6. illustrate
   reelect
   occult

   _____

7. irregular
   ilegible
   innumerable

   _____

8. spraying
   buding
   building

   _____

9. exit
   examination
   exibit

   _____

10. truely
    truthfully
    trustworthy

    _____

11. believable
    presidental
    forcible

    _____

12. incomplete
    completion
    completness

    _____

13. glorifyed
    marrying
    prettiness

    _____

14. advisement
    arguement
    efficient

    _____

15. employed
    buyer
    plaied

    _____

16. timeless
    timely
    timeliness

    _____

17. semiannual
    disservice
    imaterial

    _____

18. disapoint
    disagree
    disappear

    _____

19. quizzmaster
    quizzical
    quizzing

    _____

20. couragous
    imagine
    originate

    _____

21. compelled
    forgeting
    preference

    _____

22. finally
    actively
    definitelly

    _____

23. trees
    bushes
    leafs

    _____

24. conceive
    releive
    mischief

    _____

25. sopranoes
    potatoes
    tornadoes

    _____

26. Wendsday
    February
    library

    _____

27. crunches
    axs
    valleys

    _____

28. children
    fish
    mothers-in-law

    _____

29. proofs
    selfs
    scarfs

    _____

30. drive-ins
    representive
    accommodate

    _____

Check your answers on page 44 in the Answer Key for Book Three. If you correctly completed 25 of 30 items, you have shown that you have mastered these skills. If not, ask your instructor for help.

Skill Unit 11
USING FREQUENTLY CONFUSED WORDS CORRECTLY

What Skills You Need to Begin: You need to have mastered dictionary skills (Skill Unit 9) and spelling skills (Skill Unit 10).

What Skills You Will Learn: After you complete this skill unit, you will be able to spell and pronounce correctly frequently confused words and to choose the word you mean to use.

Why You Need These Skills: Many English words sound alike or almost alike, but are spelled differently and have different meanings. The words to, too, and two sound the same, for example, but are spelled differently and have different meanings. The words accept and except sound almost alike, but are also spelled differently and have different meanings. If you want to express yourself clearly, you must be able to say and write what you mean.

How You Will Show What You Have Learned: You will take the Self-Check at the end of this lesson on page 307. The Self-Check contains 20 items. If you correctly answer 16 of 20 items, you will have shown that you have mastered these skills.

If you feel that you have already mastered these skills, turn to the end of this unit and complete the Self-Check on page 307.

Subskill 11A: Identifying Possessive Pronouns and Contractions

When you complete this subskill, you will be able to distinguish between possessive pronouns and contractions.

Possessive pronouns such as his, hers, yours, its, ours, their, and whose **indicate ownership by their spelling.** They never have apostrophes.

Contractions are words formed by combining two words into one. They do have apostrophes. The apostrophe shows where one or more letters have been omitted when the two words are combined.

I am → I'm	The apostrophe takes the place of the missing a.
You are → You're	The apostrophe takes the place of the missing a.
It is → It's	The apostrophe takes the place of the missing i.
It has been → It's been	The apostrophe takes the place of the missing ha.
We are → We're They are → They're	The apostrophe takes the place of the missing a
Who is → Who's	The apostrophe takes the place of the missing i.

When you use an apostrophe with a pronoun, you are usually using a pronoun-verb combination.

To avoid confusion between possessive pronouns and contractions, substitute the missing letters in the contraction and read both words.

It's getting late.

If you substitute the missing letter, the sentence will read:

It is getting late.

Therefore, you use the apostrophe.

It's sad because its paw hurts.

If you are not sure whether or not to use an apostrophe, try adding the missing letters.

It is sad because it is paw hurts.

Now you know that the first it's is a contraction; the second its is a possessive pronoun.

Compare the following sentences:

Who's hat is this?
Whose hat is this?

The first sentence is incorrect. The apostrophe means that there has been a contraction of the words Who is. We would not say "Who is hat is this?" In the second sentence, whose is used correctly. Whose is already a possessive form, so an apostrophe is never used.

Check your ability to distinguish between possessive pronouns and contractions by completing the following exercise.

Exercise for Subskill 11A

Write the possessive pronoun or contraction needed in each of the sentences on page 296.

EXAMPLE: (Who's) coming to our house for the holidays?

1. I think (the_____) house is beautiful.

2. (Wh_____) paper is this?

3. She lost (h_____) gloves.

4. Where do you think (you_____) going?

5. (The_____) late again.

6. (It_____) (you_____) turn to do the dishes.

7. (Who_____) going on the trip to Mexico?

8. We took (h_____) car instead of ours.

9. What did you do with (you_____) homework?

10. I hope (it_____) been a nice day.

Check your answers on page 44 in the Answer Key for Book Three. If you correctly answered all 10 items, go to Subskill 11B. If not, do the Supplemental Exercise for Subskill 11A.

Supplemental Exercise for Subskill 11A

You can shorten words by combining them. When you combine words, an apostrophe is substituted for the missing letters. These combined words are called contractions.

who + is → who's

Some contractions sound like possessive forms. When you use contractions in written sentences, you must distinguish them from possessive pronouns that are pronounced in the same way. If you are not sure which form is correct, try adding the missing letters.

Who's (who is) the new secretary?

Now do this exercise.

Write the correct possessive pronoun or contraction needed in each of the following sentences.

EXAMPLE: The land is (theirs).

1. The bird had finished building (it_____) nest.

2. The police officer said that (it_____) five miles to the nearest gas station.

3. (It_____) a marvelous idea!

4. Has the jury reached (it_____) verdict?

5. (Th_____) constantly arguing about money.

6. The children took (th_____) toys to grandmother's house.

7. (Th_____) to be married this summer.

8. (Wh_____) responsible for the bill?

9. Do you know (wh_____) suitcase this is?

10. The person (wh_____) car is parked by the fire hydrant is getting a ticket.

Check your answers on pages 44 and 45 in the Answer Key to Book Three. If you correctly completed 8 of 10 items, go to Subskill 11B. If not, ask your instructor for help.

Subskill 11B: Distinguishing Meanings of Common Homonyms

When you complete this subskill, you will be able to distinguish between the different meanings and spellings of common homonyms.

Homonyms are words that sound alike when pronounced but have different spellings and meanings. When you speak, an error in the use of a homonym would not be noticed. But when you write, homonyms can cause spelling and usage problems.

Study the following sets of homonyms carefully, noting the meaning and spelling of each word. Consult a dictionary for additional or more detailed definitions.

aisle: passageway
isle: island

allowed: permitted
aloud: spoken with a normal voice

all ready: everyone prepared
already: at or before this time

ascent: going up; slope
assent: agree

band: something that ties together; group of musicians; group of
people joined for common purpose
banned: forbidden

blew: past tense of blow
blue: color

capital: most important, first rate; chief city or town; money used
in business
Capitol: building

coarse: rough
course: part of a meal; place for game or games; a group or series
of studies

complement: something added to complete a whole
compliment: something said in admiration, praise or flattery

dear: beloved, highly thought of
deer: wild animal

desert: abandon
dessert: last course of dinner

die: lose one's life
dye: color

find: discover
fined: penalized

for: preposition
fore: in or at the front
four: two plus two

groan: moan
grown: past participle of grow

guessed: past tense of guess
guest: visitor

hall: passageway
haul: pull

hear: listen
here: in this place

heard: past tense of hear
herd: group

hoarse: having a rough voice
horse: animal

hole: cavity
whole: entire

knew: past tense of know
new: not old

know: understand
no: negative

lead: heavy metal
led: past tense of <u>lead</u>

loan: thing lent
lone: single

meat: flesh
meet: come together

one: a single unit
won: past tense of <u>win</u>

passed: past tense of <u>pass</u>
past: time gone by

principal: head of school; chief; main
principle: fundamental rule or truth

right: proper; opposite of left
rite: ceremony
write: to draw letters and words on paper

road: highway
rode: past tense of <u>ride</u>
rowed: past tense of <u>row</u>

sea: ocean
see: observe

stationary: fixed
stationery: writing paper

there: place
their: possessive pronoun
they're: contraction of <u>they</u> + <u>are</u>

threw: past tense of <u>throw</u>
through: from end to end

to: in the direction of
too: also; very
two: number

weather: condition of the atmosphere
whether: an expression of choice; if

who's: contraction of <u>who</u> + <u>is</u>
whose: possessive pronoun

wood: timber
would: past tense of <u>will</u>

Check your understanding of the meanings and spellings of common homonyms by doing the following exercise.

Exercise for Subskill 11B

Part A. Write the correct homonym(s) to complete each of the following sentences.

EXAMPLE: Put the plate over (th__ere__).

1. Bismarck is the (capit_____) of North Dakota.

2. He was (t_____) tired to go to the meeting last night.

3. Talking is not (al_____) during classes.

4. The bride walked down the (_____sle) next to her father.

5. After the ceremony she (thr_____) her bouquet of flowers to her friend.

Part B.   Give a verb homonym for each noun that is listed. Then compose two sentences. In the first sentence, use the noun form of the homonym. In the second sentence, use the verb form.

EXAMPLE:

Noun	Verb
cell	sell

The cancerous <u>cell</u> growth was rapid.

Walter wants to <u>sell</u> his motorcycle.

6. weight   _____

    _____

    _____

7. road   _____

    _____

    _____

8. maid   _____

    _____

    _____

9. steel   _____

    _____

    _____

10. deer _____

_____

_____

Part C. Match each form of the homonym in Column A to the meaning that best fits it in Column B. Write the letter for the meaning of each homonym on the line next to it. Use your dictionary if necessary to make sure of the meaning of a word.

Column A   Column B

EXAMPLE: time   _g_   a. to implore

thyme   _c_   b. a rush of power

11. serial   _____   c. an herbal plant used to season food

12. cereal   _____   d. strap used to control a horse

13. pray   _____   e. a story given in successive parts

14. prey   _____   f. a grain used for food

15. wail   _____   g. every moment there is

16. whale   _____   h. an animal hunted for food by
                                  another animal

17. reign   _____   i. royal power

18. rein   _____   j. to make long, loud, sad cries

19. surge   _____   k. warmblooded fishlike mammal

20. serge   _____   l. a strong twilled fabric

Check your answers to Part A and Part C on page 45 of the Answer Key for Book Three. Ask your instructor to evaluate your sentences in Part B. If you correctly completed 16 of 20 items, go to Subskill 11C. If not, complete the Supplemental Exercise for Subskill 11B.

Supplemental Exercise for Subskill 11B

Homonyms are words that sound the same but whose meanings and spellings are different. Study the list of homonyms on pages 297–299. Then do this exercise.

Part A. Write the correct homonyms to complete each of the following sentences.

EXAMPLE: I (wo __ul__ d) love to go with you.

1. The main (co_____rse) was baked chicken.

2. I would like to know (w_____ther) you are coming or not.

3. What are the (princip_____) parts of the verb speak?

4. Did you hear him (compl_____ment) me?

5. Save me your (des_____rt).

Part B. Give an adjective homonym for each noun that is listed. Then compose two sentences. In the first sentence, use the noun form of the homonym. In the second sentence, use the adjective form.

EXAMPLE:

Noun	**Adjective**
mane	main

The horse's mane was plaited.
The main event was a dance contest.

6. reel _____

_____

_____

7. rite _____

_____

_____

8. hole _____

_____

_____

9. plane _____

_____

_____

10. pear _____

_____

_____

Part C. Match each form of the homonym in Column A to the meaning that best fits it in Column B. Write the letter for the meaning of each homonym on the line next to it. Use your dictionary if necessary to make sure of the meaning of a word.

Column A		Column B
pail	_h_	a. an opening in a fence or wall
pale	_j_	b. to invert stitches in knitting
11. sensor	_____	c. a body of people associated in some work
12. censor	_____	d. for or about a navy
13. pearl	_____	e. device to detect and record physical phenomena
14. purl	_____	f. to prohibit the use of something
15. naval	_____	g. the central part of anything
16. navel	_____	h. container for liquids
17. gait	_____	i. a smooth, hard gem found in oysters
18. gate	_____	j. colorless, whitish complexion
19. corps	_____	k. manner of walking or running
20. core	_____	l. small depression in abdomen

Check your answers to Part A and Part C on page 45 in the Answer Key for Book Three. Ask your instructor to evaluate your sentences in Part B. If you correctly completed 16 of 20 items, go to Subskill 11C. If not, ask your instructor for help.

Subskill 11C: Learning the Differences Between Words That Are Often Confused

When you complete this subskill you will be able to use correctly common problem words whose spellings and pronunciations are similar but not quite the same, and whose meanings are different.

The pairs of words listed on the following pages are often confused even though they are pronounced and spelled differently and have different meanings. If you pronounce them carefully you will be more likely to use and spell them correctly.

accept: to take
except: left out

advice: opinion
advise: to give advice

affect: to influence
effect: a result

among: in a group of several (three or more)
between: in or connected to two items or people

breathe: (verb) to draw air into the lungs
breath: (noun) air drawn into the lungs

bring: to carry something from another place to "here"
take: to carry something from "here" to another place

choose: (present tense) to select
chose: (past tense) selected

clothes: wearing apparel
cloths: pieces of material

conscience: ideas and feelings within a person
conscious: being aware, able to feel

continually: repeated, interrupted action
continuously: uninterrupted action

credible: believable
credulous: believing even unlikely things

eligible: properly qualified
illegible: impossible to read

emigrate: to leave one's country to settle in another
immigrate: to come into a foreign country to live

human: having the form or qualities of a person; a human being
humane: merciful

idea: a thought or opinion
ideal: a standard of perfection or excellence

later: comparative form of late
latter: the second of the two

legislator: a member of a legislative body
legislature: a group of persons that has been granted the authority to make laws

loose: not close together
lose: suffer a loss

moral: good in character
morale: mental condition; spirit

persecute: oppress; harass
prosecute: bring before a court of law

personal: individual
personnel: people employed in the same place

precede: go before
proceed: more forward

quit: stop
quiet: silent
quite: very; completely

respectfully: with respect
respectively: referring back to several things in the order in which
they were mentioned

stature: height
statue: image of a person or animal

than: in comparison with
then: at that time

Study the words on the above list carefully. Then check your ability
to use these words by doing the following exercise.

Exercise for Subskill 11C

Underline the correct words to use in each of the following sentences.

EXAMPLE: What (effect, affect) will the rain have?

1. Maria (chose, choose) her furniture last June.

2. The graduation speaker will (advise, advice) you.

3. The singer said his father was (quite, quiet) a man.

4. The i (proceeds, precedes) the e in the word niece.

5. The librarian asked us to be (quite, quiet).

6. Mr. Stevens works in the (personal, personnel) office.

7. I don't like to carry (lose, loose) change.

8. The tree was higher than the (stature, statue).

9. Anne Frank was (prosecuted, persecuted).

10. The committee had to (chose, choose) a new president.

11. Do your students (continuously, continually) interrupt you.

12. I am (illegible, eligible) for a tax rebate.

Check your answers on page 45 in the Answer Key for Book Three. If you correctly completed all 12 items, go to the Self-Check. If not, complete the Supplemental Exercise for Subskill 11C.

Supplemental Exercise for Subskill 11C

Study the list of word groups that are often confused on pages 304 and 305. Note that the words in each group are pronounced differently, spelled differently, and have different meanings. Then do the following exercise.

Underline the correct word to use in each of the following sentences.

EXAMPLE: Pat had a wonderful (idea, ideal) for the party.

1. Dentists and construction workers fill (holes, wholes).

2. After the wreck, the driver's (moral, morale) was low.

3. Last night we (choose, chose) to go to the movie.

4. The (human, humane) shelter provided homes and care for the abandoned puppies.

5. Mr. Anderson's house is bigger (than, then) mine.

6. The report was far from (credible, credulous).

7. Nick believes everything because he is (credible, credulous).

8. My box of new (stationery, stationary) is here.

9. Leave your umbrella in the (haul, hall).

10. In order to be (eligible, illegible) to vote, you must be registered.

11. Once the light turns green, you may (precede, proceed).

12. My mother is (quit, quiet, quite) beautiful.

Check your answers on pages 45 and 46. If you correctly answered 10 of 12 items, go to the Self-Check. If not, ask your instructor for help.

SELF-CHECK: SKILL UNIT 11

Read each group of sentences. One of the four underlined words in each group is incorrect. Circle the letter of the sentence which contains the incorrect word. Rewrite the sentence on the line provided substituting the correct word to complete the sentence.

EXAMPLE: a.   That report is on file in the personnel department.
            ⓑ.   She was so private a person, she was nicknamed the "Loan Ranger."
            c.   The herd of cattle stampeded.
            d.   What was your lucky find?

            She was so private a person, she was nicknamed the "Lone Ranger."

1.   a.   I have to leave early.
    b.   You're a good student.
    c.   The compliment of 30° is 60°.
    d.   The principal parts of the verb are listed in the dictionary.

_____

2.   a.   Smoking is not aloud.
    b.   Don't use coarse language.
    c.   I didn't order dessert.
    d.   Frank Clark was a member of the state legislature for many years.

_____

3.   a.   This truck is for military personal.
    b.   Mike was called to the principal's office.
    c.   I was going fifty miles an hour when the truck passed me.
    d.   The library is a quiet place to study.

_____

4.   a.   They're going with us.
    b.   John is older then Mike.
    c.   Harrisburg is the capital of Pennsylvania.
    d.   The management is not responsible for personal property.

_____

5. a. Dogs are not permitted to run <u>loose</u> in the park.
    b. The <u>morale</u> of the team was high.
    c. They <u>immigrated</u> from Poland in 1938.
    d. After I finish, you may <u>proceed</u>.

    _____

6. a. His handwriting is not <u>eligible</u>.
    b. The queen's <u>reign</u> was sixty years.
    c. The children toured a <u>dairy</u>.
    d. He is the state <u>legislator</u> from District Ten.

    _____

7. a. Personification gives <u>human</u> qualities to animals, objects, and ideas.
    b. What did the doctor <u>advice</u> you to do?
    c. The inscription was <u>illegible</u>.
    d. I cannot <u>accept</u> the invitation.

    _____

8. a. I ordered <u>steak</u>, not catfish.
    b. I would like to know <u>weather</u> you are going.
    c. His performance was <u>affected</u> by the rain.
    d. He was a man of <u>principle</u>.

    _____

9. a. Tommie likes camping, <u>too</u>.
    b. The wash tubs are <u>stationery</u>.
    c. The stars have <u>shone</u> brightly.
    d. Did the speaker <u>cite</u> Emerson or Thoreau?

    _____

10. a. Learn from your <u>past</u> mistakes.
    b. Jane wrote an <u>advice</u> column.
    c. Meet me at the <u>statue</u>.
    d. I wonder <u>whose</u> been invited?

    _____

11. a. The state <u>legislator</u> will convene in January.
     b. Put the <u>clothes</u> in the washing machine.
     c. The <u>personnel</u> office is closed on Mondays.
     d. It's best to <u>proceed</u> slowly.

12. a. Does this medication have any side <u>affects</u>?
     b. The case will not be <u>prosecuted</u>.
     c. The parade was postponed because of adverse <u>weather</u>.
     d. Because of his <u>humane</u> nature, the man could not dispose of the puppies.

13. a. The obstacle <u>course</u> was completed yesterday.
     b. Jane received many <u>complements</u> on her new dress.
     c. The puppy dug a <u>hole</u> in the garden.
     d. My cousin plans to <u>immigrate</u> next year.

14. a. Whose <u>cloths</u> are in the closet?
     b. My son is <u>eligible</u> to vote.
     c. Please <u>accept</u> my thanks.
     d. The test was <u>quite</u> difficult.

15. a. I have been extremely busy the <u>past</u> few weeks.
     b. The lawyer will <u>advise</u> you.
     c. Alcohol has an <u>affect</u> on reaction time.
     d. We toured the <u>capitol</u> building.

16. a. Sam won <u>fourth</u> prize in the essay contest.
     b. The gears are <u>loose</u>.
     c. The baby's <u>breath</u> is sweet.
     d. Everyone came <u>accept</u> Paul.

17. a. He <u>deserted</u> his family.
     b. <u>Breathe</u> deeply when you are cold.
     c. Read the letter in the <u>Personal</u> Column.
     d. Mark is an <u>illegible</u> bachelor.

18. a. Since John wanted the former, I took the <u>latter</u>.
     b. You <u>guest</u> wrong!
     c. The company has personalized <u>stationery</u>.
     d. Who <u>heard</u> the siren?

19. a. Time <u>past</u> slowly.
     b. Who <u>won</u> the game?
     c. The driver was <u>fined</u> ten dollars.
     d. The <u>principal</u> led students out during the fire drill.

20. a. The new machine in the hospital helps some people <u>breath</u>.
     b. Two pictures are out on <u>loan</u>.
     c. Review the <u>preceding</u> questions.
     d. We're spending a week near the <u>sea</u>.

Check your answers on pages 46–48 of the Answer Key for Book Three. If you correctly answered 16 of 20 items, you have demonstrated mastery. If not, ask your instructor for help. At the end of the book is a Posttest that can indicate which topics from all the Skill Units you might need to review.

Posttest

WRITING SKILLS

The following test will help you find out how much you have learned about writing skills. The test will also help you to see which English skills you need to review.

The test is divided into eleven parts, one part for each unit in the book. You may want to take the test all at once or one unit at a time, depending on what you and your instructor decide. When you complete the test, check your answers starting on page 48 in the Answer Key for Book Three. Then turn to the Skills Correlation Chart on pages 336 and 337 in this book and circle the number of any questions you missed. The chart will show you which parts of this book covered the English skills that gave you the most trouble. You should review the parts that match the questions you missed.

Skill Unit 1:   Writing Simple Sentences

Part A.   Read sentences 1–5 and do the following:
· Circle the simple subject.
· Circle the verb.
· On the space provided after the sentence, tell whether the underlined word is an object, a predicate nominative, or a modifier.
Review your work to be sure you have completed each step.

EXAMPLE: My three adventuresome (cousins) (found) a place to live. _____ **object** _____

1.   The staff gave <u>Thomas</u> a surprise birthday party. _____

2.   I felt <u>uneasy</u> about the decision. _____

3.   Marilyn and Chris finished the report on <u>time</u>. _____

4.   Pete is the best <u>worker</u> in the factory. _____

5.   Margaret told me the whole, <u>sad</u> story. _____

Part B.   Underline the verbal or verbal phrase in each of the following sentences. Then identify what kind of verbal is being used by writing <u>participle</u>, <u>gerund</u>, or <u>infinitive</u> in the blank provided.

EXAMPLE: The **running** team is getting ready for the race. _____ **participle** _____

6.   A registered letter is being sent to your house. _____

311

7. The only solution was to drive an extra fifty miles. _____

8. She likes jogging in the park. _____

9. Bernice hates fried eggs for breakfast. _____

10. When are you going to be back from vacation? _____

Part C. Underline the verb in parentheses that agrees in number with the subject.

EXAMPLE: Most of the staff members (has, **have**) read the memo.

11. My pants (is, are) made from brushed cotton.

12. Each of the members (has, have) a task to complete before the next meeting.

13. The team (practice, practices) every day.

14. Measles (is, are) a childhood disease.

15. This sheep (has, have) wandered away from the rest of the flock.

Part D. For each sentence, circle the subject and underline the verb in parentheses that agrees in number with the subject.

EXAMPLE: (Erica or her sisters) (has, **have**) the key.

16. Alone on the road (was, were) a boy and his dog.

17. The boy next to the pinball machines (has, have) been here all day.

18. There (is, are) still many apples left in the basket.

19. Cookies and a cake (was, were) all the refreshments at the birthday party.

20. Where (has, have) Penny and Alice put the newspapers?

Skill Unit 2:   Writing Compound Sentences

Part A. Read each of the compound sentences on the following page and perform the following steps:
- Write S1 and S2 over the first and second subjects, respectively.
- Underline the verbs and/or verb phrases and write V1 and V2 over them.
- Circle the connective and write C over it.

Review your work to be sure that you have completed each step.

EXAMPLE: Martin **was wearing** a new suit, (and) he **looked** great.

1. The show would begin at 6:30; therefore, they had little time for dinner.

2. Kevin took the subway; Maria walked.

3. Brenda had enjoyed the party; however, she was glad to be home.

4. Carl doesn't know anything about cars; nevertheless, he tried to fix his car.

5. Murray took a different route home, for he wanted to avoid Frank.

Part B. Some of the following sentences are compound sentences, and some are not. Read the sentences and do these steps:
- Rewrite the sentences in the spaces provided, adding commas or semicolons where they are needed; and
- If a sentence does not need any additional punctuation, write no punctuation change on the space provided instead of rewriting the sentence.

EXAMPLE: Jenny had bought a new kite and she was hoping to fly it that weekend.
Jenny had bought a new kite, and she was hoping to fly it that weekend.

6. Wilma had had a long summer so she welcomed the return of winter.

_____

_____

7. George had a sore throat nevertheless he went to work.

_____

_____

8. Paul and his friends went to see the car show.

_____

_____

9. Sheila was late nonetheless she stopped for a cup of coffee.

_____

_____

10. Andy had some money but he wanted to save it for the weekend.

_____

_____

Part C. Correct the following run-on sentences using the conjunction or conjunctive adverb provided in parentheses.

EXAMPLE: Jennifer just got a raise, now she can afford to eat out when she wants. (therefore)

Jennifer just got a raise; therefore, now she can afford to eat out when she wants.

11. The meeting had lasted the entire morning, they had not made any major decisions. (but)

_____

_____

12. Gordon was confused, he thought they should turn left. (for)

_____

_____

13. It rained most of the day, they had a nice time. (nevertheless)

_____

_____

14. The temperature was rising, it was time to go in. (and)

_____

_____

15. The temperature was below zero, I had to wear a heavy coat. (therefore)

_____

_____

Skill Unit 3: Writing Complex Sentences

Part A. Read the sentences on page 315. In each sentence, underline the independent clause and put brackets around the dependent clause.

EXAMPLE: **The person [who has the most money] will have to pay.**

1. The 83rd person who buys a ticket will win a prize.

2. The comedian picked on the man who jeered at him from the front row.

3. Carla, who had been on a diet, wanted a piece of candy.

4. The employee who clocked the most overtime got the raise.

5. If you have a hard time sleeping, you should try counting sheep.

Part B.   Read each of the following sentences and do these steps:
   · Underline the correct relative pronoun from the two given in parentheses;
   · Underline the adjectival clause;
   · On the space provided, write whether the adjectival clause is restrictive (giving essential information) or non-restrictive (adding extra information); and
   · Add commas where necessary.
Review your work to be sure you have completed each step.

EXAMPLES: The car   (that, which)   has Florida plates is mine.   **restrictive**
   Your car,   (which, that)   needs a tune-up by the way, is parked out back.   **nonrestrictive**

6. The man   (who, that)   is wearing a white coat will be helping you.   _____

7. The job belongs to the person   (who's, whose)   name is called.   _____

8. This record player   (which, that)   is the best available still doesn't play loud enough.   _____

9. The store   (which, that)   always had soda, unfortunately, was closed.   _____

10. The people   (that, who)   really care about Christmas start buying gifts in August.   _____

Part C.   Read the following sentences, and do these steps:
   · Put brackets around each adverbial clause;
   · Draw an arrow to the word the clause modifies; and
   · Underline the subordinating conjunction.

EXAMPLE: Paul will **leave [when Andy returns.]**

11. As soon as you get home, give me a call.

12. While you watch the children I'm going to run to the corner.

13. Although you have Friday off, you will find a way to complete the project on time.

14. Give me your phone number so I can call you when I'm ready.

15. I will write you as soon as I have an address.

Part D. Read the following sentences and do these steps:
- Put brackets around each noun clause; and
- From the pair of choices given in parentheses, underline the words that describe the function of the clause in the sentence.

EXAMPLE: Thelma knew [**what to do**].   (subject, **direct object**)

16.   That they showed up at all is to their credit.   (direct object, subject)

17.   Whoever left this package here will be sorry.   (subject, predicate noun)

18.   I asked him whether he liked the movie.   (direct object, predicate noun)

19.   Ask whomever you like.   (object of a preposition, direct object)

20.   Jake doesn't know where his books are.   (direct object, indirect object)

Skill Unit 4:   Using Sentence Punctuation

Part A.   Put the correct punctuation at the end of each of the following sentences.

EXAMPLE: Full speed ahead!

1.   How old are you

2.   My, what a gorgeous morning

3.   Please be seated

4.   Not on your life

5.   Why are you laughing

Part B.   Punctuate each of the following sentences by adding any necessary commas. If the sentence is correct as written, write C in the space provided.

EXAMPLE: Janet Henderson my new neighbor gave me a ride.
_____

Janet Henderson, my new neighbor, gave me a ride.
_____

6.   Bill as many of you know will be retiring soon.   _____

7.   Turn at the next light Dad.   _____

8.   My husband Chris works nearby.   _____

9.   My new address is 1505 Walnut St. Springfield Connecticut.
_____

10.   Santa Claus has a white fluffy beard.   _____

Part C. Read each of the following sentences. For each underlined phrase, use the space provided to write a phrase that uses an apostrophe and has the same meaning.

EXAMPLE: I wish I had the luck of Peter Jones. **Peter Jones's luck**

11. <u>You are</u> the first person I called. _____

12. This is <u>the car that belongs to them</u>. _____

13. <u>It is</u> a long story. _____

14. I came at <u>the invitation of my boss</u>. _____

15. He has <u>the good looks of his sisters</u>. _____

Part D. Rewrite each of the following sentences in the spaces provided, using commas, periods, quotation marks, exclamation points, and capital letters where they belong.

EXAMPLE: lauren said molly please let me know when you arrive
"Lauren," said Molly, "please let me know when you arrive."

16. did you ever find your wallet again asked martin

_____

17. luckily said miguel it was returned with my driver's license still in it

_____

18. the man nudged his son and told him to say how do you do

_____

19. where in the world margaret said angrily have you been

_____

20. hurry up eileen exclaimed

_____

Skill Unit 5: Using More Sentence Punctuation

Part A. Rewrite the following sentences if necessary, adding any needed semicolons. In some cases, you will change commas to semicolons. If the sentence is correct, write a C in the space provided.

EXAMPLE: Sue already had a driver's license, however, she had to reapply for a license when she moved.
<u>Sue already had a driver's license; however, she had to reapply for a license when she moved.</u>

1. I thought the food was mediocre at that restaurant, and, as a matter of fact, the service was not very good, either.

2. The trip took them through Boston, Massachusetts, Albany, New York, and Scranton, Pennsylvania.

3. Once they had agreed on a price, the tension between them disappeared.

4. Terry's car was in the parking lot, Martha's was in the street.

5. Tony had finished eating, therefore he was full.

Part B. Following are 5 sentences. In some sentences, the colon is used correctly; in others it is used incorrectly. Put a C in the space provided next to each sentence that is correctly punctuated. Put I in the space provided next to the sentence that is incorrectly punctuated.

EXAMPLE: The only way out was: down the fire escape. __I__
               Helen likes two flavors of ice cream: vanilla and strawberry. __C__

6. The keys to success are: motivation and perseverance. _____

7. Dear Mr. Stevens:
     I am writing to offer . . . _____

8. Maria understood: the same thing had happened to her. _____

9. These are games for a rainy day: checkers, solitaire, and gin rummy. _____

10. Beware: of the bumps. _____

Part C. Rewrite each of the following sentences in the spaces provided, using dashes or parentheses where needed.

EXAMPLE: Robert eyed the pastries hungrily he hadn't eaten all day.
Robert eyed the pastries hungrily (he hadn't eaten all day).

11. Cool colors such as blue, green, and lavender are best for the reading room.

_____

_____

12. I'm surprised by your reaction I thought you would understand.

_____

_____

13. After a brief delay perhaps 15 minutes the demonstration began.

_____

_____

14. Eat well every day or pay the consequences.

_____

_____

15. Janet would be leaving soon for Ottawa the capital of Canada.

_____

_____

Skill Unit 6:   Using Modifiers in Sentences

Part A. Rewrite the following sentences so that the adjectives and adverbs in parentheses clearly modify the underlined words.

EXAMPLE: When George <u>got</u> home, they sat down to supper. (finally)
<u>When George finally got home, they sat down to supper.</u>

1. Marcia got rid of her <u>sweaters</u> when she packed. (frayed)

_____

2. <u>Jean</u>, who emigrated from Haiti, spoke French. (only)

_____

3. She <u>starts</u> the coffee at the diner on Sundays. (always)

  _____

4. The boys felt ashamed and <u>embarrassed</u>. (very)

  _____

Part B. The following sentences are unclear or confusing due to mis-placed phrase modifiers. Rewrite each sentence to make it clear; you may add or change words as needed. There may be more than one way to rewrite a sentence correctly.

EXAMPLE: Burying his bone in the rose garden, Maurice finally found the dog.
<u>Maurice finally found the dog burying his bone in the rose garden.</u>

5. Jim kept dropping the tools building the bookcase.

  _____

6. The recipe was easy for Florence to follow in the cookbook.

  _____

7. Joaquin waved to his brother on his way to work. (The brother is going to work.)

  _____

8. The girls smiled at the usher entering the theatre. (The girls are going in.)

  _____

Part C. The following sentences are unclear due to misplaced adjective clauses. Rewrite the sentences so that they are clear. There may be more than one way to rewrite a sentence.

EXAMPLE: The tires are still getting bald that I rotated.
<u>The tires that I rotated are still getting bald.</u>

9. She insisted on wearing shoes on her feet that were too small.

  _____

10. Hank stuffed the papers into his pocket that he needed for the meeting.

  _____

11. He was here to discuss the new policy for a few minutes that he had developed.

_____

12. He picked up the record from the floor that I had just bought.

_____

Part D.   Some of the following sentences contain dangling modifiers. If a sentence contains a dangling modifier, rewrite it. If a sentence is correct, write <u>Correct</u> in the space provided. Note that there are many possible ways to rewrite these sentences.

EXAMPLE: Riding on the expressway, the map was hard to read.
<u>Riding on the expressway, I found the map hard to read.</u>

13. To get the best results, the chicken should cook for an hour.

_____

14. Working late, I wondered if the stores were still open.

_____

15. Listening to the radio, the weather report came on.

_____

16. Going to the park, the thermos fell and broke.

_____

Skill Unit 7:   Writing Effective Sentences

Part A.   Each of the following sets of sentences includes two sentences with incorrect parallel structure and one correct sentence. For each set, decide which sentence is correct and write <u>C</u> in the space provided.

EXAMPLE: Reading books is more relaxing than squash.   _____
Reading books is more relaxing than playing squash.
<u>C</u>
To read books is more relaxing than playing squash.
_____

1. Kevin likes to meet new people and making friends.   _____

Kevin likes meeting new people and making friends.   _____

Kevin likes meeting new people and to make friends.   _____

2. During a snowstorm, warm clothes and hot soup are welcome. _____

During a snowstorm, warm clothes*and eating hot soup are welcome. _____

During a snowstorm, wearing warm clothes and hot soup are welcome. _____

3. Linda is both scholarly and an athlete. _____

Linda is both scholarly and athletic. _____

Linda is both a scholar and athletic. _____

4. Skating is as fun as to dance. _____

Skating is as fun as dancing. _____

To skate is as fun as dancing. _____

5. The application was more a challenge than threatening. _____

The application was more challenging than a threat. _____

The application was more a challenge than a threat. _____

Part B. Each of the following sets of sentences includes two sentences with incorrect or inconsistent uses of verbs and one correct sentence. For each set, decide which sentence is correct and write C after it.

EXAMPLE: Wanda had turned around and driven home. ___C___
Wanda has turned around and drove home. _____
Wanda turned around and driven home. _____

6. If Pedro had studied harder, he will pass the exam. _____

If Pedro had studied harder, he would have passed the exam. _____

If Pedro had studied harder, he passes the exam. _____

7. The magician waved her wand and "abracadabra" was said. _____

The wand was waved by the magician and she said "abracadabra." _____

The magician waved her wand and said "abracadabra." _____

8. While Kurt was talking to his mother, Juanita called a friend. _____

While Kurt was talking to his mother, Juanita had called a friend. _____

While Kurt was talking to his mother, Juanita calls a friend. _____

9. The installation was checked and approved by the inspector.
_____

The installation was checked and the inspector approved it.
_____

The inspector checked the installation and it was approved by him. _____

10. Margot could tell that Larry hadn't prepared for the meeting.
_____

Margot could tell that Larry hasn't prepared for the meeting.
_____

Margot could tell that Larry will not prepare for the meeting.
_____

Part C. Read each of the following pairs of sentences. Decide which sentence shows correct pronoun reference and agreement, and put a C in the space provided.

EXAMPLE: Everyone could remember their code. _____
Everyone could remember his or her code. __C__

11. Enrico's mother, who is wearing the blue dress, is scolding him.
_____

Enrico's mother is scolding him, who is wearing the blue dress.
_____

12. Somebody lost their hat. _____
Somebody lost his or her hat. _____

13. Each of my uncles has his favorite restaurant. _____
Each of my uncles has their favorite restaurant. _____

14. Gwen wore her old coat to the church bazaar, which has holes in the pockets. _____
Gwen wore her old coat, which has holes in the pockets, to the church bazaar. _____

15. Melinda told Alicia she needed a new place to live. _____
Melinda needed a new place to live, and she told Alicia. _____

Part D. The following sets of sentences contain sentences that are complete and sentences that are sentence fragments. Put a C next to sentences that are complete.

EXAMPLE: The clock, which was losing three minutes every day, needed to be replaced. However, the historic society wanted it. To be repaired. _____
The clock, which was losing three minutes every day, needed to be replaced. However, the historic society wanted it to be repaired. __C__
The clock, which was losing three minutes every day. Needed to be replaced. However, the historic society wanted it to be repaired. _____

16. The horror movie came to a bloody end. After the last person had filed out of the movie theater. The usher, who had seen the movie 10 times, breathed a sigh of relief. _____

The horror movie came to a bloody end. After the last person had filed out of the movie theater, the usher, who had seen the movie 10 times, breathed a sigh of relief. _____

The horror movie came to a bloody end. After the last person had filed out. Of the movie theater. The usher, who had seen the movie 10 times. Breathed a sigh of relief. _____

17. Grandpa was in a good mood last Friday night. He told us the story about last summer's fishing trip. Giving us the latest version. _____

Grandpa was in a good mood. Last Friday night. He hold us the story about last summer's fishing trip, giving us the latest version. _____

Grandpa was in a good mood last Friday night. He told us the story about last summer's fishing trip, giving us the latest version. _____

18. Take a left at the light. Go about five miles, and take another left at the intersection. Before you get to the Post Office. _____

Take a left at the light. Go about five miles, and take another left at the intersection before you get to the Post Office. _____

Take a left. At the light. Go about five miles, and take another left at the intersection before you get to the Post Office. _____

19. Ursula was getting tired of listening to her neighbors. Fighting and carrying on every night. She knew that the time had come to look for a new apartment. _____

Ursula was getting tired of listening to her neighbors fighting and carrying on every night. She knew the time had come to look for a new apartment. _____

Ursula was getting tired. Of listening to her neighbors fighting and carrying on every night. She knew the time had come to look for a new apartment. _____

20. Joshua finally received a phone call from the manager asking him to come back to work after a long lay-off. As a result, Maria could cut back her hours at the plant. _____

Joshua finally received a phone call from the manager. Asking him to come back to work after a long lay-off. As a result, Maria could cut back her hours at the plant. _____

Joshua finally received a phone call from the manager, asking him to come back to work. After a long lay-off. As a result, Maria could cut back her hours. At the plant. _____

Skill Unit 8: Writing Unified Paragraphs

Part A. Read each of the following paragraphs. Locate the topic sentence, the sentence that sums up the details expressed by the other sentences in the paragraph. Underline the entire topic sentence. The topic sentence is not necessarily the first sentence of a paragraph.

EXAMPLE:

When a canary bathes, it first immerses itself in water. When it comes out, it spreads its wings with special muscles to expose as many feathers as possible to the air, shaking its body forcefully to expel droplets of water. After several minutes of this, the bird relaxes its wings and begins a tedious process of rearranging all its feathers with its beak. <u>The canary is indeed a meticulous groomer.</u> The procedure never fails to restore a silklike sheen to the bird.

1. He went on tour performing throughout Europe at age six. At age 12, he wrote two operas. He was knighted by the Pope at age 14. Wolfgang Amadeus Mozart was an established musician by the time he was a teenager.

2. The origin of the term "Adam's apple" is unknown. The Adam's apple is a projection of cartilage in the human throat that moves up and down during swallowing, especially noticeable in males. According to legend, the Adam's apple developed because a piece of forbidden apple that Eve gave to Adam stuck in his throat. In fact, however, the Biblical story of Adam and Eve never mentions apples. In this story, God warns only of the fruit of the tree in the garden, telling Adam and Eve that if they touched or ate it they would die.

3. Each year in the United States, some 1,500 children under age 5 die in automobile accidents. Thousands more suffer injuries. Many unnecessary deaths and injuries can be prevented with the correct use of car seats. In fact, most states require child safety restraints. Manufacturer's instructions for installing car seats must be followed carefully; a child using an improperly installed car seat is not much better off than a child without one.

Part B. Each of the following topic sentences is ineffective because it is either too narrow or too broad. In the space provided, write <u>TN</u> after the sentence if it is too narrow; write <u>TB</u> if it is too broad.

EXAMPLE: Beethoven composed nine symphonies. __**TB**__

4. In 1984, 136 people officially declared their candidacy for the presidency. _____

5. Although nearly half of the American astronauts who have traveled in space have suffered from motion sickness, none have discussed it in public. _____

6. Peanut butter is nutritious. _____

Part C. Read the following paragraphs and decide which two methods are used to develop the controlling idea. In the space provided, write 1 if the method of supplying relevant facts is used; 2 for the use of examples; 3 for contrasting or comparing; or 4 for supplying reasons showing cause and effect to explain the main idea.

EXAMPLE:

People have little control over what they may receive in the mail. A company or organization can send you whatever it wants. Consumers are legally protected from commercial abuses of the mail, however. For example, if you receive merchandise that you did not order, and then a bill, you do not have to pay. You do not have to return the merchandise, either. By law, this merchandise is a gift, and nothing is required from you in return.   **2, 4**

7.   Onions have been cultivated from the earliest times. The Greek historian Herodotus wrote that the Egyptians worshipped the onion. The builders of the Great Pyramid at Giza, he wrote, survived mainly on garlic and onions. In contrast, the people of ancient India hated onions and had laws against eating them in certain places. Down through the ages, the onion has played an important role in cooking. _____

8.   Scientists have ways of tracking changes in the chemical content of the air we breathe. The amount of carbon dioxide in the air has been growing rapidly. To find out how much carbon dioxide was in the air in the 1800s and even earlier, researchers from Los Alamos National Laboratory are collecting artifacts, such as telescopes and glass vials, that may have trapped ancient air in them. By determining the amount of carbon dioxide in the atmosphere at different points in history, they hope to estimate its rate of increase. _____

9.   People can get seasick at the top of a skyscraper. The top of the World Trade Center in New York, for example, can move three feet or more in a high wind. Such movement may be troubling and uncomfortable to people, but it is not a threat to the building as a whole. As architects and engineers plan taller and lighter buildings, the wind sway factor becomes a more difficult problem. _____

Part D. Each of the paragraphs on the following page contains a sentence that is irrelevant to the main idea of the paragraph. Read the paragraphs and underline the irrelevant sentences.

EXAMPLE:

Many devices have been developed to allow handicapped people to drive cars. Hearing aids are also becoming more advanced. Among the most common driving aids are hand controls, which allow the driver to accelerate and brake with one hand. The least expensive of these is the push-pull control, which makes the car accelerate when the driver pulls it and brake when the driver pushes it. The only problem with this control is that starting on a hill is difficult because the driver cannot brake and accelerate at the same time.

10. Something like acupuncture has been used on corn in the Northwest. Corn is popular at picnics. When you insert a toothpick into the ear stem of a sweet corn plant and through to the main stalk above the joint, you will make the corn mature faster and taste sweeter. The silk must still be green when you do this. The method seems to work because the plant naturally sends sugar to its wounds.

11. During the summer, the kids are out of school. There are several things you can do to keep your home cool in the summer. Keep your blinds and shades drawn when you're not home, especially those on an east or west wall. Don't cook, bathe, or do laundry during the hottest part of the day. If you have a central cooling system or an air conditioner, there is no need to leave it on when no one is home; it doesn't take long to cool a space down.

12. The mbira, or thumb piano, is an African musical instrument related to the xylophone. It is a small wooden box with a bridge nailed onto it. Tied to the bridge are several flat iron pieces that resonate when plucked with the thumbs to make a soft, melodic sound. Much African music is polyrhythmic.

Part E. Each of the following paragraphs is ineffective for two of the following reasons: (1) the topic sentence is too broad or too narrow; (2) the sentences are not arranged in a logical order; (3) the sentences do not flow smoothly for lack of transition words or appropriate repetition; and (4) there are sentences that are not related to the topic sentence, or irrelevant details are included. In the space provided, use the numbers to identify these problems.

EXAMPLE:
   Pineapples should be eaten as soon as possible after they are harvested. They do not ripen or sweeten any more after picking. Christopher Columbus brought pineapples to Europe in 1493. The best pineapples are available from March through June and have fresh, dark green leaves. If you cannot smell the fragrance of a good-looking pineapple, it is probably only because it is cold.   **1, 4**

13. Each year, England recalls Fawkes' failure to blow up Parliament in 1605. On November 5, in addition to celebrating the occasion with bell-ringing, bonfires, and parades, the English serve up a ginger cake known as parkin. The day is also known as Parkin Day in some English towns. Just as turkey goes with Thanksgiving in the United States, parkin goes with Guy Fawkes Day in England. England's parliamentary system has been in place since the 13th century. _____

14. Thousands of researchers around the world are involved in radio astronomy. Computers are being used to send systematic signals into space and to alert humans when a systematic signal comes in. Radio astronomers hope to pick up radio signals from extraterrestrial beings. The astronomers themselves used to have to sit by their machines and wait for a message from outer space. _____

15. Germs are everywhere. When you are handling food, you should take steps to cut down the numbers of "bad" bacteria you allow to come in contact with the food. You should always wash your hands before handling food. You should wash your hands after handling raw meat so that you don't transfer the germs to something else. Keep hot foods above 140 degrees Fahrenheit. Hot foods taste better when they are served piping hot. Keep cold foods refrigerated. _____

Skill Unit 9: Using the Dictionary

Part A. Alphabetize each of the following sets of words by placing 1 next to the word that should appear first in each set, 2 next to the second word, and so on.

EXAMPLE:

4	irony
3	indigo
6	irritate
2	indeed
1	idea
5	irrigate

1.
_____ flour
_____ algebra
_____ necessary
_____ relax
_____ industry
_____ often

2.
_____ shadow
_____ singer
_____ shame
_____ shin
_____ syndicate
_____ sandwich

3.
_____ translation
_____ terrible
_____ trapezoid
_____ terrain
_____ trampoline
_____ turmoil

Part B. Choose the correct phonetic spelling for each of the following words by putting a check next to your choice.

EXAMPLE: bury
  a. _____   bur′ē
  b. ✓   ber′ē

4. knowledge
  a. _____   näl′ij
  b. _____   nōl′ej

5. practice
  a. _____   prak′təs
  b. _____   prak′tis

6. reflex
  a. _____   rē′fleks
  b. _____   ri′flecks

Part C. Each of the following words is misspelled. Find the correct spelling for each word on the sample dictionary page on page 330. In the space provided, rewrite each word, showing the correct spelling and using hyphens to show syllable division.

EXAMPLE: dolerous   **do-lor-ous**

7. doller   _____

8. domestick   _____

9. dolfin   _____

Part D. Part One: For each of the following dictionary entries, use the spaces provided to write all the different forms of the word that are given. Then in parentheses write the part of speech the dictionary entry gives for each form.

EXAMPLE:

re·im·burse (rē′im burs′) *vt*. -bursed′, -burs′ing [RE- + archaic *imburse*, to pay, after Fr. *rembourser* < *re*-, again + *embourser*, to pay < *en*-, in + *bourse*, a PURSE] 1. to pay back (money spent) 2. to repay or compensate (a person) for expenses, damages, losses, etc. —*SYN.* see PAY[1] —re′im·burs′a·ble *adj.* —re′im·burse′ment *n.*

reimburse (verb)
reimbursing (verb)
reimbursed (verb)
reimbursable (adjective)
reimbursement (noun)

dole   416   **domesticity**

2. *a)* equatorial ocean regions noted for dead calms and light fluctuating winds *b)* such calms and winds

dole¹ (dōl) *n.* [ME. *dol* < OE. *dal*, a share, parallel to *dæl*: see DEAL²] **1.** a giving out of money or food to those in great need; relief **2.** that which is thus given out **3.** anything given out sparingly **4.** a form of payment by a government to the unemployed, as in England **5.** [Archaic] one's destiny or lot —*vt.* doled, dol'ing to give sparingly or as a dole (usually with *out*) —SYN. see DISTRIBUTE —**on the dole** receiving government relief funds

dole² (dōl) *n.* [see ff.] [Archaic] sorrow; dolor

dole·ful (dōl'fəl) *adj.* [ME. *dolful* < *dol*, grief (< OFr. *doel* < VL. *dolus*, grief, pain < L. *dolere*, to suffer, prob. < IE. base *del-*, *dol-*, to split, cut) + *-ful*, -FUL] full of or causing sorrow or sadness; mournful; melancholy: also [Rare] **dole'some** —SYN. see SAD —**dole'ful·ly** *adv.* —**dole'ful·ness** *n.*

dol·er·ite (däl'ə rīt') *n.* [Fr. *dolérite* < Gr. *doleros*, deceptive < *dolos*, deceit (for IE. base, see TALE): from its close resemblance to diorite] **1.** a coarse, crystalline variety of basalt **2.** loosely, diabase or any of various other igneous rocks whose composition cannot be analyzed without microscopic examination

dol·i·cho·ce·phal·ic (däl'i kō'sə fal'ik) *adj.* [< Gr. *dolichos*, LONG¹ + -CEPHALIC] having a relatively long head; having a head whose width is less than 76 percent of its length: also **dol'i·cho·ceph'a·lous** (-sef'ə ləs); see also CEPHALIC INDEX —**dol'i·cho·ceph'a·ly** (-sef'ə lē) *n.*

dol·i·cho·cra·ni·al (-krā'nē əl) *adj.* [< Gr. *dolichos*, LONG¹ + -CRANIAL] long-skulled, with a cranial index of 76 or less: also **dol'i·cho·cra'nic** (-nik) —**dol'i·cho·cra'ny** (-nē) *n.*

doll (däl) *n.* [< *Doll*, nickname for DOROTHY] **1.** a child's toy made to resemble a human being **2.** a pretty but frivolous or silly young woman **3.** a pretty child **4.** [Slang] any girl or young woman **5.** [Slang] any attractive or lovable person —*vt.*, *vi.* [Colloq.] to dress carefully and stylishly or showily (with *up*)

dol·lar (däl'ər) *n.* [LowG. & Early ModDu. *daler* < G. *thaler* (now *taler*), contr. < *Joachimsthaler*, coin made (orig. in 1519) at (St.) *Joachimstal*, Bohemia < (St.) *Joachim* + *thal*, *tal*, valley (see DALE)] ☆**1.** the monetary unit of the U.S., equal to 100 cents: symbol, $, as, $1.00 **2.** the standard monetary unit of various other countries, as of Canada, Australia, Liberia, Ethiopia, etc.: see MONETARY UNITS, table **3.** the Mexican peso **4.** any of several monetary units used only in trade, as the British Hong Kong dollar, the Straits Settlements dollar, etc. **5.** a coin or piece of paper money of the value of a dollar **6.** [Obs.] a Spanish coin (piece of eight) used in American Revolutionary times

☆**dollar diplomacy** the policy of using the economic power or influence of a government to promote in other countries the business interests of its private citizens, corporations, etc.

☆**dol·lar·fish** (-fish') *n.*, *pl.* **-fish'**, **-fish'es**: see FISH² a saltwater food fish (*Poronotus triacanthus*) with a short, compressed body and small, smooth scales, occurring along the Atlantic coast of the U.S.

☆**dollar sign, dollar mark** a symbol, $, for dollar(s)

dol·lop (däl'əp) *n.* [< ?] **1.** a soft mass or blob, as of some food; lump **2.** a small quantity of liquid; splash, jigger, dash, etc. **3.** a measure or amount [a *dollop* of wit]

dol·ly (däl'ē) *n.*, *pl.* **-lies** [dim. of DOLL] **1.** a doll: child's word **2.** a tool used to hold a rivet at one end while a head is hammered out of the other end **3.** [Dial.] a stick or board for stirring, as in laundering clothes or washing ore; dasher ☆**4.** any of several kinds of low, flat, wheeled frames for transporting heavy objects, as in a factory ☆**5.** a narrow-gauge locomotive for railroad yard work ☆**6.** *Motion Pictures & TV* a low, wheeled platform on which the camera is mounted for moving it about the set —*vi.* **-lied**, **-ly·ing** to move a dolly forward (*in*), backward (*out*), etc. in photographing or televising the action —☆*vt.* to move (a camera, load, etc.) on a dolly

Dolly Var·den (vär'd'n) [after the character in Dickens' *Barnaby Rudge*] **1.** a dress of sheer figured muslin worn over a bright-colored petticoat **2.** a woman's flower-trimmed hat with a large brim ☆**3.** a kind of red-spotted trout (*Salvelinus malma*) found in streams west of the Rocky Mountains and in E Asia

dol·man (däl'mən, dōl'-) *n.*, *pl.* **-mans** [Fr., earlier *doloman* < Turk. *dolama*, parade attire of the Janizaries] **1.** a long Turkish robe **2.** a hussar's showy, gold-braided jacket worn like a cape with the sleeves hanging free **3.** a woman's coat or wrap with dolman sleeves

dolman sleeve a kind of sleeve for a woman's coat or dress, tapering from a wide opening at the armhole to a narrow one at the wrist

dol·men (däl'mən, dōl'-) *n.* [Fr. < Bret. *taol*, table + *men*, stone] a prehistoric tomb or monument consisting of a large, flat stone laid across upright stones; cromlech

do·lo·mite (dō'lə mīt', däl'ə-) *n.* [after the Fr. geologist Déodat de *Dolomieu* (1750–1801)] **1.** a common rock-forming mineral, $CaMg(CO_3)_2$,

DOLMEN

often occurring in extensive beds **2.** any of several rocks similar to dolomite in composition

Dol·o·mites (dō'lə mīts', däl'ə-) division of the E Alps, in N Italy: highest peak, 10,965 ft.: also **Dolomite Alps**

do·lor (dō'lər) *n.* [ME. & OFr. *dolour* < L. *dolor* < *dolere*, to suffer: see DOLEFUL] [Poet.] sorrow; grief

Do·lor·es (də lôr'əs) [Sp. < *Maria de los Dolores*, lit., Mary of the sorrows] a feminine name

‡**do·lo·ro·so** (dō'lô rō'sô; E. dō'lə rō'sō) *adj.*, *adv.* [It.] *Music* with a sorrowful or plaintive quality

do·lor·ous (dō'lər əs, däl'ər-) *adj.* [OFr. *dolerous* < LL. *dolorosus*: see DOLOR] **1.** very sorrowful or sad; mournful **2.** painful —**do'lor·ous·ly** *adv.*

do·lour (dō'lər) *n. Brit. sp. of* DOLOR

dol·phin (däl'fən, dôl'-) *n.* [ME. *dolfin* < OFr. *dalphin* < VL. *dalfinus*, for L. *delphinus* < Gr. *delphinos*, gen. of *delphis*, akin to *delphys*, womb < IE. base *gwelbh-*, whence Av. *garewa*-] **1.** any of several water-dwelling mammals (family Delphinidae), with numerous teeth and often a beaklike snout, common in warm seas **2.** either of two swift marine game fishes (genus *Coryphaena*), with colors that brighten and change when the fish is taken out of the water **3.** *Naut.* a buoy or spar for mooring a boat —[D-] *Astron. same as* DELPHINUS

dolphin striker a small spar under the bowsprit of a vessel, helping to form a truss which supports the jib boom; martingale

BOTTLE-NOSED DOLPHIN (70–160 in. long)

dolt (dōlt) *n.* [prob. < ME. *dolte*, pp. of *dullen*: see DULL, *v.*] a stupid, slow-witted person; blockhead —**dolt'ish** *adj.* —**dolt'ish·ly** *adv.* —**dolt'ish·ness** *n.*

Dom (däm) *n.* [Port. < L. *dominus*, a lord, master] **1.** a title given to certain monks and clerics **2.** a title of respect formerly given to gentlemen of Brazil and Portugal: used with the given name

-dom (dəm) [ME. & OE. *dom*, state, condition, power: see DOOM¹] *a n.-forming suffix meaning:* **1.** rank or position of, domain or dominion of [*kingdom*, *earldom*] **2.** fact or state of being [*wisdom*, *martyrdom*] **3.** a total of all who are [*officialdom*]

dom. 1. domestic **2.** dominion

do·main (dō mān', də-) *n.* [ME. *domein* < MFr. *domaine* < L. *dominium*, right of ownership, dominion < *dominus*, a lord: see DOMINATE] **1.** territory under one government or ruler; dominion **2.** land belonging to one person; estate **3.** supreme ownership: see also EMINENT DOMAIN, PUBLIC DOMAIN **4.** field or sphere of activity or influence [the *domain* of science] **5.** *Math. a)* the set of those values of a variable which can be used as arguments for a given function *b)* the set of all integers, or a set of elements whose combinative properties are the same as those of the integers

do·mal (dō'm'l) *adj. same as* CACUMINAL

dome (dōm) *n.* [sense 1 < L. *domus*, house (< IE. *domu*- < base *dem*-, to build); others < Fr. *dôme* < Pr. *doma* < LL.(Ec.), roof, building, cathedral < Gr. *dōma*, housetop, house, temple < same IE. base: cf. TIMBER, DOMINATE] **1.** [Poet.] a mansion or stately building **2.** a hemispherical roof or one formed by a series of rounded arches or vaults on a round or many-sided base; cupola **3.** any dome-shaped structure or object **4.** [Slang] the head **5.** *Geol. a)* an anticlinal structure of circular or broadly elliptical form *b)* a form produced by a pair of corresponding planes parallel to one crystal axis but inclined to the other two —*vt.* domed, dom'ing **1.** to cover with or as with a dome **2.** to form into a dome —*vi.* to swell out like a dome

domes·day (dōōmz'dā', dōmz'-) *n. same as* DOOMSDAY

Domesday Book [said to be so named because it judged all men without bias, like the Last Judgment] the record of a survey of England made under William the Conqueror in 1086, listing all landowners and showing the value and extent of their holdings

do·mes·tic (də mes'tik) *adj.* [ME. < OFr. *domestique* < L. *domesticus* < *domus*: see DOME] **1.** having to do with the home or housekeeping; of the house or family [*domestic* joys] **2.** of one's own country or the country referred to [Canada's *domestic* affairs] **3.** made or produced in the home country; native [*domestic* wine] **4.** domesticated; tame: said of animals **5.** enjoying and attentive to the home and family life —*n.* **1.** a servant for the home, as a maid or cook **2.** [*pl.*] native products —**do·mes'ti·cal·ly** *adv.*

do·mes·ti·cate (də mes'tə kāt') *vt.* **-cat'ed, -cat'ing** [< ML. *domesticatus*, pp. of *domesticare*, to tame, live in a family < L. *domesticus* < *domus*: see DOME] **1.** to accustom to home life; make domestic **2.** *a)* to tame (wild animals) and breed for many purposes of man *b)* to adapt (wild plants) to home cultivation *c)* to introduce (foreign animals or plants) into another region or country; naturalize **3.** to bring (a foreign custom, word, etc.) into a region or country and make it acceptable —*vi.* to become domestic —**do·mes'ti·ca'tion** *n.*

do·mes·tic·i·ty (dō'mes tis'ə tē) *n.*, *pl.* **-ties 1.** home life; family life **2.** devotion to home and family life **3.** [*pl.*] household affairs or duties

10.

di·ver·si·fy (-fī') vt. -fied', -fy'ing [ME. *diversifien* < OFr. *diversifier* < ML. *diversificare*, to make different < L. *diversus* (see DIVERSE) + *facere*, DO¹] 1. to make diverse; give variety to; vary 2. to divide up (investments, liabilities, etc.) among different companies, securities, etc. 3. to expand (a business, line of products, etc.) by increasing the variety of things produced or of operations undertaken —*vi.* to undertake expansion of a line of products or otherwise multiply business operations —di·ver'si·fi·ca'·tion *n.*

_____

_____

_____

_____

11.

touch·y (tuch'ē) *adj.* touch'i·er, touch'i·est [TOUCH + -Y²: also (sense 1) altered < TECHY] 1. easily offended; oversensitive; irritable 2. sensitive to touch; easily irritated, as a part of the body 3. very risky [a *touchy* situation] 4. highly flammable or readily ignited —*SYN.* see IRRITABLE —touch'i·ly *adv.* —touch'i·ness *n.*

_____

_____

_____

_____

_____

12.

pur·ism (pyoor'iz'm) *n.* [Fr. *purisme* < *pur*, PURE] 1. strict observance of or insistence on precise usage or on application of formal, often pedantic rules, as in language, art, etc. 2. an instance of this —pur'ist *n.* —pu·ris'tic, pu·ris'ti·cal *adj.* —pu·ris'ti·cal·ly *adv.*

_____

_____

_____

_____

_____

Part Two: Read the four definitions in the following dictionary entry for the noun <u>plot</u>. Then read the following sentences and choose the correct definition for each sentence by writing the number of the definition in the space next to each sentence.

plot (plät) *n.* [ME. < OE., a piece of land: some meanings infl. by COMPLOT] 1. a small area of ground marked off for some special use [garden *plot*, cemetery *plot*] 2. a chart or diagram, as of a building or estate 3. a secret, usually evil, project or scheme; conspiracy 4. the plan of action of a play, novel, poem, short story, etc. —*vt.* plot'ted, plot'ting 1. *a)* to draw a plan or chart of (a ship's course, etc.) *b)* to mark the position or course of on a map 2. to make secret plans for [to *plot* someone's destruction] 3. to plan the action of (a story, etc.) 4. *Math. a)* to determine or mark the location of (a point) on a graph by means of coordinates *b)* to represent (an equation) by locating points on a graph and joining them to form a curve *c)* to draw (the curve thus determined) —*vi.* to scheme or conspire —

EXAMPLE: ___2___ The rooms seem smaller than they looked on the plot.

Den Helder   377   dentistry

Den Hel·der (dən hel′dər) seaport in NW Netherlands, on the North Sea: pop. 54,000

de·ni·a·ble (di nī′ə b′l) *adj.* that can be denied

de·ni·al (di nī′əl) *n.* 1. the act of denying; a saying "no" (to a request, etc.) 2. a statement in opposition to another; contradiction [the *denial* of a rumor] 3. the act of disowning; repudiation [the *denial* of one's family] 4. a refusal to believe or accept (a doctrine, etc.) 5. *same as* SELF-DENIAL 6. *Law* the opposing by a defendant of a claim or charge against him

de·nic·o·tin·ize (dē nik′ə ti nīz′) *vt.* -**ized**, -**iz′ing** [DE- + NICOTIN(E) + -IZE] to remove nicotine from (tobacco) —**de·nic′o·tin′i·za′tion** *n.*

de·nier[1] (də nir′; *for 2,* den′yər) *n.* [ME. *dener* < OFr. (Fr. *denier*) < L. *denarius,* DENARIUS] 1. a small, obsolete French coin of little value 2. a unit of weight for measuring the fineness of threads of silk, rayon, nylon, etc., equal to .05 gram per 450 meters

de·ni·er[2] (di nī′ər) *n.* a person who denies

den·i·grate (den′ə grāt′) *vt.* -**grat′ed**, -**grat′ing** [< L. *denigratus,* pp. of *denigrare,* to blacken < *de-,* intens. + *nigrare,* to blacken < *niger,* black] 1. to blacken 2. to disparage the character or reputation of; defame —**den′i·gra′tion** *n.* —**den′i·gra′tor** *n.* —**den′i·gra·to′ry** (-grə tôr′ē) *adj.*

den·im (den′əm) *n.* [< Fr. (*serge*) *de Nîmes,* (serge) of NÎMES, where first made] a coarse, twilled, sturdy cotton cloth used for overalls, uniforms, etc.

Den·is (den′is) [Fr. < L. *Dionysius*] 1. a masculine name 2. Saint, 3d cent. A.D.: patron saint of France: his day is Oct. 9

de·ni·trate (dē nī′trāt) *vt.* -**trat·ed**, -**trat·ing** to remove nitric acid, the nitrate radical, the nitro group, or nitrogen oxide from —**de′ni·tra′tion** *n.*

de·ni·tri·fy (-trə fī′) *vt.* -**fied′**, -**fy′ing** 1. to remove nitrogen or its compounds from 2. to reduce (nitro groups, nitrates, or nitrites) to compounds of lower oxidation —**de·ni′-tri·fi·ca′tion** *n.*

den·i·zen (den′i zən) *n.* [ME. *denisein* < Anglo-Fr. *deinzein* < OFr. *denzein,* native inhabitant < *denz,* within < VL. *deintus* < L. *de intus,* from within] 1. *a*) an inhabitant or occupant *b*) a frequenter of a particular place 2. [Brit.] an alien granted specified rights of citizenship 3. an animal, plant, foreign word, etc. that has become naturalized —*vt.* [Brit.] to naturalize

Den·mark (den′märk) country in Europe, occupying most of the peninsula of Jutland and several nearby islands in the North and Baltic seas: 16,615 sq. mi.; pop. 4,758,000; cap. Copenhagen: Dan. name, DANMARK

Denmark Strait strait between SE Greenland & Iceland: c. 180 mi. wide

☆**den mother** a woman who supervises meetings of a small group (**den**) of Cub Scouts

Den·nis (den′is) a masculine name: *var.* of DENIS

de·nom·i·nate (di näm′ə nāt′; *for adj., usually* -nit) *vt.* -**nat′ed**, -**nat′ing** [< L. *denominatus,* pp. of *denominare,* to name < *de-,* intens. + *nominare:* see NOMINATE] to give a specified name to; call —*adj.* designating a number that represents a unit of measure [3 lb. and 15 ft. are *denominate* numbers]

de·nom·i·na·tion (di näm′ə nā′shən) *n.* [ME. *denominacioun* < OFr. < L. *denominatio:* see prec.] 1. the act of denominating 2. a name; esp., the name of a class of things 3. a class or kind (esp. of units in a system) having a specific name or value [coins of different *denominations*] 4. a particular religious sect or body, with a specific name, organization, etc.

de·nom·i·na·tion·al (-′l) *adj.* of, sponsored by, or under the control of, a religious denomination; sectarian —**de·nom′i·na′tion·al·ly** *adv.*

de·nom·i·na·tion·al·ism (-′l iz′m) *n.* 1. denominational principles 2. a denominational system 3. acceptance or support of such principles or system 4. division into denominations

de·nom·i·na·tive (di näm′ə nə tiv, -nāt′iv) *adj.* [LL. *denominativus*] 1. denominating; naming 2. *Gram.* formed from a noun or adjective stem [to eye is a *denominative* verb] —*n.* a denominative word, esp. a verb

de·nom·i·na·tor (-nāt′ər) *n.* [ML.] 1. [Now Rare] a person or thing that denominates 2. a shared characteristic 3. the usual level; standard 4. *Math.* the term below or to the right of the line in a fraction; the term that divides the numerator [7 is the *denominator* of 6/7]

de·no·ta·tion (dē′nō tā′shən) *n.* [LL. *denotatio*] 1. the act of denoting 2. the direct, explicit meaning or reference of a word or term: cf. CONNOTATION 3. an indication or sign 4. [Rare] a distinguishing name; designation 5. *Logic* all the individuals or objects to which a given term applies

de·no·ta·tive (dē′nō tāt′iv, di nōt′ə tiv) *adj.* 1. denoting; indicative 2. of denotation —**de′no·ta′tive·ly** *adv.*

de·note (di nōt′) *vt.* -**not′ed**, -**not′ing** [Fr. *dénoter* < L. *denotare,* to mark out, denote < *de-,* down + *notare,* to mark < *nota,* NOTE] 1. to be a sign of; indicate [dark clouds *denote* rain] 2. to signify or refer to explicitly; stand for; mean: said of words, signs, or symbols, and

distinguished from CONNOTE 3. *Logic* to be the name for (individuals of a class) —**de·not′a·ble** *adj.*

de·noue·ment, dé·noue·ment (dā noo′mān; *Fr.* dā noo mäN′) *n.* [Fr. < *dénouer,* to untie < *dé-* (L. *dis-*), from, out + *nouer,* to tie < L. *nodare,* to knot < *nodus,* a knot: see NODE] 1. the outcome, solution, unraveling, or clarification of a plot in a drama, story, etc. 2. the point in the plot where this occurs 3. any final revelation or outcome

de·nounce (di nouns′) *vt.* -**nounced′**, -**nounc′ing** [ME. *denouncen* < OFr. *denoncier* < L. *denuntiare:* see DENUNCIATION] 1. to accuse publicly; inform against [to *denounce* an accomplice in crime] 2. to condemn strongly as evil 3. to give formal notice of the ending of (a treaty, armistice, etc.) 4. [Obs.] to announce, esp. in a menacing way —*SYN.* see CRITICIZE —**de·nounce′ment** *n.* —**de·nounc′er** *n.*

‡**de no·vo** (dē nō′vō) [L.] once more; anew; again

dens. density

dense (dens) *adj.* [ME. < L. *densus,* compact < IE. base *dens-,* thick, whence Gr. *dasys,* thick (used of hair), Hittite *dassus,* strong] 1. having the parts crowded together; packed tightly together; compact 2. difficult to get through, penetrate, etc. [a *dense* fog, *dense* ignorance] 3. slow to understand; stupid 4. *Photog.* opaque, with good contrast in light and shade: said of a negative —*SYN.* see CLOSE[1], STUPID —**dense′ly** *adv.* —**dense′ness** *n.*

den·sim·e·ter (den sim′ə tər) *n.* [< L. *densus,* DENSE + -METER] any instrument for measuring density or specific gravity

den·si·tom·e·ter (den′sə täm′ə tər) *n.* [< ff. + -METER] 1. a device for measuring the optical density of a photographic negative 2. *same as* DENSIMETER

den·si·ty (den′sə tē) *n., pl.* -**ties** [Fr. *densité* < L. *densitas*] 1. the quality or condition of being dense; specif., *a*) thickness; compactness *b*) stupidity *c*) *Photog.* degree of opacity of a negative 2. quantity or number per unit, as of area [the *density* of population] 3. *Elec. same as* CURRENT DENSITY 4. *Physics* the ratio of the mass of an object to its volume

dent[1] (dent) *n.* [ME., var. of DINT] 1. a slight hollow made in a surface by a blow or pressure 2. an appreciable effect or impression, as by lessening —*vt.* to make a dent in —*vi.* to become dented

dent[2] (dent) *n.* [Fr. < L. *dens:* see DENTAL] a toothlike projection as in a gearwheel, lock, etc.

dent. 1. dental 2. dentist 3. dentistry

den·tal (den′t′l) *adj.* [ModL. *dentalis* < L. *dens* (gen. *dentis*), a tooth, akin to Cym. *dant,* OHG. *zan,* OS. *tand,* ON. *tönn,* Goth. *tunthus,* Pre-OE. *tanth,* OE. *toth,* TOOTH] 1. of or for the teeth or dentistry 2. *Phonet.* formed by placing the tip of the tongue against or near the upper front teeth —*n. Phonet.* a dental consonant (th, *th*) —**den′tal·ly** *adv.*

☆**dental floss** thin, strong thread for removing food particles from between the teeth

☆**dental hygienist** a dentist's assistant, who cleans teeth, takes dental X-rays, etc.

den·ta·li·um (den tā′lē əm) *n., pl.* -**li·a** (-ə) [ModL., the type genus (< L. *dentalis,* DENTAL) + -IUM] any of a genus (*Dentalium*) of marine mollusks

den·tate (den′tāt) *adj.* [ME. *dentat* < L. *dentatus < dens:* see DENTAL] 1. having teeth or toothlike projections; toothed or notched 2. *Bot.* having a toothed margin, as some leaves —**den′tate·ly** *adv.*

den·ta·tion (den tā′shən) *n.* 1. the quality or state of being dentate 2. a toothlike projection, as on a leaf

☆**dent corn** a strain of Indian corn in which the mature kernel develops a hollow at the tip

den·ti- (den′tə, -ti) [< L. *dens:* see DENTAL] a combining form meaning tooth or teeth [dentiform]: also, before a vowel, **dent-**

den·ti·cle (den′ti k′l) *n.* [L. *denticulus,* dim. of *dens:* see DENTAL] a small tooth or toothlike projection

den·tic·u·late (den tik′yoo lit, -lāt′) *adj.* [L. *denticulatus*] 1. having denticles 2. having dentils 3. *Bot.* finely dentate Also **den·tic′u·lat′ed** —**den·tic′u·late·ly** *adv.*

den·tic·u·la·tion (den tik′yoo lā′shən) *n.* 1. the quality or condition of being denticulate 2. a denticle

den·ti·form (den′tə fôrm′) *adj.* [DENTI- + -FORM] tooth-shaped

den·ti·frice (-fris′) *n.* [ME. *dentifricie* < L. *dentifricium,* tooth powder < *dens* (see DENTAL) + *fricare,* to rub] any preparation for cleaning teeth, as a powder, paste, or liquid

den·tig·er·ous (den tij′ər əs) *adj.* bearing teeth

den·til (den′til) *n.* [MFr. *dentille,* dim. of *dent* < L. *dens:* see DENTAL] *Archit.* any of a series of small rectangular blocks projecting like teeth, as from under a cornice

den·tin (den′tin) *n.* [< L. *dens* (gen. *dentis*): see DENTAL & -INE[4]] the hard, dense, calcareous tissue forming the body of a tooth, under the enamel: also **den′tine** (-tēn, -tin)

den·tist (den′tist) *n.* [Fr. *dentiste* < ML. *dentista* < L. *dens:* see DENTAL] a person whose profession is the care of teeth and the surrounding tissues, including the prevention and elimination of decay, the replacement of missing teeth with artificial ones, the correction of malocclusion, etc.

den·tist·ry (-rē) *n.* the profession or work of a dentist

13. _____ I could read the book quickly because it had a fast-moving plot.

14. _____ It was nothing more than an underhanded plot to get more money from the old man.

15. _____ Wendy reserved a large plot for tomatoes.

Part E. Find each of the following words on the sample dictionary page on page 332. In the space provided, write the etymology of each word.

EXAMPLE: dental   **ModL. dentalis < L. dens (gen. dentis), a tooth**

16. denote _____

17. denim _____

18. denizen _____

Skill Unit 10: Spelling

Part A. Write each of the following words correctly by filling in the blanks with either *ie* or *ei*.

EXAMPLE: consc**ie**nce

1. c_____ling   2. gr_____ve

3. sl_____gh   4. w_____rd

Part B. Combine one of the prefixes in List A with a word base from List B to form the new word that best fits the meaning of each sentence. Write the word in the space provided.

	List A	List B
Prefix	Meaning	Word Base
dis	the opposite of	circular
im	not	informed
mis	wrongly	jointed
semi	half	lease
sub	under	mature

EXAMPLE: The governor gave a long **disjointed** speech.

5. A half moon is _____ in shape.

6. Jenny and Martin showed up late because they were _____ about the time.

7. Hilda's neighbors are going to _____ their apartment while they are away.

8. Bob and his friends reminisced about the _____ pranks they used to enjoy when they were young.

Part C. Add the suffixes to the word bases as directed. You may have to add, drop, or change letters before the suffix can be added.

EXAMPLE: sincere + ity = **sincerity**

9. waste + ful = _____

10. happy + ly = _____

11. argue + ment = _____

12. wed + ing = _____

Part D. Write the correct plural of each of the following nouns in the space provided.

EXAMPLE: shelf   **shelves**

13. deer _____

14. son-in-law _____

15. watch _____

16. hero _____

Part E. Each of the following words is incorrectly spelled. Write the correct spelling in the space provided.

EXAMPLE: vetran   **veteran**

17. privlege _____

18. disasterous _____

19. temperture _____

20. mischievious _____

Part F. Each of the following words is spelled incorrectly. Write the correct spelling in the space provided.

EXAMPLE: envirement   **environment**

21. labratory _____

22. assinement _____

23. colum _____

24. bookeeper _____

Skill Unit 11: Using Frequently Confused Words Correctly

Part A. For each of the following sentences, underline the correct possessive pronoun or contraction from the pair of words in parentheses.

EXAMPLE: Martin and Juana have finished (they're, **their**) dinner.

1. Let me know when (you're, your) ready to go.

2. The volcano blew (it's, its) top.

3. (Who's, Whose) the next president going to be?

4. Eric and Jean painted (they're, their) living room pink.

5. (It's, Its) time to go home.

Part B. For each of the following sentences, underline the correct homonym from each pair in parentheses.

EXAMPLE: Peter read his part (allowed, **aloud**) until he had it memorized.

6. Larry was (hoarse, horse) from cheering during the football game.

7. The scarf had faded so badly that Laura decided to (die, dye) it.

8. Susan didn't care so much about the $6; it was the (principal, principle) of the thing.

9. Jake read the (hole, whole) book in three hours.

10. Wanda could not participate without her parents' (assent, ascent).

Part C. For each of the following sentences, underline the correct word from each pair in parentheses.

EXAMPLE: You will have to (except, **accept**) my apology.

11. Lenny and Paula went out to (chose, choose) curtains.

12. The new policy won't (affect, effect) Manuel.

13. Gordon felt (persecuted, prosecuted) by the neighborhood gang.

14. Martha took her grievance to the (personnel, personal) committee.

15. Try not to (lose, loose) your temper.

Skills Correlation Chart for Posttest

After you check your answers, look at the following chart. Circle the number of each question you missed. Then review the subskill in which the skills for the questions you missed are explained.

		Question Number	Subskill Number	Subskill Name	Page Number
Skill Unit One	WRITING SIMPLE SENTENCES	1 2 3 4 5 6 7 8 9 10 11 12 13 14 15 16 17 18 19 20	1A 1B 1C 1D	Recognizing the Parts of a Simple Sentence Identifying Verbals in Simple Sentences Making Subjects and Verbs Agree in Number Choosing a Verb to Agree With Special Subjects	pages 30–37 pages 37–46 pages 46–54 pages 54–60
		If you correctly answered 15 or fewer questions, you should review the subskills in Unit One for the questions you missed. If you correctly answered 16 or more of the questions in Unit One, go to Skill Unit Two.			
Skill Unit Two	WRITING COMPOUND SENTENCES	1 2 3 4 5 6 7 8 9 10 11 12 13 14 15	2A 2B 2C	Constructing Compound Sentences Punctuating Compound Sentences Revising Run-On Sentences	pages 64–70 pages 70–75 pages 75–81
		If you correctly answered 11 or fewer questions, you should review the subskills in Unit Two for the questions you missed. If you correctly answered 12 or more of the questions in Unit Two, go to Skill Unit Three.			
Skill Unit Three	WRITING COMPLEX SENTENCES	1 2 3 4 5 6 7 8 9 10 11 12 13 14 15 16 17 18 19 20	3A 3B 3C 3D	Identifying Dependent Clauses and Complex Sentences Using Adjective Clauses in Complex Sentences Using Adverb Clauses in Complex Sentences Using Noun Clauses in Complex Sentences	pages 85–89 pages 90–99 pages 100–105 pages 105–112
		If you correctly answered 15 or fewer questions, you should review the subskills in Unit Three for the questions you missed. If you correctly answered 16 or more of the questions in Unit Three, go to Skill Unit Four.			
Skill Unit Four	USING SENTENCE PUNCTUATION	1 2 3 4 5 6 7 8 9 10 11 12 13 14 15 16 17 18 19 20	4A 4B 4C 4D	Using Periods, Question Marks, and Exclamation Points Using Commas Using Apostrophes Punctuating Quotations	pages 115–118 pages 118–125 pages 125–130 pages 130–134
		If you correctly answered 15 or fewer questions, you should review the subskills in Unit Four for the questions you missed. If you correctly answered 16 or more of the questions in Unit Four, go to Skill Unit Five.			
Skill Unit Five	USING MORE SENTENCE PUNCTUATION	1 2 3 4 5 6 7 8 9 10 11 12 13 14 15	5A 5B 5C	Using Semicolons Using Colons Using Parentheses and Dashes	pages 137–142 pages 142–146 pages 146–152
		If you correctly answered 11 or fewer questions, you should review the subskills in Unit Five for the questions you missed. If you correctly answered 12 or more of the questions in Unit Five, go to Skill Unit Six.			
Skill Unit Six	USING MODIFIERS IN SENTENCES	1 2 3 4 5 6 7 8 9 10 11 12 13 14 15 16	6A 6B 6C 6D	Positioning Single-Word Modifiers Positioning Phrase Modifiers Positioning Clause Modifiers Correcting Dangling Modifiers	pages 156–163 pages 163–169 pages 169–172 pages 172–177
		If you correctly answered 11 or fewer questions, you should review the subskills in Unit Six for the questions you missed. If you correctly answered 12 or more of the questions in Unit Six, go to Skill Unit Seven.			

		Question Number	Subskill Number	Subskill Name	Page Number
Skill Unit Seven	WRITING EFFECTIVE SENTENCES	1 2 3 4 5	7A	Using Parallel Structure	pages 182–190
		6 7 8 9 10	7B	Using Verb Tenses and Voices Correctly	pages 190–198
		11 12 13 14 15	7C	Using Correct Pronoun Reference and Pronoun Agreement	pages 198–202
		16 17 18 19 20	7D	Avoiding Sentence Fragments	pages 202–206

If you correctly answered 15 or fewer questions, you should review the subskills in Unit Seven for the questions you missed.
If you correctly answered 16 or more of the questions in Unit Seven, go to Skill Unit Eight.

		Question Number	Subskill Number	Subskill Name	Page Number
Skill Unit Eight	WRITING UNIFIED PARAGRAPHS	1 2 3	8A	Recognizing Topic Sentences	pages 210–218
		4 5 6	8B	Writing Effective Topic Sentences	pages 218–223
		7 8 9	8C	Identifying Methods of Paragraph Development	pages 223–232
		10 11 12	8D	Recognizing Irrelevant Details	pages 232–236
		13 14 15	8E	Writing Unified Paragraphs	pages 236–241

If you correctly answered 11 or fewer questions, you should review the subskills in Unit Eight for the questions you missed.
If you correctly answered 12 or more of the questions in Unit Eight, go to Skill Unit Nine.

		Question Number	Subskill Number	Subskill Name	Page Number
Skill Unit Nine	USING THE DICTIONARY	1 2 3	9A	Finding Words in the Dictionary by Using Alphabetical Order and Guide Words	pages 244–250
		4 5 6	9B	Using the Dictionary to Pronounce Words Correctly	pages 250–254
		7 8 9	9C	Using Entry Words to Spell and Divide Words Correctly	pages 255–257
		10 11 12 13 14 15	9D	Identifying Parts of Speech and Selecting the Correct Definition	pages 257–262
		16 17 18	9E	Locating the Etymology of a Word	pages 262–264

If you correctly answered 13 or fewer questions, you should review the subskills in Unit Nine for the questions you missed.
If you correctly answered 14 or more of the questions in Unit Nine, go to Skill Unit Ten.

		Question Number	Subskill Number	Subskill Name	Page Number
Skill Unit Ten	SPELLING	1 2 3 4	10A	Spelling Words with ie and ei	pages 266–269
		5 6 7 8	10B	Spelling Words Formed by Adding Prefixes	pages 270–273
		9 10 11 12	10C	Spelling Words Formed by Adding Suffixes	pages 274–280
		13 14 15 16	10D	Spelling Plurals	pages 280–284
		17 18 19 20	10E	Pronouncing Words Correctly to Aid Spelling	pages 284–286
		21 22 23 24	10F	Using Memory Aids to Improve Spelling	pages 286–292

If you correctly answered 18 or fewer questions, you should review the subskills in Unit Ten for the questions you missed.
If you correctly answered 19 or more of the questions in Unit Ten, go to Skill Unit Eleven.

		Question Number	Subskill Number	Subskill Name	Page Number
Skill Unit Eleven	USING FREQUENTLY CONFUSED WORDS CORRECTLY	1 2 3 4 5	11A	Identifying Possessive Pronouns and Contractions	pages 294–297
		6 7 8 9 10	11B	Distinguishing Meanings of Common Homonyms	pages 297–303
		11 12 13 14 15	11C	Learning the Difference Between Words That Are Often Confused	pages 303–306

If you correctly answered 11 or fewer questions, you should review the subskills in Unit Eleven for the questions you missed.
If you correctly answered 12 or more of the questions in Unit Eleven, you have achieved mastery.